THE EURO AND ITS RIVALS

NEW ANTHROPOLOGIES OF EUROPE

Daphne Berdahl, Matti Bunzl, and Michael Herzfeld, founding editors

THE EURO AND ITS RIVALS

Currency and the Construction of a Transnational City

GUSTAV PEEBLES

Indiana University Press
Bloomington and Indianapolis

This book is a publication of

Indiana University Press
601 North Morton Street
Bloomington, Indiana 47404-3797 USA

iupress.indiana.edu

Telephone orders	800-842-6796
Fax orders	812-855-7931
Orders by e-mail	iuporder@indiana.edu

Library of Congress Cataloging-in-Publication Data
Peebles, Gustav.
The euro and its rivals : money and the construction of a
transnational city / Gustav Peebles.
p. cm. — (New anthropologies of Europe)
Includes bibliographical references and index.
ISBN 978-0-253-35638-3 (cloth : alk. paper)
ISBN 978-0-253-22320-3 (pbk. : alk. paper)
1. Euro. 2. Europe—Economic integration. 3. Money.
4. International economic relations. I. Title.
HG925.P44 2011
332.4'94—dc22
2010046612

1 2 3 4 5 16 15 14 13 12 11

To my parents,

who have inspired me and
supported me every step
of the way.

CONTENTS

PREFACE

This book is *not* about the yen and the dollar, the most obvious rivals to the euro. Instead, it is about the underreported ways in which daily monetary usage and public debates about monetary policy play a role in constructing the boundaries of community. It is an attempt to look at the euro through a specifically anthropological lens, since the lion's share of work on the euro has been within the fields of economics and political science.

There is a metaphysics of money that is swept aside by the fields that typically study it, and that sometimes turns too magical when studied by people outside those fields. I have tried to ground the power that money has outside the economic sphere by relying on standard ethnographic techniques—watching what people say and do about money on a daily basis—and not succumbing to a more Baudrillardean approach that sees it as all fictitious, diaphanous, and endlessly recursive. I take seriously the idea that money can create communal attachments, even when rational economic actors insist that it is a purely scientific instrument. This book bridges the typical gap that keeps these two distant wings of research around money from even speaking to one another. Each view can inform the other, but there must be more of a common language to bring the two together.

The time is ripe for such an approach to money. As this book goes to press, the world is awash in monetary chaos, and every day brings a sense of foreboding that the entire edifice of monetary stability will collapse in a sea of worthless paper. In early 2010, Greece was at the brink of such a collapse, which illuminated the precise sort of monetary community that I use as a conceptual apparatus in this book. Europeans of all stripes were challenged with the question of just how much solidarity they felt with their fellow EU citizens from Greece. Were they hopeless spendthrifts? Or had they fallen on hard times because of an unforeseeable business cycle?

Fascinatingly, the euro and its sociolegal underpinnings meant that these questions had been answered already. Because all of the euro-zone countries had their fate soldered to Greece's with the founding of the euro, they were largely compelled to act in solidarity with their Greek neighbors. Sweden and Denmark—both outside the euro zone—were under no such compunction. Because they are outside of the vast monetary community of the euro, they had no need to show compassion or solidarity to the Greeks. It was left to the members of the euro zone to part with their hard-earned money and use it to prop up Greece. To save the euro from collapse, they had to treat the Greeks as members of their community who were in need of aid, regardless of whether the problems were the result of an objectively vicious business cycle or subjectively dubious behavior.

This story is similar to the stories I trace here. How did Swedish bankrupts and vagrants come to be treated differently than non-Swedish bankrupts and vagrants as the country gradually built a sense of national solidarity over the nineteenth and twentieth centuries? What sociolegal instruments make it possible to see a similarity in the legal and moral treatment of vagrants and bankrupts? Seen through the lens of daily currency practices and infrastructure, these two groups have much in common.

Money is almost like language—a fact remarked upon since at least Marx—but I don't mean this in the typical sense. Instead, I am referring to the fact that both money and language somehow present frictionless surfaces to history and society. In their ubiquity, they are frequently viewed as neutral forces. This makes them hard to study, for people often do not see currency (or language) usage as a value-laden act.

The debate about joining the euro in both Sweden and Denmark changed all that. But so did two other variables that form the backbone of my story. The novel attempt to build the transnational Øresund Region opened up new possibilities for grasping the meanings of monetary usage in Sweden and Denmark. The region sought to destroy a border that had been in effect since 1658 by bringing together two big cities—Malmö and Copenhagen—by way of a giant bridge-tunnel complex. The bridge spawned vast dreams of an entirely new world, at least for Malmö, which had long suffered as Sweden's least-sophisticated city. The ease of reaching Copenhagen would usher in a new era of success in a variety of fields, including industry and education. People would be happier with the bridge; life would be easier and more fun.

Additionally, the bridge was a physical instantiation of the "new Europe." Just as the European Union had eliminated countless legal barriers to the movement of capital, goods, and labor, the bridge would facilitate a radical leap in space and time, suddenly allowing these same factors of production to flow more smoothly and more rapidly across dated, cumbersome boundaries. The bridge would make the complex aspects of European integration—determined in faraway Brussels and Luxembourg—a daily, lived experience.

The bridge is in many ways just like the euro. Both are far from mere symbols; they are mundane tools in the shaping of a new reality. As everyday tools, they are meant to disappear in their ubiquity, just like language. But instead, the euro and the bridge (they emerged on almost identical time lines) were both contested. Some people were in favor of the new region and the new currency, both of which would provide opportunities for the transgression of ancient boundaries of cultures, economies, and states. Some people were opposed and sought either to preserve the status quo or even to introduce slower times. But either way, the seemingly separate debates about the bridge and about money were compellingly isomorphic —that is, proponents of the bridge were invariably proponents of the euro, while opponents of the bridge were invariably opponents of the euro. Simmel long ago showed an interest in both bridges and money, and here was living confirmation of his suspicion that there might be metaphysical harmonies shared by these two sociological devices for creating connections.

Mostly, the opponents of the euro were in favor of the respective national currencies on each side of the Øresund. Meanwhile, a number of smaller fringe groups were laying the groundwork for a local iteration of the world's ongoing battle over globalization. These people were in favor of so-called local currencies, which aim to circumscribe the movement of money to an almost self-defeatingly small dimension. Like their far more successful counterpart, the slow food movement, these people represent what is typically glossed as the antiglobalization movement. But like their slow food counterparts, they are, ironically, part of a global movement. This suggests that popular terminology is sorely misrepresentative of the facts on the ground. Proponents of local currencies are not necessarily opposed to a globalized world that is interlinked in complex ways. They do, however, hope that the connective tissues are not derived from the tendrils of capitalism. Instead, new global connectivities should be woven from more humanistic fibers, and local-currency advocates are often motivated by a concept of global solidarity with all humans.

Whereas most advocates for globalization and space-time compression see the monetary policies of such fringe groups as deeply muddled thinking, I take them seriously. In putting up a mirror to dominant monetary policy, they help us think about money more generally. In particular, their practices and policies help to illuminate the ways in which money can succeed—or fail—at circumscribing the movement of labor, goods, and capital, just like the Øresund Bridge. This bounded movement, whether facilitated by the euro, the kronor and kroner of Sweden and Denmark, or the local currencies, then plays a role in the social construction of community. Just as the creation of a public sphere can produce a feedback mechanism for consolidating itself as a deeper and more lively public sphere, a currency can produce a self-fulfilling snowball effect if more and more people subscribe to its usefulness. Money and language—they both give us a common frame of reference in which to get things done, everyday.

Given the world today, anthropologists are forced to understand the intricacies of central banks and monetary policy. We need to develop a critical approach to these vital social institutions by turning to the tools and theories in our methodological toolkit rather than those of other disciplines. Jane Guyer, Keith Hart, Douglas Holmes, Bill Maurer, and Janet Roitman, among others, have been leading the charge on this. Building on their insights, I have used qualitative research methods to focus intimately on the power of currency to create boundaries and to constitute groups, delineating native and foreigner from one another.

We need to probe the ways in which currency—as an economic tool rather than as a non-economic symbol—binds individuals and groups together. When a wealthy Argentine can store her economic value in a currency that differs from the currency that her compatriots must use for economic storage, does this have consequences for one's sense of national belonging? When the Icelandic government attempts to bail out Icelandic depositors, but not foreign depositors, in Icelandic private banks, does this have any consequences for the consolidation of group cohesion? When a state treasury accommodates debtors instead of creditors, does it carry consequences for social hierarchy?

Such questions can be best addressed by embracing a renewed détente between the insights of economics and of anthropology, rather than by refusing to let one or the other into the same public sphere. By telling the story of the Øresund Region and its battling currencies, I hope this book contributes to bridging such divides.

Acknowledgments

During this project, which took many years, I received significant financial and social support. An attempt to enumerate all who helped me would almost surely fail to account for everyone, but there are a number of people and institutions that deserve special mention.

On the financial side of matters, my research benefited from assistance provided by a National Science Foundation Graduate Student Fellowship, a Markovitz Fellowship, the American Scandinavian Foundation, the Council on European Studies, and the Council for Advanced Studies in Peace and International Cooperation. I thank NYU's Center for European Studies, Columbia's Anthropology Department, and The New School for all lending a hand with financial support, and I thank my colleagues at these institutions for their intense intellectual feedback. I want to extend special thanks to Marty Schain, Beth Povinelli, Julia Foulkes, Isabelle Frank, Timothy Quigley, and Almaz Zelleke for both their empathetic grasp of the difficulties of juggling life with work and their generous efforts to provide institutional support. Nick Dirks also seems to have a particular knack for ensuring that no souls get lost when they're in his charge.

Various sections of the book were assessed and scrutinized by thoughtful and incisive colleagues at LSE, Columbia University, Concordia University (Montreal), University of Pennsylvania, MIT, Stockholm University, and Oslo University. I am thankful for all the comments I received during these seminars, and the book bears their mark.

I owe a great deal to the enduring support of the three series editors, Daphne Berdahl, Matti Bunzl, and Michael Herzfeld, who always had faith that a book on Scandinavia could circulate beyond a small sphere of specialists. Since I know that Daphne was an early supporter, I am sad that I can no longer reach out to her personally, as she left us all far too early in life. Both American and European academics miss her voice greatly.

I must also thank the diligent and insightful people at Indiana University Press, especially my editor, Rebecca Jane Tolen, who had the wisdom, honesty, and experience to say when something needed to be entirely rewritten. Her collaboration and effort on this book and her vision for its potential audience provided a steady foundation throughout the process. Several anonymous reviewers offered their time and careful criticism. Merryl Sloane provided copyediting the likes of which I'd never seen before.

An earlier version of chapter 4 was originally published as "A Geography of Debauchery: State-Building and the Mobilization of Labor versus Leisure on a European Union Border," *Focaal: European Journal of Anthropology* 51 (2008): 113–131, © Berghahn Books.

This project began with Susan Gal, who took me under her wing at the beginning of my time at the University of Chicago, even though we shared only a common interest in that vaguely defined continent known as Europe. All of my work since meeting her has been marked by her influence, and over the years she has always been ready to help me through any problem. John Comaroff, James Fernandez, and John Kelly have also been pivotal influences on both this book and the trajectory of my life.

I owe many thanks to the incredibly hospitable and stimulating people in Sweden and Denmark who have been affiliated either loosely or intimately with the University of Lund's Ethnology Department. In particular, Anders Linde-Laursen has proven to be a long-standing friend and mentor, and Orvar Löfgren has continually provided enlightenment with both his writings and his personal energy. Researchers Fredrik Nilsson and Tom O'Dell were doing amazing work on the Øresund Region long before I stepped foot there, and my work has relied on their insights and labor. In Stockholm, Christina Garsten, Ulf Hannerz, Anna Hasselström, Monica Lindh de Montoya, Johan Lindquist, and Brian Palmer have always provided a welcoming and collaborative environment. Parts of the book have also benefited from the sharp eyes of colleagues in the rest of Europe: Matthew Engelke, Chris Fuller, Keith Hart, Deborah James, Don Kalb, Charles Stafford, and Michael Stewart.

Back in America, I have drawn strength from the excellent friends I have met within academia, including Gabriella Coleman, Drew Gilbert, Jessica Greenberg, Rachel Heiman, Andrea Muehlebach, Rashmi Sadana, Miriam Ticktin, Hylton White, and Caitlin Zaloom. And I have told the story many times how, long ago, John Watanabe opened up the life of scholarship to me for the first time and sent me down this path. Finally, Emily Sogn and Rhea Rahman both proved essential in bringing the book to completion.

My many informants were spread across both sides of Øresund Sound. The insights they gladly provided form the backbone of all the analysis in this work, and my anthropological approach to studying the euro would have been much harder without their cooperation. I thank them for allowing me access to their daily lives, opening their doors despite their hesitations regarding being an object of anthropological inquiry.

I owe much to my friends and family. My long-time friends from New York, Chicago, and Washington have always been supportive and willing sounding boards. I'm thinking especially of Jake Waletzky, who was the glue that bound many of us together, and we all dearly miss him. Even though he cantankerously disagreed with me much of the time, his impact was so great on my life that I can conjure his voice without any problem.

My parents and sister have stood by me throughout this entire process, even while all the other neighborhood kids sped past me in the attainment of home mortgages and monthly paychecks. My choices must have been a bit mystifying to them, but I hope that this book in some measure makes them proud. Finally, my wife, Amanda Pollak, needs the most special of mentions: for putting up with me during all these years and being there to listen at any moment. She even provided a steady and essential stream of both grammatical and substantive critiques while we tried to pull this all together. Along the way, we had two wonderful kids to whom I owe a hearty thanks for their kind toleration of my missing far too many bedtime readings.

THE EURO AND ITS RIVALS

ØRESUND REGION

Map by Ben Ostrower

Introduction

Straddling a watery border in northernmost Europe lies a transnational space called the Øresund Region. As one newspaper headline confirmed, "The Øresund Region Is a Utopia" (Magnusson 1997) and, for many reasons, it could have readily fallen within the parameters of Thomas More's witty double entendre, simultaneously denoting both "good place" and "no place." But, unlike more openly fictional utopias, the Øresund Region was envisioned as a transnational marketplace coming into being; in the process, it confronted the older utopian visions of Sweden and Denmark, two well-regulated, Social Democratic nation-states held dear by their citizens, who were now being asked to usher in the new project.

Promising to meld the cities of Copenhagen, Denmark, and Malmö, Sweden (as well as each town's surrounding hinterlands), the Øresund Region was meant to be a concrete incarnation of the European Union's (EU) more abstract boundary-destroying mission, a place where transnationalism would become so normalized that it would no longer be noted. A swirling market of mobile goods, services, capital, and people would slip away from national constraints and transform the body of water that separates the two countries into a transcendent link.

Not surprisingly, these visions, which were proclaimed during the years leading up to the completion of the Øresund Bridge—marking the informal commencement of the Øresund Region in 1999–2000—also had many detractors. As such, the border separating Sweden and Denmark has served as the fulcrum of a debate about divergent models of the future. Some of these models have been transnational, some national, and some post-national.

Despite a project to build a giant bridge-tunnel complex that would connect the two cities and despite the creation of a binational bureaucracy dedicated to building the transnational Øresund Region, at the turn of the millennium it could not be said to yet fully exist. Unlike the Swedish or Danish nation-states themselves, or even the EU, the region was still embryonic during the fifteen months I spent there in 1999–2000 when I began my research. It was supported by some vital infrastructural scaffolding, to be sure, but it remained mostly a vision of the future for broad segments of Swedes and Danes. To complicate matters, some people, such as the proponents of local currencies, who will be discussed at length below, were opposed to the region altogether. They preferred instead a more localized vision of the future, wherein people would not seek to transcend borders on a daily basis merely for the sake of transcending them. Rather, they wanted to construct new borders, circumscribing ever smaller, subnational spaces. In the face of the EU's drive to expand people's horizons of mobility, these groups were seeking instead to shrink them.

The Øresund Region, therefore, offers the tantalizing possibility that we can ethnographically document dueling attempts to build new socio-political spaces (one transnational, one subnational) after the supposed weakening of the typical nation-state form. These imagined new spaces relied on new organizing principles and underlying philosophies. At the same time, they were being attempted in two of the most steady and stalwart members of the nation-state club, Sweden and Denmark. Consequently, the success of these new projects was far from assured, and some visions of the future in the Øresund Region have not come to full fruition. But following Herzfeld and his notion of "social poetics" (Herzfeld 1997), such failures might nonetheless be necessary. In other words, the argument over the future is essential to producing it, and the task of the ethnographer is to document the debate as it unfolds. In the case of southern Sweden and eastern Denmark, some groups were honing their portrayal of the future from an idealized picture of the Social Democratic past, while others were developing theirs by turning to an idealized vision of the Smithian free market.

These different visions of the future proved easy to trace ethnographically because they mapped onto debates about monetary policy that were occurring at the same time in the region. As Swedes and Danes were arguing over whether and how to construct the Øresund Region, they were simultaneously arguing over how to organize their monetary systems. On the one hand, I encountered people who believed that money and the market in which it must circulate were sullying and dehumanizing influences upon social life; these were forces that needed to be tamed and constrained by regulation in order to render the social world both moral and livable. On the other hand, I met people who promoted the power of money as efficiency incarnate; such people continually proclaimed the limitless promise of the market, if left unfettered by the regulatory constraints of a meddling and moralistic government.

These positions represented two sides of the utopian imagination in the Øresund Region. In the former case, where the market was seen as sullying to the human spirit, the community was envisioned as built upon sacrifice. In the latter case, the community was built by way of the efficiency of the division of labor—people coming together out of self-interest, and precisely in an effort to avoid sacrifice.[1] Understanding how these two common appeals to community-building related to monetary and political boundaries will help a great deal in grasping the debates in the Øresund Region and, I would argue, many other debates about nationalism and globalization.

Gradually, I became aware that these opposed groups had already organized themselves around specific plans for monetary organization. The people interested in promoting the region were simultaneously hoping that Sweden and Denmark would agree to start using the European Monetary Union's (EMU) euro, the vast pan-national currency that now circulates as legal tender in seventeen (Estonia joined on January 1, 2011) countries of the European Union. In 1999, neither Denmark nor Sweden had taken a stance on joining yet, but they were in the process of deciding. Meanwhile, some people who sought to tame money had attached themselves to a relatively new global movement that aimed to create new, "local" currencies that would operate at an almost infinitesimal scale, at least in comparison with the euro. These local-currency proponents hoped that, via a new organization of currency, money could be rehumanized, so as to no longer be a sullying and dangerous force. In addition, the Øresund Region also contained proponents of the existing national currencies—people who had little interest in subscribing to either radical reconfiguration of money and instead happily defended the status quo.

Given these positions, documenting the building of the Øresund Region offers a compelling example of the role that currency can play in the construction of social space. Both the opponents and the proponents of the Øresund Region were aiming to build new senses of belonging, via money, in a space long divided by a classic national border. The euro proponents envisioned a new, fluid citizenry of the region who would embrace cultural difference and a transnational identity that would gain its strength from the power of the market and the tempting ease provided by an efficient division of labor. Alternatively, the local-currency proponents imagined a return to the pre-national village, built on mutual sacrifice and care for one's neighbors. Meanwhile, defenders of each national currency typically saw little need for either the region or the local currencies' villages, and usually did not harbor any strong desire to radically rework the reigning Social Democratic nation-state model or the currencies that upheld it.

The Øresund Region

In order to properly grasp the Øresund Region as a goal of policy makers, one first has to understand the reality that this vision was trying to transform. The regionalist movement promoted the future cultural and bureaucratic melding of two large portions of each country, the areas known as Hovedstaden and Sjælland in Denmark and the area known as Skåne in Sweden. That said, generally in the public's mind, the region was composed of a smaller space, hugging the borderland a bit more than the map on page xx would suggest. Part of the reason for that perception was the overwhelming focus on ensuring a vibrant connection between the two cities of Malmö, Sweden, and Copenhagen, Denmark.

If the two cities are considered as a single entity, the area becomes the largest city in the Scandinavian countries, surpassing Stockholm's approximately 2 million inhabitants. Copenhagen alone has 1.7 million people. In the new transnational city of Øresund, connected by the ten-mile-long Øresund Bridge, there are around 2.3 million people. The entire region has a population of 3.7 million, with 2.5 million on the Danish side and 1.2 million on the Swedish side.[2] One-quarter of Denmark's and Sweden's combined population lives inside the Øresund Region, making it a formidable force.[3] Interestingly, only a small percentage of the Swedish and Danish populations has permanently migrated to the "foreign" sides of the sound, though there is more daily commuting.[4] But all these numbers are growing, which suggests that the EU programs and the bridge are having an impact, though not with the speed that regionalists had imagined.

This was historically a transnational space, but one radically different than the space that the regional proponents were hoping to conjure forth.[5] While Swedes traveled to Denmark with great frequency and Danes also made trips to Sweden, each of these places typically remained very much within the ambit of its respective nation-state. All technical and bureaucratic regulations, including those related to schooling, health care, and commercial trade, emanated from each national capital. Consequently, each side felt very Swedish or Danish, and not some mixture of the two (especially on the Danish side, because Copenhagen is the national capital).

Prior to the development of the dream of an Øresund Region, each national group typically saw the other side as an instrumental space rather than as a "normal" space; the city on the other side of the sound served as an escape valve from problems at home, whether financial or moral. Thus, as many people explained to me, each national group tended to see the other side's citizens as a generally uninteresting body of natives, but not as a possible group of compatriots. The opposite side of the sound was a space to be used, rather than a space to be committed to as part of one's potential community. For example, one local expert on demographics told me that the few Danes who choose to live on the Swedish side generally fail to integrate into the daily culture of Sweden. Rather, they stand as a small, Danish outpost on Swedish territory. They choose to live there primarily for economic reasons, as it is far cheaper to live in the Swedish city of Malmö and commute to Copenhagen every day than pay to live in Copenhagen itself. He explained that this outpost mentality is so pervasive that many Danes refuse to live in Sweden merely because of the schooling available there. They apparently think that Sweden's educational philosophy promotes too much egalitarianism; he suggested that if someone opened a Danish school on the Swedish side, more Danes would come flooding over. In other words, they want to live on the Swedish side in order to save money, but they want to raise their children as Danes even though they would grow up within Sweden.

Similarly, Swedes rarely live on the Danish side. They do, however, travel to Copenhagen in droves, a phenomenon that I will document in this book. My ethnographic research showed that the Danish side is a place to let loose. Whereas Danes come to Sweden to save money, Swedes go to Copenhagen to spend money. And they spend it in ways that are frowned upon at home. Much like crossing the Mexican border for Americans, Copenhagen embodies a space of decadence for Swedes, where they can free themselves from moral strictures and avoid the gaze of their country-men at home.

The Øresund Region was designed to gradually change all of this. It was aiming to make both sides of the sound a space of humdrum normality for Swedes and Danes, rather than an escape from it. People would live, work, and play on both sides of the sound just as if the other city were a neighboring town in the home country. To achieve this, people would need to see themselves and the foreigners on the other side of the sound as "Øresundians," rather than exclusively as Danes or Swedes. As the vision of the region first took root, some people even discussed the possibility that the region could create this normality quickly and with ease, for it was suggested that the populations on both sides of the sound were "brother peoples," with much in common already.[6] Indeed, a fringe group of Danish nationalists pushed the idea that southern Sweden could now return to its "rightful" home, as it had been severed from Denmark in a peace treaty between the two countries in 1658.

Such beliefs were partly shared, I learned, by a group of "Scanish" nationalists on the Swedish side of the sound. (Skåne, the southernmost province of Sweden, is called Scania in English.) This fringe group, which met in local Malmö watering holes, also set its sights on the momentous date of 1658, which they believed marked the beginning of a Swedish cultural genocide of Scanish culture. By returning to Denmark via the newly imagined Øresund Region, they would cast off the overlords in Stockholm and would be free to pursue their national culture unhindered.[7] From the perspective of these people, Skåne itself was already a transnational space, even prior to the vision of the Øresund Region. It was transnational not only because it had occasional Danes in its midst, but because it had Swedes mingling daily in its Scanish midst.

What is interesting for the purposes of the argument here is the way in which these proponents of a regional ethnic solidarity were quickly banished to the sidelines of the debate; their utopian vision of a restored Denmark or a pure Skåne never gained much traction at the level of policy and infrastructure. For example, no mainline regionalist with whom I spoke ever promoted the idea that Skåne's children should be learning about "Mother Denmark" in the classroom in order to help build the new region, though this is a highly common nation-building technique. Indeed, it was one of the premier tactics employed by Sweden to transform Skåne's population into Swedes after 1658 (see Ehn, Frykman, and Löfgren 1993). Regionalists hoping to be taken seriously rarely indulged in this sort of nationalist or subnationalist rhetoric, though jabs at Stockholm were certainly thrown occasionally. Instead, nationalists and subnationalists of this sort on both sides were readily dismissed as cranks. Proponents far preferred to acknowledge, even to highlight, the distinctions between Sweden and Denmark, and how these differences enriched the region itself.

Thus, having dismissed the possibility of relying on some sort of already-existing ethnic solidarity across the sound, the lion's share of regional proponents set out to build the region via the rhetoric of efficiency and ease rather than the idea of sacrifice toward a common good. In Durkheimian terms, proponents were seeking to build organic solidarity (unity through economic dissimilarity, i.e., the division of labor) rather than mechanical solidarity (unity through mental or ethnic similarity; see Durkheim 1984 [1893]). Following this logic, movement within the Øresund Region needed to be made attractive and easy, not challenging. For example, workers at Øresund Business Integration (one of many nonprofits designed to promote the region) often saw their job as directed toward either dismantling or harmonizing the regulatory barriers that separated the two countries. Efforts to frame regulation itself as a "barrier" stands as an important index of the ideological debates that were afoot in the Øresund Region. Regional proponents saw barriers as self-evidently problematic hindrances to economic growth. Historically, however, the Swedish and Danish Social Democratic visions have vitally relied on the idea that regulation is not a barrier at all, but a mode of defending and building citizen (or business) freedom from potentially menacing or unfair competitive logics; given proper and sound regulation, citizens and companies of the Social Democratic welfare state are more free to do as they please, rather than less.

Beyond efforts to change the dominant regulatory regimes, regional proponents also aimed to make the region attractive for hesitant businesses in other ways. They began by constructing a new statistical unit, reimagining the two separate sides of the sound as one giant labor market, educational market, transportation network, innovation hub, and the like. Such technical descriptions were designed to make the region more attractive to both individuals and businesses; in making it more attractive, proponents were hoping that the imagined region would transform into reality by way of daily practice.

Armed with this new description, regionalists began to spread the word and to develop on-the-ground projects that promoted the region in many spheres of everyday life. The new subway system being built in Malmö would no longer be promoted as something to help Malmö-ites get around their own town, but would connect them more speedily with Copenhagen; the local governmental employment agencies adopted a joint project to promote labor migration; the Danish business press hosted conferences to inform their readers of the benefits of the region; a new interstate bureaucracy was formed to address regionalist concerns that were not attended to by local bureaucracies; and consulting projects aimed to harmonize best practices in business, tourism, education, and other fields of common human endeavor on both sides of the sound. Whatever field of activity they addressed, all of these endeavors operated by repeating the common refrain that, once the region was finalized, life would be much better, easier, and more efficient. All these efforts and others like them formed much of my ethnographic data, and more detail will be provided as this study progresses.

With such techniques, regional advocates were hoping to conjoin the two welfare states, previously separated by the sound, into one market, with harmonized regulations, mobile labor, and heavy competition. According to these regionalists, once it was completed, the Øresund Region would not only conquer the Scandinavian hegemony of Stockholm, but also outpace many higher-profile powerhouses of Europe, such as Berlin and Hamburg (Øresund Business Integration n.d.: 6).[8]

Europe

Via the EU, the regionalists received vital political, legal, and financial support. In this sense, the region must be seen through a much wider lens, as part of EU-wide movements to transform everyday life across the continent. In other words, the regionalists' vision of a transnational future was itself the result of the transnational flow of ideas and practices.

And those ideas, as the EU's founders would readily agree, largely focused on the goal of achieving solidarity via efficiency rather than via sacrifice. The EU began as a trade treaty, focusing exclusively on the movement of goods, services, labor, and capital (see Peebles 1997). Like the Øresund Region writ large, it has always been committed to expanding and integrating Europe into one giant marketplace. By now, the EU has gone a long way toward creating a borderless Europe. In the fifteen states that joined prior to the 2004 wave of Eastern European accessions, few technical obstacles remain to the flow of the four components of the market; many people think that the main obstacle remaining is the one created by culture (Shore 2000). To wit, though the legal means to do so have long been in effect, many Europeans still fail to move to other countries within the EU for work, fail to switch over to many foreign products, fail to seek the services of a nonlocal bank. It is as if citizens of the EU are oddly clinging to some sort of mechanical solidarity even though they have been presented with all the infrastructure necessary to build a broader and more efficient organic solidarity.

In the face of such intransigence on the part of the consumers and producers who were supposed to happily benefit from the disintegration of national boundaries, the EU has embarked on several programs to promote its transborder regions. These regions are spaces that receive special funding and support in order to promote the growth of a local market that eradicates national borders in everyday life. Although previously the EU had often been scorned as a byzantine bureaucracy located in cosmopolitan Brussels, it is now embarking on boundary-destroying projects that go beyond the market liberalizations that the Treaty of Rome and the European Court of Justice have guaranteed to all EU citizens and their goods and capital. The regions are designed to be microcosmic EUs, attempting to convince local inhabitants to abandon their ties to the nation-state and instead adopt the same cosmopolitan spirit that allegedly prevails in the Brussels bureaucracy.

Andrew Asher (2005) provides a rich ethnographic description of one such transborder region on the Polish-German border. Focusing on the debate over whether Poland should join the EU or not (it did join in 2004), he discerns a similar utopian rhetoric about the limitless possibilities of "becoming European" that I describe throughout this book. As he shows, the regionalization[9] effort on the Polish-German border represented an attempt to "bring the EU home" by making it palpable and meaningful to the people who live within its bounds.

Implicit within much regionalization theory is the idea that nation-states have been encumbering allegedly natural flows of goods, capital, and labor for too long. According to this logic, the market is real and true whereas the nation-state is artificial and arbitrary. Thus, regionalization processes across Europe will finally release these flows from the regulations determined by the arbitrary borders of nation-states. Only the EU can provide the overarching infrastructure to deliver this new, *smaller* community (for the regions are frequently composed of smaller sections of the nation-states to which they belong). In other words, connecting with the broader EU entails moving toward a smaller regional infrastructure and away from the national one. People—nationalists in Scotland, Basque Country (Aretxaga 2005), and Italy's Friuli (Holmes 2000), or regionalists in Sweden and Denmark—voice this paradoxical fact frequently. If, then, the regions are the places where the first kernels of Europeanization will thrive, this new sense of pan-national belonging will have come about, ironically, because of a system of governance claiming to be committed to ever-smaller administrative units, far from anything as broad as "Europe."[10]

Several scholars have shown the many ways in which EU projects have tried to build community solidarity via sameness, so that the scales would fall from people's eyes and they would recognize their alleged always-already-there "Europeanness."[11] Techniques for building a common European culture have included schooling and the creation of new symbols, such as the euro and a flag.[12] Explaining that the EU is both an embryonic state and also a "novel political system," Shore writes that "the EU's supranational organisations are engendering a new type of European subjectivity" (2005: 237, 241). The EU stands as "an embryonic state without a corresponding nation: it has created the political roof for a new system of European governance, but it has yet to create 'Europeans' beyond the elite enclaves of its own institutions" (ibid.: 249).[13]

The regionalization effort in the Øresund Region appears to be one response to this problem. However, regional proponents do not exclusively follow the standard model, outlined by Shore and others, of building a sense of community by crafting a shared identity. Instead, they seem to acknowledge that Europeans living in transborder regions must also bind themselves together via the division of labor and the flow of goods. This was Jean Monnet's vision long ago when he and Robert Schuman proposed the European Coal and Steel Community, the very first step in integrating Europe into one peaceful marketplace. One could even posit, schematically, that Monnet believed that Europe had been riven by war for so long *because* of the mechanical solidarity that dominated each national group; a new infrastructure to build organic solidarity would finally allow peace to prevail. The regionalization efforts are but the latest incarnation of this decades-old agenda.

The Euro

The plan to build a new transborder region overlapped with the plan to introduce a pan-national currency. We should not be surprised, then, to find that people opposed to the region were also opposed to the euro. One stark manner in which the EU could be seen to be promoting Europeanization as well as "domesticating the nation-state" (Shore 2000) was through the introduction and circulation of the euro. The EMU project may well be one of the most impressive accomplishments of the EU to date. Years in the making, the new currency moved into the daily life of hundreds of millions of users with relative ease and no crises (until Greece's in 2010). As a highly trusted object, today it traipses across the globe, well beyond its initial target audience. The political achievement of building the euro is all the more impressive when one remembers that the lion's share of European integration has been achieved undemocratically, through the European Court of Justice. Further, introducing the euro meant that all the participating national banks had to relinquish monetary sovereignty to the European Central Bank, and adopting the euro also involved losing at least a degree of command over fiscal policy. Greece's sizable budget cuts and tax increases of 2010, enacted after deep and sustained pressure from the ECB and euro-zone countries, attest to this loss of control. As if that were not enough, at the time of its unveiling, the euro transcended the daily use of many older currencies in eleven nation-states, and therefore required a huge educational apparatus to train citizens in its value and use (see, e.g., Malaby 2002).

As this study documents ethnographically, the vast array of information dispersed by groups and individuals in favor of the euro in Sweden and Denmark focused on it as part of a general progress toward greater efficiency, economic well-being in a globalizing world, and ease in day-to-day life. Only on exceedingly rare occasions did I hear an appeal to any idea of sacrifice, such as when one wing of the Social Democratic Left would speak of it as a means of rebuilding social democracy at the European level, since it had been dismantled at the national level by the forces of globalization.

Contrariwise, it was much more common for opponents of the euro in both Sweden and Denmark to rely on a rhetoric of sacrifice in order to convince people to reject it; in so doing, they seemingly admitted defeat in the debate on efficiency and ease, and instead tried to convince voters that they should retain the krona (Sweden) or krone (Denmark) because those currencies represented values beyond the realm of the market. For example, proponents of the euro frequently told me that interest rates would be lower if the euro were adopted, thereby making the national economy more vibrant. But more than once when I probed opponents' opinions about this claim, they responded that, if the commitment to the Social Democratic welfare state required a "payment" to the international banking community in the form of higher interest rates, then that would be a sacrifice that the nation should be willing to bear in order to preserve its values.

In the end, both Denmark and Sweden opted out of the remarkable and ambitious new currency union, thereby leaving the Øresund Region with its monetary border long after the new bridge transcended its watery one. Though members of the EU must agree to join the EMU and adopt the euro, Sweden and Denmark are under no actual pressure to do so. And contrary to the ceaseless and emphatic threats in the lead-up to each country's referendum on adopting the euro, their economies seem to be humming right along despite the continued use of their kronor and kroner. The projected doomsday scenarios that were supposed to result from rashly rejecting the euro have yet to materialize.

The Øresund Region's proponents were mightily aware of the dangers of this monetary border to their vision of a transnational future, one even saying that adopting the euro in the region was at least as important as the bridge itself. One high-level worker involved in harmonizing banks across the sound said to me, "In my biased opinion, we are now in the thick of this thing called the region, so the euro only makes it easier, I mean, better. Having only one currency is only a good thing for us." This sort of clear and obvious overlapping between those in favor of the region and those in favor of the euro was what sparked my interest in the relationship between building communities and building currencies.

The Local Currencies

The national debates over the role of money in building (or destroying) community borders were not confined to a choice between the euro and the krona. On the Swedish side of Øresund in 1999–2000, several local currencies were cropping up, which were all designed as Local Exchange and Trading Systems (LETS). Unlike "scrip" money (see Maurer 2005) that can move from person to person and store to store much like a standard currency but within a smaller ambit, these local currencies relied on a catalog of goods and services provided by members of the community. Transactions were effected by filling out a check issued by the community and sending it to the treasurer, who then tabulated the credits and debits in the accounts of the two people involved in the transaction. Consequently, watching the money "change hands" was different from witnessing a typical currency transaction; there was no cash register or making change. This fact highlights an intriguing and important aspect of the local currencies to which I will return: with such currencies, there is no anonymity at all because one has to be a member in order to use them, and one's transactions are recorded by a third party. This unique aspect of local-currencies monetary policy has important consequences.

Local currencies are part of a global movement that has been explored by many scholars to date.[14] Maurer (2005: 45–47) reports that the local-currency movement was first conceptualized and put into practice by Michael Linton in British Columbia, Canada (see his website, www.openmoney.org). He had watched his community's economy decline, consistently reading in the press that the area was simply not attractive to global capital. He began a new local currency, arguing that global capital simply failed to properly measure the capital that he knew remained healthily within his town. A local currency would allow the people in a precisely delimited community to make their own assessments of the monetary price of goods and services. Further, he believed that the local currency would encourage resources to remain in the local area. News of his project spread, and local exchange rings can be found today in many states (see Hart 2001: 272–285).[15]

The local-currency movement stands as an example par excellence of what has come to be known as the antiglobalization movement. Not surprisingly, then, local currencies tend to be popular in spaces that have seen the rapid contraction or exportation of capital. The local currencies are seen as a method to enclose capital's otherwise global movement.

Significantly, as Maurer (2005) details in his ethnographic work on the local-currency movement in Ithaca, New York, the movement also has "homegrown" theorists, who have published treatises on local currencies that explore why they are good at sustaining communities, why they are ethically superior to national money, and how to help them spread (Douthwaite 1996; Greco 1994; Kennedy 1995; Lietaer 2001). As if on cue, I encountered some of these same treatises when I first met local-currency advocates. In other words, it is a self-conscious movement, aware of the need to both propagate and theorize its actions.

Generally speaking, people attracted to the local-currency movement in Sweden were drawn to it out of either an environmentalist ethos or a communitarian one, or both. They came from all walks of life, generations, and career paths, but they all shared this foundation. My first encounter with the local-currency movement occurred when I stumbled onto a self-published magazine by a group of ecologically minded roommates. Here was sacrifice incarnated as tabloid: their journal required much effort to produce and it was not for sale, but rather just scattered for free across potential reading sites in Malmö, such as cafes. In no possible fashion could this journal have made money for them; rather, they labored to produce the magazine in order to promote their vision of the future. After reading a few articles, I decided to contact them.

Notably, even sharing an apartment in Sweden constitutes idiosyncratic behavior.[16] But here were four grown men all sharing living space and political views; in fact, the sharing of the living space, they explained, was itself a political statement. Brandishing some of the central texts of the global local-currency movement, they told me of a future of small autarkic villages, where money would no longer be hoarded for personal gain and instead would be used exclusively to facilitate the exchange of other goods. In these villages, consumption would be reduced, as would class hierarchy. Such a life would entail sacrifice: everything would require a bit more work, and temptations would need to be denied.

This radical vision of a much more rural future was mostly inspired by certain elements within the global environmentalist movement. Theorizing a special kind of currency to circulate in such villages was merely a means to an end. Still, the currency was essential. Only by embracing a local currency could temptations be kept in check; it was too easy for internationally recognized currencies to flit away on any passing whim. Currency must be controlled anew by the local community, otherwise, consumption and class distinction would increase. In Marxian terms, the community would reestablish its control over capital, rather than being controlled by it.

Sitting in Malmö on the eve of the Øresund Bridge's completion, it was inevitable that this group would have opinions about the region. I learned that the region was opposed to all in which they believed. For them, it was oriented toward overconsumption, waste, speed, and a needless proliferation of choices provided by a globe-spanning market. The autarkic village and its local currency would seek out slower times. Hearing all this and comparing it to the rhetoric of the euro-loving proponents of the Øresund Region confirmed my belief that one could study the Øresund Region by studying currency choice.

Once I knew of the existence of this movement, I found other local-currency rings. Four such rings were either formed or in the process of being formed in Sweden, and I participated in the initial planning of one of them; others existed in Denmark, with which the Swedish ones were in diffuse contact. The local currencies were, in many ways, the anti-euro. As the euro promised to exponentially expand people's monetary boundaries, the local currencies proposed to shrink these boundaries down to almost Lilliputian dimensions. But both the euro and the emergent local currencies emanated from disappointment with the nation-state's regulations. I was witnessing what Roitman (2004) would call a "pluralization of regulatory authority." Some people were actively looking for alternatives to what they viewed as the failed efforts of the nation-state to generate a sense of bounded community via everyday monetary transactions.

Methodology

Sweden, because of its prominence as a beacon of the modernist spirit, turned out to be a particularly appropriate vantage point from which to view the factors that would contribute to the success or failure of these bold experiments. During the twentieth century, Swedes became famous for their mixed socialist economy, fondly dubbed the "People's Home." By modeling the entire country as a giant home, the social welfare state strove to protect its citizens from the irrationalities and vicissitudes of the market. As with much smaller homes, the influence of monetary value was supposed to be minimized or even hidden. Moral values, instead of the quantitative economic values indexed by money, were supposed to guide individual decision making. As such, the People's Home was intended as a space of regulation and order—a place that often mapped the dangers of the market onto notions of "the foreign." Indeed, the Swedish People's Home was so successfully regulated that foreign space achieved a liminal status for Swedes: traveling abroad granted a freedom to embrace the dangers and wilds of the market that were tamed in the home.

This bifurcation of homes and markets has a long history in capitalist modernity, and is not unique to Sweden. As Keith Hart writes: "The modern economy consists of two complementary spheres that have to be kept separate, despite their interdependence. One of them is a zone of infinite scope where things and, increasingly, human creativity are bought and sold for money, the market. The second is a protected zone of domestic life where intimate personal relations hold sway, home" (Hart 2001: 211–212). Sweden merely implemented this folk logic at the national level, thereby embedding the distinction even more profoundly in the lives of its citizenry. By ethnographically detailing both the use and the monetary policy of the multiple currencies in circulation in the Øresund Region, I hope to provide insights into the ways in which this distinction between homes and markets may be undergoing shifts today.

Because Sweden is so famously described as a "home" and the Øresund Region (and the EU) so famously described as a "market," I will ground this ethnography by studying the successes and failures of Swedes in integrating with their Danish counterparts. I am interested in how they are using the new space of the Øresund Region, as well as how they fought for and against it.

In order to show what people were fighting for or against, the historical background is crucial to this story. Therefore, each chapter will provide a brief historical investigation of the topic being covered—whether it is the idea of utopia or the manner in which bankrupts used to hide money in the past. Providing this background allows me to gradually detail the history of the building of a paradigmatically modernist nation-state— Sweden—in order to show how it confronted some paradigmatically post-modernist challenges from the EU and the transformations that its proponents hoped to usher in.

Beyond this historical evidence, my ethnographic evidence relies on multiple vectors of data. I tracked and traced the activities of both the local-currency movements and the many Øresund Regionalization efforts, interviewing members of both groups and attending many conferences and meetings. I attended informational sessions (of which there were endless opportunities in the lead-up to the bridge opening), meeting leaders there and also in their offices. I spoke with friends and strangers alike about the Øresund Region, which was an easy topic of conversation at the time, with the bridge construction afoot. I assembled a wide range of opinions on the regionalization effort and currency use, which I supplemented by gathering documents from political parties, interest groups, and the press. Beyond this, I also spoke with people not involved in the debate, for example, talking to travelers and vendors in stores about currency usage and the types of consumption to which it was attached.

To develop a consistent approach to all these data, I traced three particular discourses about monetary usage and rhetoric that emerged frequently in the divergent visions of the future of the Øresund Region. I will argue that people use each currency I am tracing (the euro, the local currencies, the Swedish kronor, and the Danish kroner) in order to enact particular commitments to (1) the hidden or transparent nature of wealth and transactions, (2) elevating either labor (or sacrifice) or leisure (or ease) as a moral good, and (3) whether goods and people should be mobile or stable.

By linking the prevalent opinions regarding these discourses with the currencies and their usage, important elements of the arguments about the euro and the Øresund Region come to light. I will be using these oppositions in order to elucidate the shifting moralities that attach themselves to currency and how people occasionally try to slip outside of these governing moralities. In this manner, I will show how each currency, as a concrete instantiation of abstract money in the lived world (see Dodd 2005), carries with it moralities that can be explicated via these oppositions. By tracing these discourses, I will show how currency structure, rhetoric, and use can help to build or erase the boundaries between homes and markets, thereby either consolidating or undermining the Øresund Region.

Because I am interested in how currencies are used in conjunction with (and to reinforce) social borders, each chapter is attuned to how different currency adherents viewed, utilized, and crossed the border separating Denmark and Sweden, and how these practices and beliefs have been changing as a result of the emerging Øresund Region. While many people in favor of the euro were excited about the region, local-currency adherents were often strongly opposed to its existence. Consequently, I detail the uses and rhetoric of the euro and the local currencies, but I also provide in-depth description of the uses and rhetoric surrounding the Swedish kronor and Danish kroner, by far the most dominant currencies on the respective sides of the sound. Chapters 1 and 2 offer background in the theory and history of the utopian "idea of Europe" and the various attempts to control capital via currency that have led to the contemporary visions of both the local currencies and the euro. These ideas and their histories will provide readers with the background needed to delve into the more detailed ethnographic case studies of chapters 3, 4, and 5, which cover, respectively, the movement of goods, the movement of people, and the movement of capital.

These discussions paint a picture of the ways in which the emerging Øresund Region stood as an emblem of the EU and its drive to solve, in novel ways, the problems posed by the separation of homes and markets. Local actors relied on EU bureaucrats, spending initiatives, and legal shifts to try to convince people that they would eventually find a new home in the Øresund Region's flowing market, while other locals were combating this drive toward building a new, transnational city. Documenting the efforts of the Øresund Region's proponents and opponents as they helped to construct these paths, or tried to stop them from emerging, will offer a window into the typically more obscured relationship between the construction of currency and the construction of social space. Along the way, I will probe into some embryonic forms of community-building, to see whether the old processes of nation-building or the new processes of region-building will translate into the formation of that currently elusive transnational, the Øresundian.

ONE

Imagining Utopia,
Constructing Øresund

From the Nation-State to the Region

If you can dream it, you can do it!

—*A "Disney maxim" cited by a Danish speaker at a business conference on the potential of the Øresund Region*

The utopian imagination, contrary to what many believe, is not dead (see Jacoby 1999; Kumar 1993; Marin 1993). Just as with past utopias, wild new dreams were projected onto the Øresund Region. As with old utopian visions, many battled against its creation, while countless others were merely uninterested—often precisely because the program struck them as fantastical. But either way, utopia, as espoused in Europe during the embryonic stages of the Øresund Region, was in many ways the inverse of past utopias. While older visions of utopia imagined spaces of order and stability, the Øresund Region relied much more on a neoliberal vision of "freeing" the flows of the forces of capitalist production.

The Øresund Region was a place notable for its "intense mythification of progress" (Coronil 1997: 5), where there was constant discussion of a potential utopian future. People attempted to craft their future in response to shifts in Sweden's relationship with a larger Europe; each camp in this debate over possible futures became one of the groups of my ethnographic inquiry. The Øresund Region served as the "heterotopia"[1] where these opposing groups of utopians attempted to fashion their respective visions of society.

Contextualizing the Øresund Region within the broader utopian tradition draws attention to the wide gaps between the ideal and the reality of the entire EU project. We can thereby notice the ways in which utopian thought has been far from inconsequential. Instead, it has been fundamental in the modernist commitment to perfection and constant progress, and as such, many utopian visions have had a substantial impact on the material world, as the epigraph above, a quote from a proponent of the Øresund Region, proclaims.[2]

Modern Europe is no stranger to these utopian visions, dreams, and attempted projects. Though utopian literature usually takes place in an imaginary world, it is no stretch to say that often these political programs are attempted on the ground. As Claeys tells us, " [U]topias helped to flesh out tentative visions of the ideal modern future, and to project imaginatively what would often later become programme, dogma and even reality" (Claeys 1994: xxviii). Europe has often found itself trying to complete some purported (r)evolutionary project in order to finally arrive at (or return to) a mythic golden age. Indeed, even the Cold War can be easily read as a debate over which side could most successfully institute the best possible society.

The modern age has thus been marked by a fixation on progress and betterment; in the case of Europe, the progress and betterment were to be achieved most often by a championing of science and rationality, though there have, of course, been romanticist and other reactions to this current that have been highly influential. This teleology, directed toward future perfection, necessarily has a utopian bent. But more detail is needed if we are to understand the ways in which certain general trends have developed over time and thereby framed the debate over how to build "perfect" societies. Kumar tries to sum up the battles among leftist utopian visions by claiming:

> Utopia was born of modernity. It was a product of that burst of thought and activity that we call the Renaissance and the Reformation. It blends Hellenic rationalism, the hallmark of Renaissance thought, with the democratizing impulse of Western Christianity that found outlet in the Protestant Reformation. . . . The two have indeed been in some kind of tension throughout the history of utopia. The rationalism of utopia has frequently led to a predilection for highly centralized and regulated, not to say regimented, social systems. The democratic and egalitarian

strands have countered with utopias that stress decentralized power and local solidarities. . . . It too embodies the often conflicting pulls of the need for order and the desire for freedom, the advantages of centralized large-scale organization and the claims of local autonomy and individual creativity. (Kumar 1991: 51)

In the Øresund Region, I found these discordant strands echoing again and again, in the debates over both the EU and the Øresund and in the past debates over how to build Sweden's People's Home that aimed to secure basic stability for its entire citizenry with cradle-to-grave welfare benefits.

That this utopian space called the Øresund Region was attempting to come into being in Sweden is highly apt and instructive, for Sweden came to be known as the foremost exemplar of a modern utopia during the twentieth century. Sweden, in so many ways, has been the paradigmatic modern Western nation-state—often considered as "perfect" a state as possible by countless theorists and supporters outside its borders. In this chapter, I will delineate the competing visions of utopia offered by Sweden and the EU / Øresund Region.

Sweden as Utopia

In addition to all the utopian literature written in Sweden since the 1770s (see Henriksson-Holmberg 1913; Ambjörnsson 1981; Quiding 1978 [1886]; Strindberg 1987 [1885]),[3] many observers, both foreign and local, have asserted that the country itself is an actual utopia. Indeed, in my opinion, it is impossible to approach a study of Sweden and the Øresund Region without grasping the extent to which it was considered the perfect land by countless writers, politicians, and cultural critics during the twentieth century.[4] Sweden had impressed so many people by the 1950s that it was standard for international teams of researchers and politicians to come on study tours to witness the intricate workings of the welfare state firsthand.[5] Sweden, a land that apparently elevated "the empirical" and "scientific knowledge" (Tomasson 1970: 276), had itself become an experiment and a well-known laboratory for the rest of the world (see Ruth 1984; Graubard 1984: v–vi). Thus, the "Swedish model" and its proponents were born.

An American named Marquis Childs began this laudatory wave in 1936 with the publication of *Sweden: The Middle Way* (a pamphlet preceded it in 1934). The book was a sleeper hit, with eight printings in 1936 alone. This was the nadir of the Great Depression, so people were looking for alternatives to the apparently massive failures and social disruptions of unencumbered capitalism. Childs began a sort of cottage industry, writing on the successes of Sweden: his book saw a total of fifteen printings by 1947. Childs lured his readership with dramatic claims: "If one were compelled to select in the present moment of flux and chaos a certain area of the earth's surface in order to show the highest good that Western civilization had up to the present achieved, one might go farther and do worse than to choose Scandinavia" (Childs 1934: 5; note Childs' assertion that flux and chaos are unattractive elements of the contemporary global order). To give a sense of the attractiveness of this model compared to others, Childs wrote bluntly:

> Sweden is almost the only country in the world in which capitalism has "worked" during recent decades. Checking the evolutionary development of capitalism at the point at which monopoly tends to distort the cycle of prosperity and depression, the Swedes seem to have interrupted the process of self-destruction which marked the economic life of other industrialized countries. In a sense it is the only country where *laissez faire* has continued to exist; where the so-called "laws" of supply and demand have not been wholly invalidated by the spread of monopoly. . . . The degree of *laissez faire* that has continued to exist in Sweden is, in a manner of speaking, hothouse *laissez faire*. It exists under a bell-jar. The state, the consumer, and the producer have intervened to make capitalism "work" in a reasonable way for the greatest good of the whole nation. (Childs 1936: 160–161)[6]

At a time when capitalism was deemed chaotic, Childs presented Sweden as the world's savior of capitalism; in high modernist fashion, this capitalism needed to be "controlled." By finding the middle ground between "the uncontrolled capitalism of America before the crash and the arbitrary Marxian communism of Russia before the Stalin modifications of a year ago" (Childs 1934: 8–9), Sweden had accomplished this better than any other country. In a variety of chapters, including studies of cooperatives and one called "Liquor Control That Works," Childs outlined the "rational" nature of the Swedish system.

Many authors followed him. Several accounts per decade came from the realms of journalism, political science, or sociology, from Childs' era to our own.[7] The many hagiographers of the state who waxed eloquent on Sweden's perfection were also enamored with its distinct moderation, another quality that made it modern, rational, and non-ideological. As the "middle way," Sweden had positioned itself as the perfect happy medium in a Europe famously divided into communist East and capitalist West.[8] Swedes themselves acknowledged and accepted this position frequently. Thus, Adler-Karlsson explained:

> Sweden has been called "the middle way." . . . We do not have any accepted theory of the middle-way economy of Sweden. One explanation for the lack of a well-established theory for our own system may be found in one of the essential points of it, namely its highly practical and pragmatic character. We do not like to play around with vague, abstract, almost meaningless concepts like capitalism or communism. Instead we try to define our concrete problems, and endeavour to solve them in a practical spirit. (Adler-Karlsson 1969: 9)

Adler-Karlsson then proceeded to advocate the Swedish model's middle way as, among other things, a means of achieving global peace and averting a third world war (ibid.: 10).

Others have agreed that Sweden has served as a model to the world.[9] For example, Peter Hall, a world-renowned expert on cities, includes a chapter on "The Social Democratic Utopia: Stockholm 1945–80" in his survey of globally and historically significant cities (Hall 1998). In this book, Stockholm (quite a small city, as he points out) enjoys the privilege of being discussed along with such world-historical cities as London, Athens, Paris, New York, Los Angeles, and Rome. It is worth studying because Stockholm "came to be seen as the living embodiment, the showcase, of a society they sought proudly to create as a model for the world. . . . [By the 1950s and '60s] it became known worldwide as the quintessence of a social philosophy [social democracy], realized on the ground" (Hall 1998: 843).

Indeed, one author suggested that Sweden may have achieved such utopian perfection that it was worth asking the question "Is Sweden Boring?" (Jenkins 1968).[10] From this perspective, we can see that the rise and fall in popularity of Sweden as a model society had little to do with the famous decline of the welfare state. Rather, it had more to do with the currents swirling outside of Sweden: the alternating excitement and disappointment with which it was viewed over the decades indexes the shifting allegiances of the global Left and Right. With Sweden's changing reputation, we witness the epistemic shuttling between the global popularity of a regulated, welfare-state modernity and of an unregulated, laissez-faire economic liberalism.

In order to build this Social Democratic utopia that was so inspiring to both detractors and proponents across the globe, several Swedish politicians seized upon the metaphorical distinction between the predictability of the home and the chaos of the market. These politicians relied on the idea that, even in turbulent times, the home remained a place where people believed that the laws of the market were nullified and inconsequential. Foreshadowing a much more famous speech by a full fifteen years, a member of parliament named Lindhagen stated in a motion that "society should be organized like a good home" (Tingsten 1941: 228). With speeches such as these, the market slowly became characterized as an amoral force, with "laws" that needed to be held at bay and relegated to special spheres; meanwhile, ethics remained in the home, and in this giant home, ethics could conquer the "science" of the economy. Social efforts could be channeled and manipulated, rather than be subservient to the tyranny of supply and demand. When reading debates from this era, one constantly comes across the word "regulate." Capitalism was productive but irrational, and a rational society must therefore regulate the economy.

Per Albin Hansson, the prime minister of Sweden from 1932 to 1946, brought this metaphor of the nation as home to legendary heights when he gave a speech to the parliament in 1928. Delineating the projected People's Home for the first time, he argued: "In the good home, equality, consideration, cooperation and helpfulness prevail. Applied to the great people's and citizens' home, this would mean the breakdown of all social and economic barriers, which now divide citizens into privileged and neglected, into dominating and dependent, into rich and poor, propertied and pauperized, plunderers and plundered" (Tingsten 1941: 307–308).

One of the essential aspects of this speech, Tingsten says, is that it marked a final departure from the fixation on "socializing the means of production" that the Social Democrats had considered a primary goal for many decades. Such nationalization programs (after much internal debate and attempted expert studies) were abandoned to the unknown future.

Nationalizations of various industries might someday happen, but it would not be a priority to bring them forth; instead, the nation would let the market take care of itself until the "conditions were right."[11] In other words, instead of exclusively focusing on controlling production with a planned economy, the Social Democrats would instead choose to develop something closer to the middle ground by focusing on organizing consumption via a slowly growing host of welfare benefits (and, during the war years, straightforward rations). In order to properly examine the Øresund Region, it is important to note the specific ways in which the modern welfare state that preceded it sought to stabilize and regulate flows in time and space, shaping over the decades of the twentieth century a "home" sphere that was safely separated from the anarchic amorality of the "foreign" economy.

The EU as Utopia

Sweden's experiences as it entered into the EU (January 1, 1995) and debated the EMU project speak particularly well to the changing debates over how to organize society in Europe today. Because much of the EU project is decidedly oriented toward promoting the benefits of the market rather than the home, Sweden's long engagement with social democracy and its middle way have been significantly impacted. Sweden's particular history, as a state that many consider to have achieved the zenith of modernity, means that the EU and EMU stand as grander challenges to the status quo there than in many other countries.

Yet even the discourse of building a pan-national Europe is older than the EU proponents typically acknowledged. Despite the continual claims of politicians that the ideals organizing the EU were "unprecedented," the cosmopolitan ideal of building organic solidarity via efficiency is a very old one indeed. Here, for example, is a quote from Saint-Simon (a central figure in early nineteenth-century utopian thought), proposing an essentially borderless Europe united by trade and industry:

> Montesquieu said that men are formed by institutions; thus, this tendency of patriotism to extend beyond the frontiers of country, this habit of considering European interests before national ones, will be an inevitable result of the establishment of a European parliament for those

called upon to form it. . . . It is therefore essential to admit to the chamber of deputies of the European parliament—that is, to one of the two active powers of the European constitution—only those men whose wider contacts, freedom from parochialism, participation in activities whose uses are not purely national but extend beyond their own country, make them better able to achieve the universal outlook, which should make up the European *esprit de corps,* and to promote the general interest which must also be the corporate interest of the European parliament. Business men, scientists, judges and administrators only should be called upon to form the chamber of deputies of the great parliament. For, indeed, everything which tends to the common good of European society can be related to the sciences, arts, legislation, commerce, administration and industry. (Saint-Simon 1976: 89–90)

This call for cosmopolitanism, written by Saint-Simon in 1814, echoes much of what one hears regarding the EU today (e.g., Shore 2000, 2005; Balibar 2004; Bellier and Wilson 2000; Berezin and Schain 2003). Further, Saint-Simon adamantly campaigned for a Europe united under one government (and his followers later advocated for a single currency; see chapter 2), yet he wanted each country to still retain some degree of national sovereignty. This was very much the model and goal of the EU as the Øresund Region was being built. Likewise, the EU pushed forward a Saint-Simonian commitment to trade and industry moving across the old borders that had previously constrained them.[12]

The EU modeled itself as a utopia for a new age, and it employed many means to promote itself to an oddly indifferent public.[13] Innumerable pamphlets, brochures, newsletters, and information centers served to alert the public to the benefits of the EU, their rights within this new regime, and the upcoming bonuses of the euro.[14] A free children's comic book entitled *The Raspberry Ice Cream War* (European Union Commission 1998) explained how the EU would be a union with no war, freedom to travel, and commendable cooperation between nations, all achieved by embracing the goal of efficiency over sacrifice.[15] More bluntly, Jacques Santer, the former president of the European Commission, stated that the EMU "only a short while ago, [would] have appeared Utopian" (Santer 1998: 1). Santer, in pointing this out along with the successes in the implementation of the EMU project, was essentially claiming that he led a project so grandiose and meritorious that it came close to successfully establishing a form of utopia in real life.

Since its founding, the EU has always claimed to be the only solution to a Europe constantly riven by war and divisive nationalities. Its integrative policy would finally bring peace and prosperity to the continent. Many a commentator has noted the utopian edicts written into the EU's Maastricht Treaty, which promises to promote a "harmonious and balanced development of economic activities, sustainable and non-inflationary growth respecting the environment, a high degree of convergence of economic performance, a high level of employment and of social protection, the raising of the standard of living and quality of life, and economic and social cohesion and solidarity among Member States" (European Union 1992: Part I, Article 2).[16] Of course, here we encounter a host of goals that are only rarely simultaneously realizable,[17] and it is equally noteworthy that these goals speak of virtually nothing beyond the economic sphere. In the EU system that existed at the time of the building of the Øresund Region, people were (legally speaking) considered primarily in their embodiment as the prototypical *Homo economicus*; the entire governing apparatus of the EU revolved around freeing the constraints upon this rational individual, who would maximize societal gains by seeking his own self-preservation. In this vision, individualism and hierarchy reigned supreme over any commitments to group solidarity or egalitarianism. Ease and the efficiency of the division of labor prevailed over the notion of sacrifice.[18]

The EU thus imagined itself quite differently from Sweden's modernist model of statehood and membership. As D'Oliveira says, the very categories of inclusion and exclusion were different in the EU. He explains that "the core and origin of Union citizenship is the right to free movement. Mobility is the central element, around which other rights crystallize" (D'Oliveira 1995: 65). This definition of citizenship is, for D'Oliveira, so novel as to be illegitimate; he calls the citizenship granted under Article 8 of the Maastricht Treaty a "gross misnomer" (ibid.: 84).[19] EU citizenship certainly remains a far cry from the traditional "soil or blood" notions of membership (Therborn 1995: 87; Shaw 2010), and also deviated from Anderson's (1983) famous claim of an "imagined community" centered around shared memory, media, or language.[20] In fact, the EU resolutely refused to be defined by common history or language;[21] instead, the community was bound together by its vision of a common future of growth, peace, and profit.

The EU thus openly embraced the values of the market. The EU's trademark was the dissolution of nation-state boundaries (though it erected new boundaries elsewhere) and often the weakening of the member states' powers of jurisdiction.[22] Within its jurisdiction, movement was prioritized over any form of Swedish stability. Capital, goods, services, and people were all encouraged to be fluid: flout common conventions and thereby innovate, leap over national boundaries and thereby expand one's business, travel to foreign lands and thereby broaden one's horizons. The EU aimed to facilitate the destruction of boundaries in social practice by removing them in legal practice and by funding their transgression in education and employment practices. I would venture to say that virtually all pamphlets produced by the EU had some mention, somewhere, of the significance of travel and movement, and how they should be lauded and encouraged in order to actualize the EU's utopian vision.

The EU is thus an emergent quasi-state apparatus trying to regulate flows of goods and people, marking new delineations of acceptable and unacceptable movement. The creation of the Øresund Region provides an excellent opportunity to witness the clash of different regimes of regulation, for in this space one could still find the older, regulated flows of credit and debt in independent Sweden and Denmark while these flows competed with the emergent ones encouraged by the EU.

Øresund Region as Utopia

The EU's regionalization programs, including the Øresund Region, were formed as a series of bi- and trinational regions scattered across Europe. The EU funded these areas with special disbursements that aimed to enhance the cultural, commercial, educational, and governmental bonds of each specific region. These areas were often claimed to have a "natural" component of an underlying common culture or economic cooperation that had merely been jaundiced by centuries of nation-state rhetoric and policy. The implicit logic of the regionalizers asserted that nation-state boundaries and policies were unnatural, whereas regionalization plans were but an expression of underlying natural coherence and commonality. Bureaucracies were set up to promote the zones, massive infrastructure projects were commissioned to tie the regions together, and local businesses banded together to create new chambers of commerce. To put it most simply, the regions were the places where the EU hoped to cultivate its most enthusiastic constituents, those who would live the EU dreams of mobility and transnationalism.[23]

The Øresund Region included a physical incarnation of transnational integration in the form of a massive bridge-tunnel complex that was inaugurated on July 1, 2000, connecting the cities of Copenhagen and Malmö (see Berg, Linde-Laursen, and Löfgren 2000, 2002). Beyond this evident scaffolding, there also existed an interstate bureaucracy, called the Øresundskomiteen, whose stated goal was to

> strengthen and illuminate the region nationally and internationally, in order to thereby build the foundation for increased growth in the region—in economic, cultural, and social perspectives. . . . The Øresund Committee builds bridges that can not be seen with the naked eye, but that for people, industries, and organizations who are near one another, opens up new roads and creates new possibilities. (Øresundskomiteen 1998: 1)

The committee worked to bring forward the common social and cultural identities of the two nationalities that comprise the region, via the encouragement of the fluidity facilitated by roads and bridges, both physical and metaphorical.[24] Once people recognized these similarities, it was believed that they would actively encourage the continued growth of the region. Swedes would naturally wish to travel to Copenhagen for work and would start to see that they had more common interest with the northeastern Danes than with their compatriots in northern Sweden. The implication was that the nation-states had actively discouraged the natural bonds that supposedly united the Øresund Region. The committee and other groups were there to restore the natural order, which had been distorted by centuries of state policy. In the rhetoric of regionalizers, there are hints of a logic that declares business activity to be natural, while any nation-state activity is unnatural. The solidaristic comforts of the People's Home were being replaced with the hierarchical strivings of the people's market.

After a century that took the nation-state to be the apex of political evolution, the emergence of these regions was nothing short of a threat to that typical form. The regions directly called into question the boundaries of the nation-state and often unabashedly undermined its sovereignty and authority. One article published by a prominent agitator for the region argued that southern Sweden would eventually be an autonomous unit within a looser Swedish federation; its future would "be decided more by cooperation with Denmark, Northern Germany and other parts of northern Europe than by cooperation with northern Sweden" (Andersson n.d.a: 3). The article asserted that taxes would stop flowing to Stockholm, that a new southern Swedish parliament would be created, and that the region would flourish in its newfound return to its "true" local heritage (ibid.). A Skånsk-Swedish-Danish dictionary was published to assert that the region even had its own distinctive language, rather than just being a mere dialect of Swedish. A reviewer insisted that "skånskan is its own language with roots in a Skåne, which existed prior to both Danish and Swedish conquerors" (Andersson n.d.b).[25]

But this sort of reliance on the Swedish-Danish border as a device for forging new political blocs is far older than this example of resistance to the nation-state. Linde-Laursen (1995, 2010) traces the creation of the boundary in Øresund from 1658 onward, and Idvall (2000) tells the tales of projects that aimed to break down the border in the past. The first agitations to establish more speedy and consistent connections emerged from the mid-nineteenth century political movement known as Scandinavism, when the countries of Norway, Sweden, and Denmark sought to work together and join their *broderfolk* (brother people) together (see Nilsson 2000).[26] Merchants were also hollering for the quicker movement of goods across the sound. The steamboat initially sufficed to meet this need. Not much later, however, people started clamoring for an "underwater bridge" through the sound, and several proposals emerged in the 1870s and '80s. Idvall tells the history of how these projects fared in each national parliament and which concerns were the order of the day (Idvall 2000: 40–91).

These proposals tied into a surging fascination of the period, railroad speculation, that demanded a fully connected European railway net. Foundationally, this was a project conceived of by Saint-Simonians; they scanned the European map, outlined centers and peripheries, and sought to ensure that all roads led to Paris. Sicily would get a bridge, England would receive a tunnel, Ireland a tunnel as well, and one François Deloncle proposed in 1886 that a tunnel be built to connect Sweden to Europe.[27] No land mass was overlooked in this pursuit of pure connectivity.

Deloncle had his competitors. Various Swedes and Danes were also putting together projects. Idvall makes the astute observation (as he does in another piece [1997] covering a different time period) that often the support or disdain a proposal received was dependent upon the interests it promoted: international, national, regional. The Saint-Simonian proposal (being a utopian vision of limitless progress and commerce and Europe-wide peace) was internationally focused, while other proposals addressed such issues as the military benefits of a tunnel for Sweden. In other words, despite the fact that the material nature of the link would be the same—a tunnel on the bottom of the sound—people at different times argued that it would serve different purposes. As Idvall (1997) shows, in the 1960s all proposals were organized around promoting a national Swedish interest, and therefore the tunnel would "naturally" be best suited if it connected the towns of Helsingør and Helsingborg, rather than the cities of Malmö and Copenhagen.[28] Despite this, today there is a bridge-tunnel connecting the latter two cities, while ferries still ply the waters between Helsingør and Helsingborg. Idvall explains that this occurred because in the 1990s the region became the paramount concern, and national concerns lost out. The focus had shifted from "how fast can we transport goods from *all* of Sweden to the European continent?" to "how well can we connect the citizens of southern Sweden with the vibrancy that Copenhagen could provide for them?"

What is quite surprising is that the EU unwittingly reproduced the original map of the Saint-Simonian railway net (see Darian-Smith 1999: 129 for a map of the planned net). Like the Saint-Simonians, the EU also adver-tised its plans to connect all of Europe, including Sicily and seemingly far-flung islands in Denmark, with a vast interconnected system of railroads, bridges, and tunnels. Here is a true Saint-Simonian fixation on pure connec-tion and the ability of a produced material world to conjure forth "commu-nity" entirely on its own. The creation of the Øresund Region obviously echoes this old utopian project and hence, as mentioned above, also meshes ideologically with the EU project itself.[29]

The Øresund Region presents a major challenge to previously well-accepted theories regarding the role of movement in the construction of social space and time. As many have insisted, the railroads of the nineteenth century were essential to the standardization of national spaces and creat-ing a sense that one was connected to a wider imagined community. As more-local space and time continua were annihilated by the railroad—its speed and its rigorous schedule—people became more accustomed to its particular domination of space and time (see Cronon 1991; Harvey 1989; Schivelbusch 1979; Frykman and Löfgren 1996 [1979]; De Certeau 1984). This is connected to a broader belief in movement's ability to create social space, best expressed by De Certeau (1984: 98–99):

> [I]f it is true that a spatial order organizes an ensemble of
> possibilities . . . and interdictions . . . , then the walker actualizes some
> of these possibilities. In that way, he makes them exist as well as
> emerge. But he also moves them about and he invents others, since the
> crossing, drifting away, or improvisation of walking privilege, transform
> or abandon spatial elements. . . . the walker constitutes, in relation to
> his position, both a near and a far, a here and a there.

Meanwhile, Virilio concerns himself more with the power of the bourgeoisie and its state apparatus in controlling this movement: "We could even say that the rise of totalitarianism goes hand-in-hand with the development of the state's hold over the circulation of the masses."[30] But taking these two respected theorists together, there is still something missing, for even if people started moving across the sound as much as some had hoped, many people remained skeptical that any new space would emerge. In fact, the same Lund scholars who insisted that the railways contributed to the creation of a Swedish national identity and communally shared sense of space and time were hesitant to claim that the new railway connection between Sweden and Denmark would promote anything similar with regard to a regional identity (personal communications; also see Löfgren 1999; Frykman and Löfgren 1996 [1979]).

Perhaps something else is at work here (and was part of the previous building of nation-states as well). Apparently, the sheer materiality of a bridge or a railroad is not enough to make people move and to create a sense of community. Human relations and shifting moral configurations are also significant. One cannot merely build a bridge. People must have a sense of why they need to cross it.

Clearly, the Øresund Region's utopian vision was tied up with the notion of mobility and flows. But in order to better grasp what obstacles lurked in the path of Øresund's ability to become a truly transnational space, it is important to fine-tune the nature of this embrace of mobility and flow. The space around Øresund, prior to its designation as a new region, had a very specific history relating labor and leisure to the construction of space and time. As Sweden's southernmost city since 1658, Malmö has always been an important port of trade. Goods and ideas have always flowed across the channel.[31] Malmö, it is worth noting, had also long been considered Sweden's classic industrial city; a common description was that it was a *trist industristad*—a dreary industrial town.

Yet, despite this intense connection with the world outside Sweden, the vast majority of goods that people consumed in Malmö were not from Denmark, and similarly, it was hard to find standard Swedish goods while in Denmark. In fact, much of the advertisement related to visiting Copenhagen revolved around the exotic goods one could consume there. A more lighthearted example of this phenomenon occurred on SAS flights to Copenhagen, which were as likely to be filled with Malmö-ites as Danes. If a passenger asked for a beer in Swedish, he would get a typical Swedish beer, but if he asked for it in Danish, he received the most famous Danish beer. Separate consumption of this sort was deeply rooted in the daily practices of Swedes and Danes in the Øresund Region. In the late 1990s and early 2000s, proponents of the region frequently complained about the lack of a network of services; cell phones, for example, failed to span the sound and thereby kept Copenhagen from feeling like home to Swedes.

For decades, travel across the sound had mostly been associated with leisure (see Linde-Laursen 1995 and 2010). As a trip to the "near-abroad," Swedes infamously let loose upon the launching of the hourly boat from their shore. A whole culture of *att tura* (touring) revolved around hopping on any boat—crossing in one of three different parts of the sound, and partying and shopping tax-free. *Att tura* was a specific rite of passage for Swedish youth (kids in Gothenburg and Stockholm still undertake these international journeys on the ferries, but they call upon different ports— either ones in Finland or Frederikshavn in Denmark). The larger boats contained discotheques and bars, and it was common to spot vomit on the carpet somewhere during the crossing (see chapters 3 and 4 for more detail on this tradition).

Other rites of passage were attached to specific rituals of consumption and purchasing. For example, as soon as passengers would board the cheaper boat from Malmö to Copenhagen (up until the year 2000, there were two ferry companies traversing the sound), no matter what the time of day, a line would form in order to buy beer, which was often accompanied by a shot of Gammel Dansk, a Danish hard liquor. (It is significant, of course, that I never spotted similar behavior on the part of the Danes.) Then, after the boat crossed a certain line in the water en route to Copenhagen, a "pling" would sound, and an attendant would announce that they were now selling cigarettes; at this announcement, another line immediately sprang into existence. One final example: for environmental reasons, all beverage cans are illegal in Denmark (only plastic and glass bottles are allowed). At this time, then, cans were only for sale in one place. When Swedes boarded the boat to travel home when leaving Copenhagen, they had one last chance to buy cheap cases of canned beer literally right before they stepped onto the boat, i.e., after clarifying that they were leaving Denmark. In this manner, the state of Denmark ensured that the unwanted trash in the form of cans would be taken abroad while the country made money at home.

Within Copenhagen itself, an entire industry of leisurely consumption was directed toward the Swedes. Indeed, once I learned the city intimately, I discovered that there were very specific places and squares where the Swedes were expected to tread. Each of these particular zones was organized around pleasure, in the forms of drinking, smoking various items of contraband that were illegal in Sweden, or shopping. Many of these specifics will be addressed in later chapters, but the point right now is to emphasize that travel across the Øresund Sound was generally related in the public mind to the pursuit of leisure.

The Øresund Region, however, aimed to change all this. Much of the interbureaucratic collaboration between the Swedes and the Danes in the Øresund Region was exclusively related to "harmonization." Interestingly, when each country was tagged as exotic, and Denmark was associated with relaxation, there was no effort to harmonize any regulations. On the contrary, the region of leisure was produced specifically because of the disharmony between the regulatory regimes, and yet this had been creating a harmonious and vibrant exchange of leisure services for decades.

With the building of the Øresund Region, the focus of the harmonization drive was specifically about harmonizing the rules of labor. The proponents of the region wished to encourage the flow of labor rather than leisure. In order to do so, they needed to harmonize the two countries' notoriously complex labor regulations. These regulations, it was often noted, were so byzantine for outsiders that they often kept people from working.[32] Once, an Albanian immigrant from Kosovo complained to me that he could never get a job in his field in Sweden, despite having Swedish citizenship, because his Albanian degrees were not accepted in Sweden (he was a civil economist); this was an exceedingly common complaint, registered in much social science literature and in the popular media. Inside Sweden, it was deemed important to have labor regulations that tightly circumscribed immigrant labor, but when building the region, the hope was precisely to pry open Danish labor markets to a vast army of supposedly ready Swedes.

Efforts such as these clarify that the region was being specifically built as a region of work, not relaxation. As Linde-Laursen (1995) shows in his chapter outlining the history of rationalizing and nationalizing the practice of dishwashing, the border was produced as a zone of difference, and activity in the home was especially distinct. As the Øresund Region now aimed to become a market, labor power needed to be equivalent, fungible, and, specifically, not nationally distinct. Following this logic, the region would only become real once it had been integrated into the psyche and movements of the average person as a zone of labor.

Not surprisingly for a region that had elevated work and the market to its raison d'être, the question of transparency also came to the fore. Things that used to be hidden needed to be drawn forth into daylight. For example, both Sweden and Denmark have had, for over a century, a nationwide dictum referred to as the Jantelagen (Law of Jante), first given expression in a Danish novel from the nineteenth century. It demands that "you should not think that you are somebody" and that one should certainly never brag. This dictum is attached to a moral demand to keep quiet about any personal successes and, furthermore, to blame all success on the rules of chance. As with so much else in the Øresund Region, this needed to change, and regional proponents were hoping that the Law of Jante would gradually fade away (as will be shown in chapter 5).

The region was already well known locally for its proleptic bluster and bravado. In the year leading up to the opening of the bridge, one could not open the daily paper without spotting some ad or article proclaiming the benefits of the region and the promise it offered. These claims were certainly hyperbolic, and some were false. For example, in an exhibit at the offices of the CityTunneln (the planned subway through Malmö that will transport people to Copenhagen even more quickly), one could read the following: "The Øresund Region is today one of Europe's most expansive. From all directions and corners interested glances turn toward what is occurring here." This was later shown to be untrue when, on the day of the bridge's inaugural, few foreign presses showed any interest in the region (see Berg et al. 2002).

Similarly, much money was expended by the Øresundskomiteen to hire public relations firms in order to develop a perfect name with which to market the region. At one point, the committee announced that the name would be S•und, a toying with letters so that the word simultaneously looked Swedish, Danish, and English, for "we must have a name that can illuminate the entire region, a name that towns and companies can utilize when they want to market themselves."[33] Another full-page advertisement in the main daily, along with providing a variety of statistical claims, informed readers, "The things that are happening down here in Skåne will change Sweden forever." When it came to the regionalization process, the well-documented Swedish taciturnity fostered by the Law of Jante had apparently given way to a more florid boasting (see Daun 1996 [1989]; Graubard 1984).

Another striking development in the drive to deliver transparency to things that used to be hidden occurred with the manipulation of statistics. Usually, statistics—the word shares the same root as the word "state"—are the preserve of the nation-state, and the manner in which data are collected has often been organized around national boundaries (see Appadurai 2006; Hacking 1990). Not so in the Øresund Region. Statistics were constantly being compiled via a sort of "border poaching"; the numbers became completely different once the region was considered as a numerically representable unit. This allowed for such claims as "There aren't really that many counterparts to the Øresund Region around the world. You could compare us with Boston, Ireland and perhaps possibly Amsterdam" (Johansson 1999: A24). The mode of calibration had shifted, and it forced the gaze itself to shift. Instead of exclusive foci on either Copenhagen or Malmö, the region (whether correctly or incorrectly) was illuminated as a functioning whole.

Finally, the bridge promised to channel material and human flows and bind the region together in a new way. There was some nationalistic rhetoric in this regard, or rather, a subnationalism of Skåne, whose advocates explained that Sweden had ruthlessly and cruelly brought them under Swedish hegemony centuries ago. For these people, the bridge would allow them to "move back" to their Danish ancestors, from whom they believed they had been violently ripped away in 1658 (see Linde-Laursen 1995). There were also Danes—although very few indeed—who remained embittered about 1658 and looked to the bridge to redraw the map not only in Denmark's favor, but somehow to its more natural state, with Skåne again a part of a sovereign Denmark.

Other less antagonistic types of connections between freedom and movement were much more commonly related to the bridge. The constant refrain revolved around space-time compression (Nilsson 1999). One of the region's earliest proponents, the Danish *framtidsforskare* (researcher of the future, or futurist) Uffe Palludan, stated that the bridge would magically bring Sweden "150 km closer to Copenhagen" (Palludan 1999: 204). The bridge would "destroy" space and time in Virilio's sense, by decreasing the effort involved in moving from one place to another. Palludan took this idea a step further than most, as did one of his colleagues whom I interviewed. They both noted how the bridge actually would bring Malmö closer to the rest of Sweden, because with the new proximity of the airport in Copenhagen, Malmö would gain many connections per day to towns in Sweden that it used to not be networked with in this manner.

Thus, for the futurists, progress lay in movement. In his writing, Palludan goes so far as to indict people who do not move as not being involved in the future. They think "statically" and are thus "blinded by the present," unaware of the benefits of the future (Palludan 1999: 167–168).[34] Just as proponents of the Øresund Region made countless arguments about the region itself moving away from Sweden and thereby gaining freedom from it, so too I will show in later chapters how individuals found a new sense of freedom in the ability to move in new directions. Often, these people saw themselves moving away from the state as well.

But as the futurists themselves noted, there were people who felt otherwise. Not everyone saw themselves as bold transgressors of boundaries in Palludan's sense. People such as these provide evidence that the moral community of the Øresund Region was far from homogeneous. It was being formed by these debates, and in turn, the competing visions were also being molded by the community itself. The utopia of the Øresund Region did not yet exist. Rather, its emergence as a potential utopia or dystopia was being debated by the many inhabitants of the zone in which it might come to fruition.

Money and Building the Future

I argue that one of the primary mediators of all these flows is currency. As I will show in the next chapter, currency depends upon a stable center as it simultaneously facilitates and constrains the movement of credit and debt relations as they work to construct a moral community. Certainly one major problem with the Øresund Region was that, as will be documented here, it had too many different currencies competing to construct this community—each with its proponents and opponents. Comaroff and Comaroff (1997) intricately detail the ways in which separate currencies can be attached to variant moral regimes, and also how one currency might "colonize" another and thereby contribute to heightened battles over the moral community: "Along the Cape frontier, cash and cows [another form of currency] became fiercely contested signs and means, alibis of distinct, mutually threatening modes of existence" (Comaroff and Comaroff 1997: 190; see also Akin and Robbins 1999; Foster 1998; Guyer 2004). We should not be surprised to find similar battles as the EMU project attempted to come to fruition in the Øresund Region.

Put bluntly, the profusion of competing currencies in the Øresund Region correlated with the fact that the utopian region remained—as yet— unsuccessful. Considering this, one sees the cohesive potential of a national (or any other successful) currency. Its ubiquitous presence makes it seem almost unimportant, and many Swedes emphatically told me that when I talked to them about the currency debates. But despite people's seeming disregard for the power of currency, my ethnographic study of daily monetary usage and rhetoric in the Øresund Region will argue that successful currencies play an important role in constructing community.

TWO

The Arts of "Scientific" Money

Monetary Policy as Moral Policy

The subject of money as a whole is a very extensive one,
and the literature of it would fill a very great library. Many
changes are now taking place in the currencies of the world,
and important inquiries have been lately instituted concerning
the best mode of constituting the circulating medium.

—*Jevons 1919 [1875]*

Because this book aims to examine the daily usage and rhetoric surrounding a variety of competing currencies, it is vital to provide a rigorous analysis of the monetary theories, histories, and structures that distinguish each currency from the others. This chapter will describe the similarities and differences among the theories and structures that organize the local-currency movement and those that organize more standard paper money, including the Swedish krona and the euro. I will argue that there are specific mechanisms by which currencies can tie people together into bounded groups. In Gaonkar and Povinelli's (2003) terminology, I am looking into the ways in which currencies can serve as a "transfiguring" device for the populations that rely on them. Knowledge of these mechanisms is essential to any ethnography that seeks to connect currency and social borders.

At the beginning of my study of local-currency movements, I was most struck by two related matters. First, they had trouble attracting members.

Second, they openly announced a desire for stringent borders to restrict monetary usage. I began to focus on the lack of a reserve system as the most idiosyncratic aspect of the local currencies' monetary theory, and posited that this specific aspect of its structure constituted not only its problem of attracting new members, but also its ability to police the borders of monetary usage.[1] In other words, the very thing that made these movements unpopular for a broader audience was precisely what they needed in order to maintain their founding goals.

It was this discovery that led me down the path of studying the role of reserves in *all* modern currencies. The reserve system (or lack thereof) illuminates a whole host of policy and moral issues related to modern paper money. Issues such as whether the money should circulate rapidly or slowly, whether it should be safely hidden in a vault or openly circulate, and whether it should represent labor (production) or leisure (consumption) all came to the fore.[2] In short, despite scientific claims to complete objectivity and moral neutrality, there are ethical concerns well outside the realm of the economy embedded within the structures and theories that undergird a currency's purported value.

Further, each wave of theorizing about money reveals a desire to finally achieve human control over money. Modernist economists treated money in much the same way as external nature was treated by modernist scientists: money was seen as a natural force external to human whims, and society required a scientific revolution in order to control it in ways that it had resisted since its birth. Money was yet another force of nature that needed to be quelled and channeled by humanity, as science has tried to conquer nature. Underlying much of these debates, therefore, is a continual drive toward seeking the "perfect," utopian money—a money that will transparently and consistently represent the material world and deliver us from corrupt governments, wily businesspeople, and an indifferent natural world.

I approach money in this way in order to develop an anthropological means of discussing the impacts and changes ushered in by the euro. A currency's relationship to boundaries makes it pertinent to the construction of spaces such as the EU, the Øresund Region, and the tiny confines of the local-currency rings. And the various methods of regulating money depend upon different moral configurations. Thus, it becomes clear that, when people are arguing about money, they may well be arguing about other things at the same time.

Early Monetary Ferment and Nation-Building

A famous Swedish economist, Knut Wicksell, asserted that Swedish "currency history until 1830 is indeed an almost uninterrupted succession of debasements and bankruptcies" (Wicksell 1935: 45; for more detail, see Peebles 2003). Such endemic problems provoked an ongoing debate over the locus of value. This debate continued for many years, and it is worth outlining briefly here, for it connects with the ethnographic details in this and later chapters. Not least, it opens up our ability to see the way in which monetary policy relates to ideas about foreignness, which is important to my discussion of nation-building and boundary transgression in the Øresund Region.

For example, an anonymous author writing in 1818 believed that it is eminently clear that the value of money hails from the "national produc-tion surplus." This results from the fact that money, in his argument, can only be metal, and the only way to gain metal to circulate in the realm is to trade goods abroad that have not been consumed locally, thereby drawing metal into Sweden. He was deeply concerned with keeping this money circulating specifically within the borders of Sweden, for otherwise shifty foreigners would be making money at "citizens' expense" (Anonymous 1818: 6).

This author's understanding of the locus of value has consequences for his politics (as all theories of value do), for he argued from this theory that all Swedes must be "free and united producers," with no leisure class aside from the necessary bureaucrats (Anonymous 1818: 49). Such a policy would allow Sweden to become an "independent nation" (ibid.) that could easily produce a surplus that would in turn give birth to a "real national currency, which would remain in the Kingdom" (ibid.: 49–50). His indictment of the leisure class (basically, the aristocracy) and his embrace of free production as the solution to all the country's problems can be seen not only as a voicing of developing bourgeois ideology, but also as a clear elevation of the value of labor over leisure. Further, this labor would produce the only true money and would thwart the efforts of foreigners, whom he believed were constantly plotting to steal value from Sweden. By advocating to keep money within national borders, he made a connection between money and boundaries, believing that the labor of the nation and the circulation of the resulting coin would build a virtuous circle that would further solidify, invigorate, and protect the independent nation.

Another anonymous author, writing only three years prior to this, believed that money was clearly only a measure of value and thus had no inherent value of its own. This is an early argument for "fiat money"[3] governed by the "quantity theory of money."[4] He boldly asserted: "In a word: The Lord of Nature has determined the value of goods in comparison to the needs of man; but the lords of the Earth and Governments determine the price of goods via a larger or smaller money supply" (Anonymous 1815: 25). He also wished to prove (echoing today's proponents of local-currency rings) that "money should not carry its own value as a good [e.g., gold]." Thus, he continued, "of all of mankind's discoveries, paper is the only serviceable material for money" (ibid.: 8). According to him, Sweden had endlessly lost out to foreigners, as the latter sucked value out of the territory because of the mystification that disallowed the state from determining the value of money (26). Further, this author was tired of the Swedish central bank's "veil of secrecy." In particular, he was driven to distraction by a hoard of silver that lay dead and immobile in the bank's coffers, wasting away at the people's expense when in actuality paper needed no metal to back itself up (17). This author, therefore, stands as an example of someone who sees consumption (rather than production) as the source of all value, determined by the way in which God composed the human body and its daily needs. Further, his concern with hidden money hoards and the dangers of immobility is an important theme that will be encountered later in this chapter and others. Although disagreeing with the pamphleteer mentioned earlier in almost every matter regarding monetary theory, he nonetheless agreed that the primary concern was the constant loss of Swedish economic value to foreign elements. Thus, both authors believed that a sound monetary policy is one that guarantees the retention of economic value within specific borders.

This is quite different from what economists assert today.[5] But either way, one can clearly see how a seemingly technical debate about the most efficient way to organize a currency can be infused with questions about building and defending borders. Debate about Swedish monetary policy has consistently reflected these concerns, sometimes focusing on a desire to sustain boundaries and sometimes, as in the case of an important debate of the 1860s, focusing on whether the country should commit to a movement to build an international currency and abandon monetary borders altogether.

The Scandinavian Monetary Union: 1874–1914[6]

The drive to create the euro was not new. The idea was broached in 1867, when utopian Saint-Simonians (see chapter 1) led European governments to gather in Paris in order to organize a pan-European currency (Einaudi 2001). The need to create an international currency, along with harmonizing all other unit measures, was apparently first noted (according to the authors of a Swedish government report on the Paris conference) in 1851 at London's Crystal Palace, where it was hard to compare the prices of the goods being displayed at the exposition (Bergström et al. 1870: 7).[7] Similar to the adamant claims of the euro's proponents, there was an alleged absence of transparency in international trade at the time, and it needed to be solved with science and rationality. However, this drive to create a pan-Western international currency based on gold failed.[8] Undaunted, the Swedes, Danes, and Norwegians went about setting up their own currency union.[9] Its status as one of the world's most successful currency unions (de Cecco cited in Henriksen and Kærgård 1995: 106; see also Cohen 1999) makes it worthy of study here.

For my purposes, the most interesting aspect of the Scandinavian Monetary Union (SMU) is the evident concern with "foreign infiltration" that seeped into the Swedish primary literature on the topic. Many pages in the 1870 Swedish government report ostensibly dedicated to the study of a pan-European currency were nonetheless devoted to a problem that had been broadly discussed at the time: the circulation of Danish and Norwegian coins in the realm. As Henriksen and Kærgård write, "the Scandinavian Currency Union was based on habit—the circulation of coins among various countries was common practice before the Union formalised it" (Henriksen and Kærgård 1995: 107).

What vexed the Swedish authorities was that the silver content of their coins was slightly higher than that of Danish and Norwegian ones, even though all three units traded at the same rate in practice. Thus, following Gresham's law (that bad money drives out good), the Swedish money was being hoarded while the Danish and Norwegian money was slowly moving north and east through the country. Because of people's demand for simplicity and fluidity of trade, the value of each country's money was, the Swedish report alleged, "falsely" measured in daily practice. As a result, "our southern provinces have a stock of currency composed of Danish royal dollars, marks, and shillings, and this comparatively worse coin reveals a clear inclination to spread from there up toward the inner parts of the country" (Bergström et al. 1870: 50). The government report argued that only professional money traders made money off the arbitrage possibilities among the coins, while regular people treated all of them as though they were identical (ibid.: 49). This situation led to the not entirely plausible theory promulgated by the authors of the report, that the Swedish mint was paying to send silver to foreigners and receiving nothing in return.[10] The report argued that Swedish silver was thereby landing— immobilized—in Denmark and Norway instead of circulating healthily in Sweden.

Lundh says that a wave of Scandinavism also aided in the creation of the SMU. This was a pan-nationalist movement that began in the 1840s with students who celebrated the shared Scandinavian roots of these countries and hoped to build a powerful bloc against Prussia and Russia (see Nilsson 2000). With the collapse of the dream of building a pan-European currency, the risk ran large that Denmark would attach itself to the new German currency system in order to facilitate trade with that neighbor. Sweden feared not only Denmark's further integration with Germany, but also German influence in Sweden. Noting that Germans had purchased a lot of industry in southern Sweden, one author wrote that Swedes should "worry that they [Germans] would follow their fellow countrymen's prejudice to spread German silver currency, which Sweden loses at least 2.5% on" (Lundh 1997: 645–646). The implication was that average Swedes would readily accept this currency. Thus, aside from clearly showing an era during which several currencies could circulate simultaneously, this argument reveals that apparently only the government saw this spread of another currency as problematic, while citizens in the southern provinces gladly accepted it.

These sorts of concerns brought forth the SMU, which was far simpler than today's EMU. The central bank of each country agreed to accept the issue of the other central banks, thereby essentially announcing that the three countries shared the same gold reserve but harbored it in three separate locales. Thus, each country could continue to print its own currency, but it was guaranteed by the gold held by all three of them together. Such an arrangement, as Cohen explains, depends upon a profound amount of mutual trust; each government (and citizenry) must believe that the other countries are not over-issuing their currency, as has so often been the case in monetary history. Cohen compares the SMU to the Latin Monetary Union and decides that the former lasted as long as it did because of "the genuine feelings of solidarity that . . . existed among their members" (Cohen 1998: 89). Meanwhile, Cohen asserts that the LMU survived because of the strong hegemonic position of France in the agreement; France essentially behaved as the monetary sovereign, dictating policies to the other members (ibid.).

Regardless of whether Cohen's analysis is correct, he clarifies how the SMU agreement was vitally dependent upon gold reserves, which controlled the central banks themselves. In other words, we need not subscribe to Cohen's view that there was necessarily strong solidarity among the Scandinavian countries, but they were all committed to an object—gold— that (they collectively believed) lay outside their control. Indeed, as soon as the gold standard collapsed during World War I (because of various import-export restrictions), the currency agreement also collapsed. The SMU stands as but one of many incarnations of an age-old theme: alienating control away from the subject (e.g., the government) and into an object (i.e., a set of currency reserves). As we will see in the next section, this wisdom began to be questioned by mainstream economists at the turn of the twentieth century.

Seeking Stabilized Money

As the twentieth century dawned, a major shift occurred in the orientation of the ferment over monetary policy. Though European governments throughout history had continually abandoned the gold standard whenever the need arose (Keynes 1960 [1930]: 299), there had nonetheless usually been a desire and promise to eventually return to "real money." Hence, withdrawals from the gold standard during times of crisis were always called "suspensions," with the guarantee that, when all had returned to normal, bills could be exchanged for gold again.[11] Within this paradigm, paper could not actually be money in and of itself; it was a mere representation of an immobilized store of value residing elsewhere. At the turn of the twentieth century, more and more economists began questioning this (as some writers had done earlier). They gradually built a set of tools that they believed would finally allow humanity to become master of the money that for so long had been an external power over it.

Not surprisingly, the desire to finally control money carried a scientific bent, seeking to wrest power away from the natural world. As Wicksell says, "Its [the establishment of a stable measure of value] fulfillment calls for every effort on the part of statesmen and thinkers. It is a thing unworthy of our generation that without pressing cause the most important economic factors are left to pure chance" (Wicksell 1936 [1898]: 194). Elsewhere, he boldly states:

> The theory of money, delimited in this way [i.e., his way], constitutes a complete and rounded whole, which eminently belongs to the province of economic science. In all other economic spheres other circumstances, such as technique, natural conditions, individual or social differences, play a role which science can only imperfectly survey and control. *But with regard to money, everything is determined by human beings themselves, i.e., the statesmen, and (so far as they are consulted) the economists; the choice of a measure of value, of a monetary system, of currency and credit legislation—all are in the hands of society, and natural conditions . . . are relatively unimportant.* Here, then, the rulers of society have an opportunity of showing their economic wisdom—or folly. Monetary history reveals the fact that folly has frequently been paramount; for it describes many fateful mistakes. (Wicksell 1935: 3–4; emphasis mine)

Wicksell, along with the famous American economist Irving Fisher, led the drive to establish, once and for all, a truly stabilized money separated from the vagaries of chance and the tyranny of nature. These factors would allegedly disappear by the pluck of human enterprise and scientific knowledge, just like the Saint-Simonians had predicted.

In particular, Wicksell failed to see the need for a gold standard. Once, while speaking of the possibility of an international currency, he said: "such a prospect need not, on closer investigation, provide cause for consternation. On the contrary, once it had come into being it would perhaps be the present system which would sound like a fairy tale, with its rather senseless and purposeless sending hither and thither of crates of gold, with its digging up of troves of treasure and burying them again in the recesses of the earth" (Wicksell 1936 [1898]: 193).[12] He also focused on currency reserves (which he considered remnants of old hoarding practices) as a general problem, even relating them to an evolutionary model, wherein the most modern peoples would not retain central banks' need for currency reserves (Wicksell 1935: 14–15, 21). Taking these positions into account, one sees that Wicksell sought a currency unencumbered by material constraints.

Such a currency could only be controlled by a powerful central bank, which Wicksell recommended could control the flow of credit by manipulating the interest rate. In making his argument that the government should take over this role as a means to control the money supply, he wrote:

> I should like then in all humility to call attention to the fact that the banks' prime duty is not to earn a great deal of money but to provide the public with a medium of exchange—and to provide this medium in adequate measure, to aim at stability of prices. In any case, their obligations to society are enormously more important than their private obligations, and if they are ultimately unable to fulfill their obligations to society along the lines of private enterprise—which I very much doubt—then they would provide a worthy activity for the State. (Wicksell 1936 [1898]: 190)

Surely he was thinking of all the past devaluations of currency that had occurred at the hands of private banks over-issuing credit.[13] Wicksell posited that private banks could not be trusted to look out for the best interests of society (compare this with Friedrich Hayek's beliefs), and instead the state would have to be given the noble task of issuing and controlling credit, and thus the money supply as well.

Fisher took much inspiration not only from Wicksell, but from the experiments of Sweden as a whole, and he spent much time studying the country's monetary policies. Fisher, it could be argued, became zealously consumed with providing the world with a stabilized money, traveling the globe on his own dime to purvey his knowledge to dictators (e.g., Mussolini) and presidents alike (e.g., Teddy Roosevelt) (du Monthoux 1987: 35–36). He also published numerous books on the topic. During the height of the movement, there were many international conferences organized in order to debate how to proceed with the task (Fisher 1935: 277ff.). Thus, like some eras preceding it, this period was fascinated with the idea of discovering a measure of monetary value that was as reliable as a meter or a pint (see du

Monthoux 1987: 52). But instead of seeking that measure in something external, such as a day's labor or a certain amount of gold, the Swedes were the first to shift the focus. One might say that the focus shifted from the idea of "discovering" a measure of value to the idea of "establishing" one. Sweden's efforts in this regard greatly inspired Fisher, and he lamented that Wicksell died before seeing his predictions come true (Fisher 1935: 94–95).

Fisher explained the watershed transformation: "Thus, for the first time in history, a country [Sweden] announced that its policy would be that of stabilizing its currency, not with regard to gold or with regard to foreign exchange, but with regard to the internal purchasing power of its money" (Fisher 1935: 320). With this move, several things occurred. First of all, there was a marked shift from believing that the locus of value resides in production. From now on, it would reside in consumption.[14] The Swedish government decided (following Keynes and the well-respected Stockholm School economists; see Lundberg 1996) that production is determined derivatively, by consumption, and this then became the source of money's value. Also, the faith that people had previously placed in gold (or silver, or a day's labor, or what have you) for millennia was now transferred to a government office,[15] where a worker tabulated statistical consumption data on scientific charts.[16]

By creating a statistical index of consumption, the Swedish central bank was able to control price levels in the country, something that Fisher excitedly insisted had been "a feat formerly declared impossible" (Fisher 1935: 407). In order to do so, the Statistical Department of the Riksbank (Royal Bank) devised a weekly retail price index (the kind we are so familiar with today). Called the consumption index, it was made up of "the average retail prices of goods and services which represent the 'cost of living' of a representative cross section of the Swedish people" (ibid.: 322).

Here we have the modernist spirit in nuce: a problem that has vexed societies since time immemorial has been solved by employing rational science and quantification. All is heroic, accomplishing hitherto unimaginable feats. Yet such heroism was performed with the desire to provide tranquility, to remove chance from human life, and to settle a representative cross-section of people into a manageable present and predictable future. This certainly stands as another of the moments—with famed Fisher promoting the cause—when Sweden became a beacon to the world. Echoing the contemporaneous comments made by Childs, Fisher declared, "If little Sweden can become an oasis in the world-wide desert of depression surrounding her . . . [and] can maintain her chosen index number almost unchanged, the same result is economically feasible almost anywhere" (Fisher 1935: 409).[17]

Of course, there were additional consequences of this momentous shift from production to consumption. By openly announcing that it would radically shift its means of controlling the currency, Sweden simultaneously ended its cooperative attitude toward the rest of the world (hence the aptness of Fisher's claim that it was an "oasis"). Insisting that stabilizing price levels was the only means to control the currency meant that Sweden no longer cared about the value of its currency vis-à-vis other world currencies. Such a move also declared that the country's gaze had shifted away from international standards of value to a national one—an idea that had been voiced as far back as the pamphlets of the 1800s.

Utilizing statistics gathered within the boundaries of Sweden both produced and reinforced a sentiment of separation. The world could be awash in chaos (as it was at this time), but Sweden would remain, via rationality and control, a space of order. It was in many ways a declaration of independence, not only from the external objects that had often exerted control over the value of money (such as gold reserves), but also from the other peoples and governments of the world. As the famous Swedish economist Gustav Cassel explained, the government believed that if it first focused on stabilizing price levels, then the external rates of exchange would fall into place as a derivative effect (Fisher 1935: 96–97). He considered this to be "a common interest of all nations" (Cassel cited ibid.: 97). In other words, following an independent monetary policy, governed directly from the nation-state, was at this point not only novel but it was allegedly in the interest of all nations to undertake the same exclusionary measures. At the time, the isolationist seed germinating within this policy was not discussed.[18]

This move from valuing production to valuing consumption also coincided with the beginnings of the People's Home. Once the source of value in economic theory had decamped from the toil and trouble of daily production, the problems upon which the state chose to focus became as technocratic as the currency's governance itself. The problem no longer lay in some morally questionable hierarchy dividing laborer and capitalist, but rather in a simple problem of rational and fair distribution.[19] Similarly, once the source of value no longer derived from human sweat or divine intervention (e.g., the amount of gold existing on the planet), the economy could be viewed more scientifically and, thus, less morally (allegedly). It is presumably not a coincidence that the People's Home is considered a wonder of technical bureaucratic achievement, providing stability from the chaos that could ensue by allowing the vagaries of the market to control one's fate.

The Hatred of Hoarding

At the same time that Wicksell and Fisher were focusing on the best way to stabilize money, Silvio Gesell sparked a movement that is regaining popularity today, in the form of the local-currency rings. Gesell, a German merchant living in Argentina, argued that the problem with money was that it was the only good that did not lose value with age. He claimed that it needed to "rust," so that it would no longer be hoarded and instead would circulate vigorously.[20] His primary insight was noticing the "unfair" balance between the movement of goods and the movement of money, and he wanted to institute a monetary system that redressed this imbalance. Gesell, although forgotten by today's economists, was influential at the time, with Fisher even instituting his theories in one experiment (see Kennedy 1995: 39) and Keynes claiming in 1936 that "the future will learn more from the spirit of Gesell than from that of Marx" (Keynes 1997 [1936]: 355).

Gesell is of concern here because of the profound influence his theories have had on the local-currency rings that are central to my discussion of money and space in the Øresund Region. Several local-currency advocates referred me to Gesell and the experiments that his ideas spawned in places such as Austria and the United States during the Great Depression. One redux of his thought can be found in Magrit Kennedy's *Interest and Inflation Free Money: Creating an Exchange Medium That Works for Everybody and Protects the Earth* (1995), a book that was cited during several interviews; it can also be gleaned directly from Gesell's book *The Natural Economic Order* (1929).

First, it is vital to note the hatred of hoarding in Gesell's monetary theory. Holding money should bear a cost, thereby forcing it into circulation. Gesell recommended a system wherein " [t]he holder of money is hunted and worried by his possession just as formerly the producer was hunted and worried by his goods until he had passed them on to someone else" (Gesell 1929: 231).[21] Note that this is the opposite of the general system in place in the West today, wherein one receives a payment for keeping cash in a bank, detached from one's immediate person and thereby socialized. Even more obviously, in the United States today (though not in Sweden), people are now often charged for putting money into circulation, in the form of an ATM fee (Peebles 2004b). Gesell wanted to encourage the movement of money, not least because he held hoarding to be the root cause of all social inequality and economic stagnation.[22]

Of course, as Wicksell pointed out, the bank itself was circulating the money that people thought they were hoarding within its vaults. The development of banking merely transferred the onerous task of surveillance and investment from the individual to the institution. Wicksell even desired the elimination of what he referred to as the national hoard (currency reserves): "In recent times, attempts have often been made and proposals put forward to render this last remnant of the old hoarding practice superfluous [the need for central banks to hold metal reserves]. We shall deal in another place with the conditions of its successful achievement" (Wicksell 1935: 14–15). Unlike Gesell, however, Wicksell approved of savings and capital investment.

This chapter is not concerned with the debate over the virtues and vices of hoarding.[23] Instead, I only wish to illuminate the fixation—from Wicksell to Gesell—with the circulation of money. Both authors insisted that, in order for money to finally come under the control of humanity, it must be forced to flow in ways that it had resisted since its birth; the hoard, they argued, must be abolished at either the individual or the state level. In this way, both authors showed a concern with regulated flows and movements, controlled by society rather than by nature. And Wicksell even related the successful regulation of these flows to movement on the evolutionary continuum toward civility.[24]

It is worth additionally noting the extent to which Gesell's theories maintained an age-old distrust of interest and usury. Kennedy's detailed explanation of the "cancerous growths" resulting from interest recalls the "diabolical growth" of money *from* money that concerned Scholastic writers during the Middle Ages.[25] In this manner, ideas about the transparent versus hidden nature of money play a role in both Wicksell's and Gesell's theories. As mentioned above, both authors abhorred hidden hoards and believed that if money circulated more rationally, society would build visible and shared social wealth. In the case of the experimenters who followed Gesell's theories, the money itself often received tags that indicated the due date by which it would need to be utilized prior to losing value.[26] Such a practice directly embedded the social authority of the community in the cash itself, and it was an idea mentioned to me often by the local-currency advocates of the Øresund Region.

Perhaps it is not coincidental that most experiments with Gesell's theories have occurred in villages, which have been associated with higher degrees of social control over individuals, for they are not as anonymous as are urban dwellers.[27] In this system, any given individual's daily movements and transactions must be watched and clearly visible; as will be shown in later chapters, this governing principle organized the exchange policy of the currency rings in today's Øresund Region.

On Hoarding and Reserves

Because the literature that indicts hoards sounds so odd to modern ears, it is important to briefly discuss the relationship, posited by famed and influential economists such as Wicksell and Keynes, between "hoarding" and the national "currency reserves." Doing so will further clarify the ways in which a national currency contributes to the construction of national boundaries, thereby directly influencing citizens' mobility by building a system of exchange that forces the international standard of value to withdraw into a state hoard.

As noted, Wicksell considered the national currency reserves to be no different than hoarding practices that other social reformers had critiqued in the past. He believed that economic science and its corresponding institutions should develop a means to circulate this value in the same manner achieved by the development of private banking with regard to individual hoards.

If we move away from the negative (and not necessarily correct) connotation that sees a "hoard" as hidden and therefore sneaky, we can recognize that, pragmatically, hoards stand as stores of value. Put simply, they are reserves against a future rainy day. This is precisely the intent of national currency reserves as well. They are held as a guarantor of value of the circulating medium within any given country. As soon as that value is called into question by the international markets (as, for example, in the Swedish currency crisis of 1992), the currency reserves are called upon to defend the

---

value of the currency. Indeed, in 1992, many Swedes complained vociferously that the national reserves were being squandered in this effort—the rainy day being merely a false production and an unnecessary outgrowth of the fixed exchange rate. Swedes complained that the national reserves were rapidly leaving the country; all that Sweden was getting in return was an added assemblage of Swedish kronor that had previously been held outside the country. Thus, while it is true that currency reserves are not a hidden store of value (though one of the early nineteenth-century pamphleteers argued that they were during his time), they are nonetheless a store of value and are intended to be used (just like a hoard) if and when bad times hit.

By specifically *not* circulating, the currency reserves guarantee the circulation of the national currency, for they assure people that somewhere lies an object that can be called upon to back up the flowing paper. Here it is essential to point out that such immobilized signs of economic value cannot be the self-same national currency. Such a tautology would provoke questions about the value of the currency; instead, there must be a perception of a stabilized international standard of value behind any given national currency.[28]

The extent of this stabilized mass is intimately tied to trust. Hence, countries with solid economies in which people want to invest can reduce the amount of their currency reserves (as Wicksell would want them to do). Contrariwise, in the 1990s and early 2000s, Argentina's failed currency board allegedly required an exact replica of the circulating value of its entire economy to be sitting stabilized in the form of American dollars: for every peso that circulated in the nation, there was supposed to be a U.S. dollar behind it, immobilized in the national coffers. Once this belief came to be questioned, the international markets tested the matter and found that there was a discrepancy between the number of pesos in circulation and the number of dollars in reserve.

Here we come to the question of currency and boundaries. Why have governments sought to draw the money out of the mattress, to release the funds lying hidden in individual hoards? In many cases in the history of monetary policy, governments or banks affiliated with governments were removing the international standard of value from the individual holder and replacing it with paper that could only circulate more locally. For example, Falkman's (1986) memoirs of growing up in Malmö in the early nineteenth century clarify that the government wanted all the citizens' silver that was "hiding" and thus helped to issue paper notes that paid handsomely for the exchange of this silver (this paper later collapsed, while the silver that had been drawn away from individual citizens retained its value).[29] It is vital to note, however, that the silver had not only been part of a personal hoard, but also was capable of being traded in virtually all quadrants of the globe at that time (similar tales abound with regard to gold). In other words, by turning from metal to paper currency, governments and banks also subtly delimit the movement of their citizens in new ways; in this sense, all national currencies are similar in spirit to the local currencies, raising the transaction costs of doing business outside of a given sphere of users.

In order to produce a vibrant, flowing national medium of exchange, governments know that they have to offer an international standard as a guarantor of value, while citizens have to use a more delimiting paper currency to which many outsiders would ultimately fail to be attracted (as the world witnessed, for example, in the Thai currency crisis of the late 1990s, when billions of Thai baht were rejected in favor of other international standards of value). Of course, when all is well with the economy and the national money, people can often convert their paper into other currencies. The point, however, is that during times of crisis governments have left their citizens with less valuable paper that constrains their physical mobility. In the aftermath of a crisis, the international standards of value must be mobilized again, moving away from the national coffers and into private hands, while the national currency is increasingly sent home, its mobility newly constrained within the borders of the country. The currency reserves (as a socialized hoard) have been individualized again, but to a different group of people.[30]

Aside from being fascinating for social scientists concerned with representations and their objects, this fact shows that a flowing currency typically necessitates a counterbalancing, stable center of value, lying immobilized somewhere. Private banks also depend on these (in the form of reserve requirements), and thus it should not be surprising that national money also requires such structures.[31] However tautological and infinitely regressive it may be, it appears that currency's value depends upon this interplay between things flowing and things stabilized.

We need not call these stabilized units "hoards," but we must recognize their significance for monetary policy. This will become especially obvious in the discussions about the local-currency rings, for what makes them so novel is their departure from this paradigm. The currency rings that I studied had no collectivized reserves,[32] and this greatly contributed to their inability to attract outsiders to exchange with them. By not providing people with a more widely established standard of value, currency rings delimit their members' movement (this is desired by the members, so it need not be indicted; this is a technical discussion about ways to organize currency). Without a signified backing up their flowing signifiers (in the language of Saussurean linguistics), currency ring members announce that they are *not* trading with the wider world. This is not unlike the consequences for Sweden when it created its consumption index as a measure for the value of currency, as described above.

Basically, currency rings are pronouncing (like the pamphleteer from 1815) that currency *is* the signified and not the signifier of some other, more stabilized value. Or, more precisely, currency ring members believe that the collective human value of their members should stand as the guarantee of the value of the currency, not some silly external object made out of metal or paper; local currencies are designed to validate (and economically value) humans and their interrelations with one another, so this should not be surprising. But, as a result of this idiosyncratic reserve system, outsiders cannot trade into the system and insiders cannot convert their local currency into some other external currency (though this is not true of all local-currency systems).

By noting this relationship between signifier and signified, it becomes clear how stable centers—hoards, reserves, deposit minimums, whatever one wishes to call them— can influence the movement of the people who carry the currency. It seems like a truism to assert that banks, nation-states, and currency rings all can channel and direct flows of money and goods, but the existence of currency reserves (or lack thereof) illuminates the ability of these social institutions to also channel and direct the flow of people.

Growing and Sustaining the Welfare State via Monetary Policy

The post–World War II era and the famously rapid growth of the Swedish welfare state have been sufficiently and expertly documented in many other places. This was also a period of massive monetary innovations, policy ferment, and convulsions (e.g., Bretton Woods and the advent of "eurodollars" in the late 1950s as a result of the Cold War). Fascinating as the extensive topic may be, I only wish to draw forth a few aspects of the ideas about monetary regulation that dominated this era, which leads up to the euro debate and the formation of the Øresund Region.

Following a lengthy period of famed "utopian" prosperity, Sweden began experiencing major problems in the 1970s with its hitherto respected model. In a nutshell, Sweden resorted to a number of well-known (among international financial markets) and somewhat embarrassing devaluations of the currency. For example, in 1977, 1981, and 1982, Sweden devalued the krona—in 1977 reducing it by 16 percent, in 1981 by 10 percent, and in 1982 by 16 percent again.[33]

Currency devaluations delineate borders between a nation and the outside world. By reducing the cost of its currency on the international markets, a country stimulates demand for its exports, thereby increasing production at home. At the same time, a devaluation makes both imports and travel abroad more expensive, thereby consigning locals to less consumption of anything foreign.[34] These are the practical, down-to-earth consequences of national currency policy—and devaluations as one of the tools within it—and they clearly show currency's ability not only to build and reinforce borders, but to manipulate them to the detriment of specific groups.

Devaluations had a bad reputation in the Øresund Region for another reason. Aside from being critiqued for being "unsolidaristic," in the sense that a devaluation unloads one's own problems onto other people (by making one's own nation's products "unfairly cheaper" on the international market and thus stimulating production at home and decreasing it abroad), I was often told that devaluations were only false fixes. Several interviewees believed that Sweden's attempt to devalue itself out of economic crises was an increasingly problematic strategy, while Lundberg simply calls it the final evidence of the failure of Keynesian demand-side policies (Lundberg 1996: 76–77).

In short, devaluations were impugned as attempts to get out of crises without laboring to do so. Just as the alchemists sought in vain to transform lead into gold to create wealth without labor, a devaluation failed to address the real problems and merely postponed them or sent them elsewhere. According to its critics, such a policy aimed to stimulate demand by magically manipulating currency, instead of confronting the problems of production, i.e., its supposedly inflexible labor market, for which Sweden was incessantly critiqued by international economists.

It is also important to note that this allegedly "leisurely" way of dealing with problems of labor (unemployment) preserved a system of welfare benefits that the outside world regarded as overly protective of leisure. Sweden, famously, had some of the most extensive holiday benefits in the world, and Swedes with whom I spoke jealously guarded them. In fact, the entire country had a distinct rhythm of labor and leisure, and it was regularly claimed that one should not expect to get anything productive done during the month of July, for the entire country was on vacation. Many stores and restaurants in major cities closed down during this time, even though it was the height of the tourist season. Reform advocates often warned that the outside world would refuse to send its capital to Sweden unless the citizenry showed itself more willing to work and adopted the general labor rhythms of the rest of Europe. Significantly, Lundberg says that Swedes, provided for so generously by the People's Home, had started staying home, refusing to move to other regions of the country in order to work. In other words, the People's Home produced an immobility of people that it defended, at least in part, by forcing the instability of its currency.[35]

I have covered this extensively elsewhere but, briefly, the Swedish krona's fixed exchange rate finally collapsed amid a pan-European currency crisis in 1992 (Peebles 2004a). This episode, I have argued, marked the end of a period when many people trusted the government, since during the crisis it so adamantly insisted that it would never allow the krona to float. As one person stated to me, it was the beginning of an era when many Swedes turned to the wisdom of businesspeople rather than government officials (the latter being a group long appreciated and respected in Sweden; see Löfgren 1988). Another person forcefully argued that the krona crisis stands as the moment when the idea of the market "strode into the living room" in Sweden. Many people cited it, along with the assassination of Prime Minister Olof Palme a few years earlier, as the end of the happy isolation of the People's Home: the citizenry was no longer protected from the alleged chaos of the unruly world outside its borders.

Via a fixed exchange rate, the state had determined the value of the Swedish currency; finally succumbing to a floating exchange rate determined by the market meant that the state now relinquished control over the value of its currency.[36] A floating exchange rate definitively opens up a country's borders to new flows of money that had previously been carefully structured by bureaucrats and central bankers and protected by the confines created by a fixed national currency. Once the currency's value was allowed to float, the order that the People's Home used to delimit gave way to the chaos of the market. The market was suddenly declared to be the more rational way to govern currency value, while government became a "distortionary" force, rather than a protective one.[37]

During the 1990s krona crisis, the media and politicians were consistently discussing the flow of capital abroad. However, while capital was flowing out of the nation (in the form of international reserve currencies), the national krona was rapidly flowing back in. In other words, during the crisis, the krona was seen as currency, but not quite as fully liquid capital. After the supply-and-demand curve shifted, the krona was once again considered a signifier of capital. But while it was being rejected and sent back to the central bank, the krona's ability to represent capital into the future was deemed tenuous by people in the market. This episode clearly elucidates that, because central banks must hoard specifically *foreign* currency as reserves, a national currency can only legitimately represent capital if it is used as an immobilized store of value outside the country while it circulates as exchange value within it. This stands as one of those generally unnoticed aspects of currency value and monetary policy structure that clearly contributes to the building of boundaries of inclusion and exclusion in daily exchange practices, and it is therefore critical for any study of how currencies were circulating in the Øresund Region.

Local Currencies

With the collapse of the fixed exchange rate, Sweden's twentieth-century isolation came to a close. It is not surprising that people refer to that event as the end of the utopian vision, for in the krona crisis there was a clear manifestation of the relationship between money and borders. The currency helped to construct the sanctum that was the nation; the value and the daily use of the national currency were intimately tied up with (and simultaneously reinforced) ideas about boundaries and their transgression.

Perhaps not coincidentally, as soon as the currency floated, new ideas about the control of money also started to stride onto the scene in the form of local currencies and the euro. Local currency was intentionally diminutive, shrinking boundaries in the face of the newly fluid borders of the nation-state, while the euro was grandiose, boldly expanding borders beyond the nation-state. Either way, proponents of each had decided, with varying degrees of seriousness, that the nation-state was doing something wrong and its command over currency was no longer readily legitimized as "natural."

Since the nation-state was alleged to be doing something wrong, then clearly new monetary policies were needed to replace the old ones. In the case of the local currencies, the differences were—not surprisingly—more striking, but very much in line with the Gesellian monetary theory outlined above. To begin with, just like Gesell, currency ring proponents often asserted that ordinary money was not a true index of goods and services. It managed to obfuscate the true value of things and people, and thus, society must look for a better—more transparent—instrument. Ring members with whom I spoke more often than not believed that the local-currency system could deliver this transparency.

While this desire for transparency was one major impetus for building a local currency, the method for delivering such transparency began with focusing on the movement of money (other aspects of the monetary theory of local currencies will be fleshed out in later chapters). Following Gesell, local-currency advocates institutionalized the dislike of the immobilized hoard. Money always needed to be circulating; hoarding was systematically discouraged and frowned upon; money must move if it was to become a true index of the actual economy. In order for money to circulate more rapidly, currency rings can even devise methods for money's value to decrease (inflation) so that it is wise to spend it today, instead of saving it for tomorrow, when it would purchase less.

Importantly, none of the currency rings with which I worked put in place such inflationary mechanisms as those advocated by Gesell. However, they all organized a system where lending at interest was disallowed, which is another way to achieve a similar purpose: one gained nothing by letting money rust, so it might as well be spent. This institutional ban on interest, while seemingly derived from scientific analysis, was also related to long-standing elevations of labor over leisure. Gesell and his global followers in our own era committed to this belief because they held that monetary sums should reflect labor sums; people should not be allowed to acquire wealth leisurely, such as by charging interest on loans. Indeed, the fact that people could acquire money in such a leisurely fashion was often cited by the people with whom I spoke as one of the reasons that money was clearly not functioning as a proper index of value.

Further distinguishing themselves from dominant monetary theory and aligning with some cameralists of old (see Small 2001 [1909]; Koerner 1999), local-currency ring members believed that money itself was the problem, whereas the neoclassical theorists and Marx all believed that money is merely a symptom or an index of other processes. This latter doctrine, called the "neutrality of money," holds that the money supply cannot impact real economic variables, only nominal ones. So, for example, adjusting the money supply can impact the nominal wage rate, but since all prices will change as a result, the real wage rate will remain the same. Consequently, believers in the neutrality of money thesis do not see monetary policy as an important space for proactive intervention in the economy. The monetary theory undergirding the local-currency movement that I studied, contrariwise, absolutely saw monetary policy as a premier avenue for guiding and impacting the economy in specific, robust directions.

Also like the views of many cameralists, the local-currency monetary theory focused on self-sufficiency. Local-currency advocates sought a world in miniature, where more things could be produced locally so that "plate" was not sent abroad in order to chase foreign objects. This thought process was precisely in line with cameralist and mercantilist doctrines that abhorred "luxuries" because they believed that everything that was necessary to life could be found at home. Thus, the cameralists and mercantilists often advocated sumptuary laws that would prevent people from buying "frivolities" from foreign spaces that could only be purchased by sending money out of the country. Similarly, local-currency proponents aimed to build a more ascetic world, where people could live with less and where crass materialism would not reign supreme. In other words, monetary policy should facilitate the creation of forms of social wealth instead of individual wealth.

The Euro

Of all the monetary theories that help to organize modern currencies, the theory underlying the euro emerged—at least in the rhetoric of the European Central Bank and its proponents during the debate over whether

Sweden and Denmark should join—as the most committed to neoliberal orthodoxy. The ECB's only stated goal was to guarantee price stability, whereas even the U.S. Federal Reserve was required to think about "maximum employment" when formulating monetary policy. In order to achieve this goal, the ECB remained committed to the quantity theory of money, which proclaims that inflation results from an excess of circulating money rather than, say, a decrease in the supply of oil (a shock that would raise the price of a major factor of production).

An organizing principle of the quantity theory is that one can achieve transparency about the amount of money in circulation, something that is very much in doubt among critics of the so-called monetarists. In other words, monetarists believe that regulating the monetary supply can be treated as a transparent science rather than an obscure art; there is, they insist, an objective criterion for making scientific decisions and the only question is how one measures it. In a further commitment to transparency, the ECB mandates that it announce its decisions and procedures openly and frequently, believing that such transparency translates into consistency and predictability.[38] Just like the Saint-Simonians, who proposed a single international currency 120 years prior to the EMU, the proponents and architects of the euro believed that chance and fate could be driven away with the shining light of science.

Much like the Swedish krona, the euro relies on a socialized hoard constituted by, among other things, the reserve requirements of participating banks. The fearful rhetoric from one side of the debate over the euro in Sweden described a potential scenario in which Swedes would be less mobile than other Europeans who joined the single currency. At the time, this fear was never presented as being related to the currency reserves in Frankfurt, but I have argued elsewhere (Peebles 2008) that the location of the hoard is, in fact, related to such mobility. Exchanging money across borders does create a transaction cost that is the result of the need to translate values that are, in part, a function of the currency reserves.

Equally significant, proponents of the euro believed that Europeans needed to start moving around more in the search for employment. They frequently voiced a concern that the euro might flow more freely than would people. Such a development could cause major inefficiencies for the EU economy, for workers would not move as rapidly to places where they were needed. This commitment to harmonizing regulatory and cultural spaces so that human intercourse could be "improved" is another example of how ECB policy is in line with the utopian vision of the Saint-Simonians. In this sense, the ECB has evidenced an embedded interest in facilitating not only the movement of workers, but also the shared sense of culture that typically aids people in integrating into new spaces.

Beyond the technical questions regarding the monetary theory underlying the euro, the debate about whether or not to join the EMU also says much about how its governance was viewed, for the debate also hinged on the same question of transparency that the monetary theorists demanded. Proponents and opponents of the euro insisted that the debate over entry must be purely rational, and thus, the first step toward deciding to join the EMU or not involved a project of illumination. Unlike the overt nationalism invoked against the euro in Denmark and Great Britain (the other two opt-outs), many Swedes prided themselves on a purely rational approach to the momentous shift in monetary governance. Often, I was gently chided that it was manifestly useless to study the cultural meanings of money in Sweden, for "it makes no difference to me whose face is on the money I use." Instead, all debate about the EMU was elevated to the level of functionality, efficiency, and pragmatics. Rather than focusing on the ideas about cultural sovereignty and heritage that were so prominent in Denmark and Great Britain, Swedes constantly discussed the economic merits and political pitfalls of the union and often showed open disdain for the nationalistic fervor with which many Danes and Britons attempted to defend their currencies.[39]

Sweden thus presents a challenge for traditional theories of both nationalism and money within anthropology. Normally, nationalisms across the globe insist that the love of country is separate and distinct from any economic pragmatism. Defending the nation is a call to blood and community, whatever the costs, rather than being about what works best, objectively. Further, myriad studies over several decades have all but consolidated a belief within anthropological theory that money can be imbued with cultural meanings and that people never treat currency simply as a means of exchange and a store of value.[40] Yet many Swedes, with their allegedly emotionless grasp of money politics, vex anthropological theory by keeping money exactly within the bounds insisted upon by the rationalistic economists. In Sweden, economic rationalism was put into play as a means to defend the nation; Sweden's pragmatic *Homo economicus* defended the national currency from foreign takeover at least as successfully as more predictable strategies relying on emotion and national pride.

Leading up to the referendum, there was a demand for data and expertise on the euro. Following a long tradition of government-sponsored research panels on any matter of national import (the *statens offentliga utredningar* [the state's public investigations]), a team of experts was assembled to analyze the question of joining the EMU. The 1996 Calmfors Commission produced not only a dense 500-page report on the political and economic pros and cons of joining the euro project, but also twenty-one additional reports that filled many hundreds of pages more. The latter were often authored by foreign experts, in order to obtain the most objective view possible on accepting the euro or preserving the krona.

In addition to the work of the Calmfors Commission, the citizenry was expected to get educated, and countless study circles (a tradition dating from the introduction of socialism to Sweden) were supposed to be organized where regular people could meet weekly to discuss the euro's implications in tempered and rational forums across the land.[41] Educational radio and TV outlets also produced several programs devoted to the birth of the euro. All these projects endeavored to perfectly inform the citizenry. Opinions about the new currency could then be based on sound argument backed by data and expert opinion so that the best possible decision could be made.

Thus, one can note a moral elevation of transparency in Swedish money politics of all stripes. Money's flows needed to be registered and clear, its origins and destinations made obvious. Money—often considered to be anonymous—needed to provide data so that things could be traced and known. The debate over the euro often revolved around which currency, the krona or the euro, would better provide a host of data about taxes, prices, and power structures.

The main reason cited for the vast majority of Swedes' trepidation regarding the euro in the lead-up to the referendum was a lack of data (i.e., proponents and opponents of the euro were on the fringe; most people claimed to not know which currency regime was better). Sweden did not opt out because of dominant fears of losing national sovereignty, but because it wanted to wait and see how the euro would fare. While other countries went out on a limb by adopting the euro before it had proven itself as both an instrument of exchange and a catalyst of political change, the Swedish Social Democrats took a fairly classic stance of moderation on the matter. A rational decision could not be made until more information was gathered. In this manner, a reliance on the future production of objective data defended the nation from potentially dangerous globalizing projects. It is important to reiterate the extent to which this differed from the rhetoric in Denmark and Great Britain. There, the EMU was dismissed out of hand by many political parties (and certainly tabloids), and no amount of data could have ever convinced them that the euro did not threaten the nation.

What remains fascinating about this reliance on data is how each side in the euro debate espoused convincing, rational arguments. Mired in discussion about transparencies and efficiencies, virtually no passion entered into the EMU debate, and Swedes were rightly confused about which monetary system to prefer. From a rationalistic perspective, several different types of monetary organization are completely justifiable, as countless economists will confirm. No one currency regime is necessarily and scientifically better or worse than another. Rather, the decision *must* contain a bit of emotion about what sort of political and economic structures one wishes to consolidate. This aspect of the monetary union was generally neglected by the public in the Swedish debate, as most people strove to focus dispassionately on conflicting expert advice.

At one debate I attended, the EMU proponent summed up this need to analyze the situation rationally by asserting that the choice to join the EMU was "a choice between the plague and cholera, not heaven and hell." In other words, precise analysis must be made of two possible trajectories (both of them bad, according to him) and how much damage could be avoided by choosing one or the other. A choice between heaven and hell, on the other hand, is more clearly a Manichaean moral choice between good and evil. Refusing to see the EMU project as a moral commitment and instead conducting a rational debate on the matter paralyzed the country and clearly differentiated Sweden from the many countries willing to make passionate—*not* purely rational—decisions about the euro.

This brief summary of the rationalized debate over the EMU has revealed an anxiety residing within Swedish attitudes toward the project. Both proponents and opponents agreed that the EMU would usher in transparencies on the economic front (e.g., no more price discrepancies or hiding money across borders) and new opacities on the political front (e.g., byzantine EU government famed for its lack of democracy). This latter point was not even denied by the project's strongest proponents. One bank referred to the EMU as a Trojan horse that would slowly force changes in European political structures to which no one knew they were agreeing at the time. At an exclusive conference in New York City on the euro designed only for bankers (which one of my informants helped me to attend),[42] a pamphlet accompanied a talk given by its author. It bluntly states:

> If the EMU process starts in 1999 as planned, much more than the operation of exchange-rate and monetary policy will change. . . . Given the political constraints on a rapid move to political union and full-scale fiscal federalism, European countries, companies and workers may be faced with no alternative but to accept very significant public-sector downsizing and supply-side reform in order to avoid the damaging consequences of being part of a single currency without any of the adjustment mechanisms required to cope with asymmetric shocks or a local loss of competitiveness. The EMU project may in this way accelerate the impact of globalisation in Europe and render more untenable the "one-nation" policies of many Continental European countries. EMU may indeed represent a Trojan horse containing the warriors of supply-side reform and deregulation. If the horse is brought within the citadel, resistance may be increasingly forlorn. A united front against the forces of supply-side flexibility looks unlikely and those countries at the vanguard of change (e.g., Ireland, Holland and perhaps Spain) may soon force the die-hards to capitulate. The political ramifications of such a process would be difficult to predict; but popular resistance to the supply-side logic of the single currency cannot be ruled out especially in Germany and France. (Bronk and Bowers 1998: 13)[43]

In contrast, the krona stood as a physical instantiation of a community committed to a politics of transparency that had reigned for many decades. As I show throughout this book, it represented a nation that valued transparency in the political realm over transparency in the economic realm. To wit, most Swedes were well aware that their strong social welfare state produced a vibrant but hidden underground economy (see chapter 3). Similarly, national currencies were believed to be part of a system that allowed for money to be hidden abroad, and it was widely believed that the euro would put an end to this practice, at least within Europe (see chapter 5). In other words, the euro would usher in an allegedly rationalized and transparent economy accompanied by an undemocratic and hidden political structure. On the other hand, the krona would preserve an allegedly irrational and hidden economy attached to a democratic and transparent political structure. Thus, we can see the anxiety caused by the advent of the euro, for it would have necessitated an inversion of the traditional moral schematics that many Swedes held dear.

Via this rational debate, the question of adopting the euro became heavily laden with nationalistic tones despite all dismissals of this possibility. In actuality, the debate was largely about the cohesion and status of Sweden's long-standing and famous (at least within Sweden) "strong state" (see Hannerz 1996: 45). The belief in a transparent and democratic state that depended upon science and the culling of data in order to make rational decisions about policy was the guiding force behind the creation of Sweden's twentieth-century welfare system.

But in the Øresund Region, there was much reference to a new governing concept: Sweden was being characterized not as a "strong state" but as a "little country." Proponents in favor of the euro frequently said that Sweden was a small country that "cannot survive on its own," thereby arguing for both EU and EMU collaboration. The krona, I was told, would be slaughtered by the new globalized market, and the only way to defend Swedish values was by hopping on board the EMU project. Sweden's cherished strong state was in retreat; indeed, one person told me that the euro was merely the "last nail in the coffin of the nation-state's ability to govern its own politics." In a society where the idea of a powerful and rational state had been a bedrock notion for most of the twentieth century, this could prove traumatic indeed. Even many people on the Left espoused the benefits of the euro precisely because they hoped that it would reconstitute the strong state at a higher level.

Monetary Belonging

The trajectory of monetary debate over two centuries reveals that a perfectly transparent money—a money that never mystifies social relations and never succumbs to the dangers of chance—stands as the endless goal. Discovering a scientific path toward a more stable money is not merely a project guided by the search for ever-increasing efficiency. A currency that maintains value into the future and across specifically delimited spaces, as I have shown here, plays a role in creating a sense of group cohesion by contributing to the creation of borders that circumscribe everyday movement.

In these endless debates over how to build the perfect money, the opposing camps that supported different currency systems can often be seen cleaving to opposing positions about which social force was distortionary upon an otherwise true world: the market or the government. Arguments about distortionary effects attempt to claim that money, if only managed properly, will someday reflect the world perfectly and thereby usher in the "right" moral world. The means to achieve modern lucidity and regulation of the social world may have been hotly contested, but the belief that such a project should and could be eventually completed was never questioned. In a manner that Comte would surely admire, there has been a consistent belief that science (as economics and political science) would deliver clarity.[44]

Certain people in the Øresund Region were attempting to bring forth their own vision of a new, right moral world. Theirs was a vision of a grand market as a new organizing principle for society and for individual behavior. This potential market, however, was challenging and inverting several of the values that were held dear during the placid reign of the People's Home. As later chapters will show, their vision asserted that the citizen should become a customer, Copenhagen should become a space of work, wealth should be more individualized, and the home was constraining while the market was welcoming.

Proponents of the Øresund Region projected these beliefs onto the euro, just as the proponents for a slower, more autarkic village life projected their views onto the local currencies, while the proponents of the Swedish and Danish nation-states maintained their faith in the krona and the krone. In this manner, all of the various currencies stood as circulating embodiments of moral and cultural values. Currency connected these values to the various stabilized centers of value that the region's proponents hoped to hold onto as they sought to navigate their way through the emerging EU and the nascent Øresund Region that stood as its localized corollary. The following chapters will follow currency usage in practice, showing how each currency governed and constituted the flow of goods, people, and capital in different ways.

THREE

Receipts and Deceits

Currency Regulation, Black Markets,
and Borders

The diversion of commodities from their customary paths
always carries a risky and morally ambiguous aura.

—*Appadurai 1986*

In Malmö, Sweden, I lived around the corner from an office furniture store.
Though I was in desperate need of a more comfortable desk chair, I could
never afford the prices. One week, I noticed that it was having a close-out
sale. Yet the prices were still, in my opinion, too high. After the sale ended, I
spotted the men whose task it was to move the remaining chairs out of the
showroom. As a dutifully bargain-hunting American, I asked how much a
chair would cost right now, since they were getting rid of them. He told me
to look around and see if I liked anything that was left. Without knowing it,
I had set the stage for a black market transaction, a sort of transaction that is
amazingly common in Sweden, but requires a good deal of insider knowledge to execute.

  Still not aware that I was engaged in shady dealings, I picked out one
that I liked, which had a price tag of 500 kronor (about $60 back then). The
man offered me the chair for 300 kronor. He then asked if I needed a *kvitto*
(receipt), to which I initially replied no. Then I recalled how hard it is to
resell goods in Sweden if one cannot provide the receipt, so I said, "Actually,
I should take one since I might sell it when I return to the United States."

He gently chuckled and clarified everything for me in a sarcastic tone: "You can't get a chair like that for 300 kronor [he used the slang term *spänn*] if you need a receipt."[1] Having already noted the seeming love affair that many Swedes have with receipts, I awkwardly tried to inject some ethnographic questions into this economic interchange, asking why I could not get a receipt. He refused to talk to me about it, simply shaking his head and saying softly, "Don't worry about it [*Det är lungt*]" several times. I walked away with my chair and no receipt, and immediately started asking other people about the situation.

Everyone I spoke with about this interaction knew immediately what had occurred; there was no debate over the nuances of the transaction. I was told that the movers would just tell their employers that a certain chair was never even there to begin with (if its absence was even noticed, which it probably was not), and suddenly they have 300 kronor for a nice lunch and a few beers that night. Furthermore, without a receipt, the money was made without any need to pay the standard value-added tax (VAT) that applied to the vast majority of goods and services traded in Sweden. In short, receipt-less transactions denied money to the state and put more money in one's own pocket. These sorts of transactions were quite standard, and the accepted delineation between legitimate and illegitimate transactions hinged on the use of the receipt.[2]

The receipt (or its absent presence) is a vital aspect of currency exchange, though it is largely unstudied by anthropologists. Receipts help to constitute legal tender per se (at least in highly regulated economies). Currency is part of a legal fabric, and when a receipt is not present, the currency is not being used in a "proper" manner; the transaction is missing a legitimizing component. Thus, a receipt indexes faith in a specific regulatory regime, whereas receiptless transactions announce a desire to evade that regulatory regime. As such, receiptless transactions become questionable and potentially illegitimate. An exchange partner can even deny in a court of law that the transaction ever took place, thereby calling into question the effectiveness of currency itself. In other words, receipts are the legal residue of our famously anonymous cash, the way in which we desperately try to trace its untraceable movements.

More specifically, within the bounds of Sweden, all transactions involving kronor theoretically required a receipt; transactions across the sound in Denmark or in the local currencies either required a different kind of receipt or could occur without a receipt at all and there was nothing *openly* immoral about them. Agreeing to a receipted transaction usually cost both individuals more, and thus often indexed a moment when people saw themselves building community via personal sacrifice. Receiptless transactions, contrariwise, were cheaper for both exchange partners, and these more individualistic exchanges stand as interesting displays of community-building via the seeking of individual ease. In other words, the absence or presence of receipts indicates a great deal about the building and transgressing of community borders in mundane daily practices.

This chapter will compare and contrast the competing currencies in their role as part of various legal and moral regimes that were attempting to regulate the movement of objects across and throughout the Øresund Region. Focusing on the use, misuse, or absence of receipts, the chapter begins with an in-depth ethnographic account of some typical, daily transactions involving Swedish kronor and Danish kroner in order to argue that making purchases in Denmark in the pre–Øresund Region era mimicked the homegrown Swedish black market in significant ways. From there, I move on to transactions that relied on the local currencies in order to show how they were asserting a new regulatory regime over many daily transactions that used to be circumscribed within the typical black market. Finally, I will look at the new Øresund Region, and how it and the euro were attempting to eliminate the classic black market aura that transnational transactions and movements used to carry in the area. By documenting this relationship between receipts and diverse modalities of exchange, I hope to show the shifting senses of belonging and exclusion in today's Øresund.

The Receipt Society

When I told people of my fascination with Swedish people's fascination with receipts, many were quick to point out to me the etymology of the word itself. In Swedish, the word for "receipt" is *kvitto,* a cognate of *kvitt,* which is the same as the English word "quit." The *kvitto* announced in material form that one was quit of a debt; it could readily be referred to as transparent evidence of a legitimate transaction where no debts were carried through time, for they were liquidated at that moment via money.

To understand why receipts became so important, one must first understand the dominant national moral compunction to be fully independent and self-sufficient and to avoid debts to individuals at all costs. There was a dominant ideology that one must "do right by oneself" (*att göra rätt för sig*) that saw personal independence as being achieved via the proper monetary liquidation of debts (a colloquial translation would be "to do one's fair share").[3] For example, on the Swedish side of the sound, the practice of buying rounds of drinks at a bar was largely nonexistent (though I was told that upper-class people were starting to do this). Though Swedish society is often accused of being highly efficient, in this case the opposite was clearly true. Even if people knew that they would have more than one drink with their friends, each individual was expected to go to the bar separately and purchase their drink. Aside from flooding the service area with more people than was necessary, this practice reveals the deep fear of gifting that I observed in Sweden. For if one were to buy a friend a drink, that person would be in one's debt, and there would be a corresponding sense of obligation and loss of individual control.[4]

This behavior was similar to that of friends who gathered for a casual dinner at a restaurant. If possible, customers asked the waiter for separate bills and, thus, separate receipts following the transaction. Barring this, the tab was divided *to the krona* depending on what each person consumed (and much effort and time could be devoted to figuring out these various sums). Upon initially encountering this behavior, I assumed—as do many others— that it resulted from a Swedish "cheapness." But after much questioning and witnessing of other instances, I realized that it results from an insistence to not be in debt to anyone else.

In other words, Swedish cultural norms dictated that everyone must constantly be cognizant of what they owe to others, and they must liquidate these debts as soon as possible. Otherwise, they would be "parasitizing" themselves by living off the kindness of others. One final example may clarify this even more. I attended a friend's wedding, and I had rented a car to get there and back. Upon hearing that I had a car, a couple asked to catch a lift back to town. As I pulled up to their residence, they both vehemently insisted that they pay me the exact equivalent of a cab fare from the wedding location. I refused their payment, and a legitimate culture clash ensued, wherein we argued for almost ten minutes about their insistence on liquidating the debt they owed for what I had believed was a free gift.

One can clearly see how, in Sweden, a strong spirit of individual independence was protected by the proper and precise dispensing of money.

Though this might sound far-fetched, it should be seen as part of the powerful legacy of over 150 years of socialist theories in Northern and Eastern Europe that indicted the "social parasite": the member of the group who threatens its very solidarity by supposedly always seeking a free ride.

For reasons such as these, receipts stood as transparent and reliable indicators that one was no longer in debt and had honorably paid for any services or goods rendered, rather than mooching off one's compatriots. Significantly, receipts also provided exact data on the precise amount of debt that had been cleared, thereby providing for perfectly equal exchanges with no fuzzy excesses or remainders, as would be the case with friends at a restaurant who merely split a bill evenly, or even with traders with whom one negotiated a price.

Further, the receipt attested to one's faith in the regulated welfare state rather than in individuals. As I mentioned above, it was hard to resell items in Sweden if one could not provide the prospective buyer with the original receipt. Without the receipt, prospective owners were wary that they were about to purchase "hot" goods; they did not trust the seller, but rather, they trusted the sanctioned receipt that accompanied the sale. But apart from being proof that the good itself was not stolen, the receipt also listed the precise contribution to the state that had occurred as a result of the transaction, by including the total of the value-added tax (*moms* in Swedish) that was paid. In both of these ways, the receipt proved that one had engaged in a legitimate transaction that would usher resources to the state and not to thieves and black marketers. Transactions with receipts cost more money, but—to put it in economistic terms—the value of the lower-priced, receipt-less transaction did not outweigh the cost of acting in an antisocial manner toward the community.

The market in secondhand bikes was interesting in this regard, not least because it was such an important market. Bikes were one of the primary transportation devices in Sweden, not used only for recreational purposes. New bikes were quite expensive, and thus many people bought used ones. In the local classifieds, I found hosts of ads for bikes that specifically announced the availability of the original receipt. Further, one could not sell a bike directly to a bike store unless one provided the receipt. Essentially, the locus of trust had moved to the regulating regime rather than between the individuals who were trading; the receipt could be called upon as evidence in the event of a conflict.[5]

It is also important to consider the way in which, aside from very large purchases such as homes and cars, the existence of a receipt marked an inability to negotiate a price. All black market transactions were eminently negotiable. In fact, this was surely one of their trademarks. Likewise, at Sweden's many *loppmarknader* (a sort of traveling garage sale of many traders who assemble together in town squares), prices were often negotiable and receipts were uncommon. Here, one was only allowed to sell petty and used goods (there was a 300 kronor maximum on sales), and the trades had the distinct feel of being part of the underground economy (some goods were sold still in their factory wrapping). Legitimate transactions, on the other hand, had "perfect" prices that delivered immediate clarity to exchange partners.

The Deceit Society

Thus, the receipt allowed the bearer to reside safely within the nation's moral space, and the Swedish People's Home relied upon this strong fear of indebtedness between individuals in order to ensure that everyone carried their fair weight (as did many other socialist regimes). A fierce commitment to individual independence was sustained by a refusal to become indebted to an exchange partner when one was within the boundaries of the national home, where everyone should "do right by themselves" *and* build lasting ties of economic indebtedness with the state via the VAT. The receipt was the material residue proving this laudatory behavior.

When neglecting or manipulating receipts, however, people were gladly abandoning these tough strictures. In these instances, social indebtedness was merely going underground. It was moving to the black market, where people affirmed social and economic indebtedness with strangers or trusted business associates rather than with the state (see Coronil 1997; Larsen 2010). The strong moral compunction to liquidate debts among friends was not common in the black market. After I started probing, I heard many stories.

People were not supposed to talk about these transactions because, as one friend told me, "It's one of the foulest things one can do." She went on to explain that the black market was a sphere that was unsolidaristic (at least to those who are committed to the Swedish model of social welfare), because it represented an open avoidance of the VAT. She had refused certain black market transactions at substantial cost to herself. A television salesman once offered to "forget" to send in the registration for her new television in exchange for, essentially, a bribe of 500 kronor. (There is a fee for television use in Sweden, and there are even inspectors who arrive at your door if they suspect you own a television and have failed to pay the fee.) She indignantly refused his offer, though his bribe would have been much cheaper than the annual TV usage fee. I know another person who refused to enter into a black market agreement in order to obtain his apartment in Malmö, and even threatened to alert the authorities to the landlord's behavior.[6]

Yet, for all this indignation, the black market was rife in Sweden. I would venture to say that a report on economic criminality occurred daily in the newspapers during my research there. Often, rich people were assumed to be particularly adept at navigating these waters. One businessman in his fifties told me, "In Sweden, we're all mafia. The Swedish people couldn't live as they do without it [the black market]." He explained that, as soon as one agrees to a black market transaction, one has saved 25 percent of one's costs in VAT.[7] But furthermore, he told me, the person receiving the money also saved because he did not report it as salary, so the money went "right down into his pocket." I was told of seemingly impossible reductions in price, all because of the lack of a receipt. One informant went to get an estimate on repairs to his car, and the figure landed at 4,000 kronor—well beyond his means. He took his business to a more local mechanic, i.e., one not affiliated with the dealership, and asked how much the work would cost if he "didn't need a receipt." The price went down to 500 kronor.

Craftspeople were a particularly storied group of black marketers. Apparently, after working for a customer three or four times, if one were trusted, a carpenter would then broach the question of whether one wanted the work done "without a receipt." Similarly, one woman told me that, as she slowly got to know the man who ran the corner quickie mart near her apartment, he started selling her black market cigarettes. Every time she asked for cigarettes, he would gesture with his hand, saying, "Do you want these Marlboros [pointing at the cigarettes openly displayed above his counter] or these Marlboros [pointing at a hidden and illegal stash below his counter]?" Buying the cigarettes below the counter, without a receipt, was much cheaper because they had been smuggled into the country and were thus outside the taxation scheme. Clearly, then, a receiptless transaction could only emerge when the locus of trust had moved into the personal relationship. The receiptless transaction between trusted exchange partners had a bit of the quality of a gift, where each person was doing the other a favor above and beyond the cold exchange of cash and services. When a receipt was *not* present, something else was traded as well (Mauss 1990).

Others told me that it was common to manipulate receipts. For example, when buying shoes, one could ask the salesperson to write "work shoes" on the receipt, which would allow the purchaser to deduct the shoes from one's annual income tax. Sometimes, two transactors will agree to write, for example, that forty chairs were purchased from the distributor, but in actuality fifty were bought. Then, ten chairs can be sold "black." One infamous businessman, Paul Klimfors, who became exceedingly wealthy via the manipulation of receipts in the taxi industry, had to move all of his ill-begotten cash across national borders. Court documents attest to his traveling to Spain with suitcases filled with cash, much of it the result of manipulated or absent receipts. He had to remove this cash from Sweden, since in the state's receipt-addled eyes, this cash could not possibly exist.

One friend's husband was an active black marketer, engaging in all sorts of receiptless black market exchanges. Once, he took me to get a cow that he had purchased under the table. When I watched the cow get butchered later, it was a display much like the gift-exchange networks evidenced in many hunting societies: a certain cut of beef was designated for the butcher, another section was given to the cattle raiser, smaller portions were offered to people who had done him other sorts of favors before. This man was a committed socialist (in his youth, he was a communist firebrand, by his own account), yet he saw his black market behavior in romanticized terms: he was recreating an old peasant lifestyle rather than evading his responsibilities to the socialist state's welfare system, which depends upon legitimate transactions.[8]

Black market transactions thus stood in an ambiguous position. On one hand, they were considered unsolidaristic at the state level, but on the other hand, they were clearly related to the return and consolidation of trust between transactors. In other words, avoiding receipts created solidaristic bonds among people at the local level while denying solidarity at a statewide level. Meanwhile, the presence of receipts was a de facto acknowledgment that social distance between transactors could be preserved, and no personal ties needed to be established or sustained. Ironically, then, the social welfare state's demand for receipts helped to constitute the cold cash nexus of anonymous exchange, one of the elements of capitalism which socialists tend to rail against most.

Therefore, seemingly in contradiction with much anthropological litera-ture to date, here we find a situation where the boundaries of the home (the People's Home) were built by a *lack* of indebtedness between exchange partners, while social indebtedness occurred in the more market-oriented sphere, where people were trying to accrue as much personal wealth and goods as possible (see Guyer 2004). By entering into an economic relationship where trust had returned to the individuals rather than being invested in the receipt, both parties were operating in a more self-interested fashion than the people who steadfastly committed themselves to the world of anonymous commodity exchange. But once the hidden third party is added to the equa-tion, this claim must be qualified: the locus of indebtedness had merely shifted. With receipts, people were sacrificing economic profit as they built and affirmed social relations with the state while they simultaneously main-tained anonymity with the immediate exchange partner. Without the re-ceipt, the state's claim to this piece of value was being called into question.[9] The credit that should have been accruing to the state was instead being spread between the illicit exchange partners during the moment of the trans-action. Thus, by engaging in black market transactions (or, as we will see below, by crossing the sound), one was denying one's position in the commu-nity and one's duties to it, but nevertheless building lasting social relations in a self-interested market sphere outside the control of the state.

Evading Blue Laws on the Deep Blue Sea

After taking many ferry rides to Denmark, I discovered that com-modity exchange across the Øresund echoed the black market in crucial ways. The sound and Denmark had been a famous zone of tax-free spend-ing for Swedes for many decades (Linde-Laursen 1995 and 2010). Both the many ferries that crossed the sound and their end destination stood as obvious and ready means to escape the Swedish state and the sumptuary laws that kept certain "decadent" products further out of reach at home.[10] The border itself was produced in part by this disharmony in consumption, and as will be shown, the EU and the region as its proxy have been making significant strides toward ending this disharmony.

Carefully looking at the types of goods carried across the sound and the manner in which they were purchased again shows how currencies can circumscribe particular moral (and, sometimes, legal) spaces. For example, because beer and cigarettes were in no way deductible from income tax, people traveling the boats and splurging in Copenhagen were less concerned with receipts.[11] Just like the black market transactions discussed above, people traveling across the sound were frequently doing so to evade the state taxation regime, for there exists no VAT on purchases made while abroad (or at least no VAT paid to Sweden, and the ferries were completely tax-free when in international waters). In an important sense, then, legal tax-free transactions outside the country were just as unsolidaristic as illegal ones within the country. In practice, if not in ethos, tax-free consumption on special purchasing journeys across the sound was identical to the unregulated exchange of the black market.[12]

One time, I took part in an exchange while crossing the sound that mimicked the sort of trust-building that occurred in the black market. When returning to Sweden, locals were often heavily laden with decadent consumables, especially beer. Back when the boats were in service (they went out of business soon after the completion of the bridge), one had to walk through a customs station, and there were specific amounts of alcohol and cigarettes per person allowed into the country; anything beyond these quotas was a sort of contraband and had to be taxed. As the boat was approaching land, two men about my age asked me and several others to help them carry their beer past the customs agents, for they had purchased well beyond the quota. As we emerged beyond the customs gate, we all returned our various portions to the two men. In exchange for our efforts in helping them to evade the taxation regime, we were offered a few beers each. As I mentioned above, it was highly unusual for Swedes to buy each other beverages, so this was truly a rare moment. This cross-sound purchasing trip had resulted in the sort of "you scratch my back, I'll scratch your back" ethos that was a necessary component of black market transactions. The casualness of the entire operation and the ease with which the others agreed to help these youth smuggle goods across the state line suggested to me that this sort of behavior was not at all uncommon.

This story brings up a point little remarked upon by Swedes regarding the similarity of the illegal goods traded on the black market and the goods acquired in special purchasing missions abroad. Without a doubt, all decadent goods that were traded on the black market were of foreign origin, including cigarettes, drugs, vodka, and the beer that was transported illegally from Denmark. A friend in the restaurant trade told me that many smaller restaurants throughout Sweden depended on Russian smuggling leagues for their alcohol; according to him, bigger restaurants had to "account for every last centiliter" of alcohol sold, so they could not get away with this illegal trade. Further, in the news and in urban legend, all the mediators of this trade in illegal goods were of foreign origin. Poles and Russians got caught smuggling liquor, while ex-Yugoslavs got caught transporting drugs. Copenhagen, aside from being associated with the imbibing of alcohol, was infamous for a part of the city called Christiania, which openly allowed the trade of drugs other than heroin (another section of town freely permitted this trade), and I heard Swedes complain that Copenhagen was fast becoming as notorious as Amsterdam. In this manner, the space within the Swedish nation-state became marked as legitimate, while corrupting influences stemmed from shadowy figures and chaotic locales outside of it.

Considering this, it is interesting to examine further the circulation of goods in Øresund. As one man who consulted businesses that wished to grow across the sound insisted, there was essentially no market in *legitimate* cross-sound goods. A woman I interviewed, who gave talks promoting the sound, would begin by telling her audiences, "There is no market today; it's a market in the process of becoming." Many standard goods of the Swedish and Danish diet, while virtually identical in content, had not managed to cross the sound to compete with each other. A system of national brands prevailed, and the only true market uniting the sound was the market in leisure or decadent goods.

There was a widespread belief in Sweden that certain non-decadent Danish food products were sullied, thus creating a further barrier to a united market in normal goods. Danish eggs, for example, were often assumed to be afflicted with salmonella. Similarly, after the country entered the EU, Sweden's beef producers began labeling their products with a Swedish flag in order to assuage people's fears about the origins of their meat. Eve Darian-Smith has an evocative discussion of the fears surrounding the Channel tunnel in England. In a chapter entitled "Rabies Rides the Fast Train," she argues that disease gets mapped onto foreign space, thereby allowing authorities to continue a regime of intense boundary control, even in the face of EU policy to the contrary: "rabies provides an acceptably neutral explanation for the maintenance and reinforcement of border controls. Rabies makes customs enforcement critical and spatial boundaries of inclusion and exclusion essential" (Darian-Smith 1999: 147–148). Over the many years prior to the arrival of the bridge, the Danish side of the sound had became marked and consolidated, via daily practice, as foreign space that was morally distinct from (in fact, morally inverse to) the governing strictures of the Swedish nation-state.[13]

It is thus worth reiterating that the only market that was harmonized across the sound was the market in decadent goods. This raises interesting questions about government claims related to the issue of cross-sound integration. There was a constant complaint that Sweden was not properly integrated with the other half of the region. Yet the black market attested to the vigorous integration of Sweden within a web of transnational markets; they just were not the markets that many Swedes who were boosters for the EU and the Øresund Region were interested in legitimizing or even discussing. As I will document below when discussing the euro, they hoped that these connections would remain hidden or be eradicated in favor of the legitimate transactions that they were having so much trouble convincing people to undertake.

Legitimizing Illicit Exchange: The Local Currencies

The ideas and practices of the local-currency advocates regarding the exchange of goods provide a fascinating contrast to those of dominant society. Therefore, I argue, they indicate much about resistance to the euro and its relationship to the building of the Øresund Region.

Arguably the most intriguing aspect of the local-currency advocates' theories (not least because they never voice it) was their almost verbatim repetition of the so-called cameralist doctrines of the seventeenth and eighteenth centuries, which were especially popular in Germany.[14] Many cameralists believed that self-sufficiency was the true mark of a strong nation, and they were strongly influenced in this belief by Aristotle (see Nielsen 1911; for more on cameralism, see Hart 1986; Small 2001 [1909]). They were thus an extreme version of mercantilists, who also chose to protect home products at the expense of foreign ones. However, many cameralists hoped to see a world without international trade altogether, a world where Swedes would trade with Swedes, and Germans with Germans, and oranges would grow against every south-facing wall in the northern hemisphere.[15] Increased self-sufficiency was one of the goals of the local-currency rings, just as it was for the cameralists a couple of hundred years ago.

And that increased self-sufficiency was directly tied to monetary policy for the local-currency advocates. While it is important to note that a range of different ideas occurs among currency ring advocates, there was a general distaste for the extraterritorial movement of money. That is to say, most local-currency advocates were opposed, as one person told me, to "these free movements of capital," the same movements of capital, it should be noted, that were widely attributed as the incipient cause of the collapse of the krona in 1992 (see Peebles 2004a). One member told me that a currency ring should never seek to expand itself over a national border, in this case, to Copenhagen. The whole idea, he explained, was to keep it local. He coupled the stability of money to the stability of production in a local society, stating, "The local currency at least stays put. It holds the companies here in the city instead of disappearing like the regular dollar can do: it can disappear over the entire world."[16] While speaking with another group of local-currency advocates, I was told that they believed that each nation should have "its own unit of exchange, non-convertible [with others]." This stringent demand also reflected their desire to create an internal market that would not need to trade with the rest of the world quite as much as the Swedish one did.

Fears about environmental degradation often came up during my interviews. These fears were then related to the seeming absurdity of the world of goods, many of which were considered unnecessary. For example, one person wondered: "Why is there Australian beer in England and English beer in Australia?" Similarly, I was told that Sweden used to make many basic things on its own that it now receives from other countries, for example, light bulbs. One person, while stating, "It's not sustainable in the long run," explained how potatoes are harvested in Germany, peeled in Italy, and then sent to the Swedish market for sale. Yet another currency ring advocate was opposed to the bridge only because it allowed cars on it; he thought there was little justification for a government to support an increase in the number of cars on the road. All these examples show a general belief held by local-currency advocates that an unnecessary commitment to capitalist trade had made people dependent upon things and processes that were completely insane, almost devilish in their skewed rationality, and causing damage to the earth with their unnecessary movements. Comments such as these evidenced a desire to curtail the forward march of the alienation of skills and knowledge occurring due to the increasingly global division of labor. Setting up a local currency could serve as a small step in the long-term attempt to recoup those skills and powers that had been lost to foreign places.[17]

The new desire to move across the sound for the alleged cornucopia offered by the bridge was seen as part and parcel of the general problem of globalization and alienation. Local-currency rings were built specifically to counteract these trends and to provide both people and goods with more stability. The consistency with which they all held to beliefs about the damaging nature of excessive trade and bizarre, irrational production chains attests to their desire for self-sufficiency and slower times. A return to such times, in their opinion, required better regulation and less boundary transgression. This vision could prove toilsome, however: one had to elevate the sweat of one's brow over the suspicious ease with which one might gain more goods from standard trade.

It is true that no one belonging to a currency ring thought that their currency would fully replace the krona, but the ideal behind the rings was to reduce their dependence on the dominant currency. As a significant part of this effort, three of the currency rings I encountered were agitating the local government to accept their currencies as partial payment for taxes.[18] This ties back to my earlier discussion of the black market in essential ways. Ordinary Swedes often accused the currency rings (if they had ever heard of them) of being merely a new way to legitimize black market transactions. When I brought this up, one interviewee responded by exasperatedly saying, "Ah, yes, the eternal question."[19] Nothing could be further from the truth in Sweden, for the local currencies in no way facilitated the evasion of taxes. No one registered the movement of goods better than a currency ring, and they all told the tax authorities that their books were open to them. So what brought forth such an accusation?

To grasp the answer, we must look at the goods that were traded in the rings. The currency rings had, indeed, basically legitimized the black market, but not in the sense that their accusers meant. The primary items that they traded among themselves were identical to the things that were exchanged on the black market—barring the market in decadent goods. They traded labor power, just like the craftspeople I referred to earlier. They traded old things lying around in their basements that someone else might make better use of, like the bicycles and the garage sales I discussed above. Yet, unlike the black market, they registered and regulated these transactions. They sought, in short, to deliver the receipt and its transparency to the transaction. They wanted to reunite elements of daily life that they thought had been unnaturally sundered by combining the social relations that incurred in gift (or black market) transactions with the regulation of trade provided by the state's demand for receipts.

By registering every transaction (they did not use receipts per se, but checks that were then mailed to the treasurer), they were theoretically keeping an eye on all transactions. In this regard, there were limits to the expenditures allowed. Thus, for example, if a negotiated price stepped over what seemed to be a reasonable limit, the board would have to approve the transaction. This, quite obviously, represented a new form of regulation over the black market. The irony is that these members of the anti-globalization Left actually endorsed the conversion of all unregulated gifts into regulated commodities. In their dislike of the power of money, they had proceeded to monetize everything in sight.

One advocate specifically insisted to me that the currency rings did not represent an attempted return to the gift economy. And I agree. Instead, currency rings, in battling the destructive potential of capitalism run rampant, recommodified and relegitimized things that otherwise fell within the purview of the black market (or gift economy) and its similar reliance on personal networks. Paradoxically, in order to banish anonymity and the cold cash nexus from the daily exchange of commodities, they were reasserting the power of the receipt. In so doing, they were keeping the locus of trust within the community as a whole and not between the specific transactors.

Ring members defended themselves against charges of economic criminality by asserting that their books were open to any authority that chose to look at them. More important, they explicitly denied any connection to the black market, for their trading, according to one member, "has the same goal as the taxation laws—to improve social welfare." By stating this, he was providing implicit evidence for my own claims. The black market was the zone of unsolidaristic transactions. Such transactions, for him, were obviously more self-interested and failed to enhance the general social welfare. The receipt would bring them back into the fold of community-spirited exchange.

But this evidence shows something much more: what they were essentially doing was attempting to create, via their currency practices, a new People's Home, the last one having disintegrated in the face of global capital and transgressed borders. Just as the Swedish state produced a currency space wherein commodity transactions were less self-interested than black market transactions, the currency rings were attempting to hold onto a zone of socialistic commodity exchange that had all too easily dissipated in the face of the escapes that were offered in places such as Copenhagen.

In their attempt to banish anonymity from commodity exchanges, the currency rings were building social boundaries, for the whole concept revolved around the idea that one needed to know one's trading partner. Indeed, one needed to know the partner well enough, for example, to know her financial circumstances so that one could negotiate a "just" price. There was, in short, an attempt to return to an alleged era when exchanges took place within community borders rather than at its margins (just as the cameralists advocated).[20] Inside these borders, monetary value was not supposed to be the reigning value and price was not supposed to be the universal common denominator. And yet, oddly, currency was the object that glued these groups together.

When we attend to the manner in which goods are exchanged in practice, we can see how these boundaries evolved. Via a commitment to transparency, bounded movement, and labor (producing one's own goods instead of relying on trade), currency rings intentionally attempted to reconstruct the exact boundaries—the boundaries of the precapitalist village —that capitalism was accused of destroying. This bounded zone of community would be marked by regulation and its accompanying receipts. In short, the rings had colonized the black market and regulated it better than the government ever could have.

Same Place, Different "Local": The Euro Advocates of Øresund

There were few elements of rhetoric more commonplace about the Øresund Region's neoliberal integration project than that it was concerned with improving the lot and power of *local* society. At first blush, then, it appeared to be highly similar to the local-currency movement. Both were hoping to replace the power of the nation-state by displacing it to a more localized society. Both were talking about increasing democracy if power devolved to the local. Both were asserting that everything would be more efficient and rational if people and governments started embracing the local.

Yet it would be absurd to assert any homology between the two projects. In spirit and ethos, they could not have been more different, though I am arguing here that they both stand as reactions to broader global processes. Advocates of the region hoped to break down nation-state boundaries; these were somehow anachronistic. The local currencies were trying to return to the imagined insularity that the nation-state had provided in the past. Regional proponents believed that many of the problems besetting their envisioned transnational space stemmed from the lack of a common currency, and thus they promoted the euro; currency ring members were trying to parse their region into a space with a variety of currencies that were, at best, cumbersome to convert.

But when it comes to the exchange of goods, all the differences become obvious. The currency rings took inspiration from the utopian visions of people such as William Morris and Charles Fourier: the outside market had wrecked a previous sense of community, and a return to simplicity and an embrace of peasant lifestyles was the solution. (They also, I would argue, took inspiration from the horrors of an imagined globalized capitalist dystopia.) As mentioned above, they were trying to reconstitute a version of the People's Home, which had been swamped by new waves of internationalism and global capital flows. Meanwhile, the people who worked to further the vibrancy of the Øresund Region shared more sensibilities with the Saint-Simonian vision of utopia. Technology, rationalized labor, and a unified currency would usher forth a new era of transnational brotherhood, cosmopolitan attitudes, and abundant material wealth.

It is hard to convey the sense of bounty and plethora that existed while people anticipated the arrival of the bridge (see Berg et al. 2000). To get started, we could turn to the apt encapsulation of these attitudes made by Steven Sampson, an anthropologist living in the region (and an expert in underground economies). When I first arrived in Øresund, he told me that people were treating the bridge as though it were "sympathetic magic." I agree and would extend this comparison further, by likening it to anthropology's classic description of cargo cults, which often deeply believed in the powers of sympathetic magic (Kaplan 1995; Worsley 1968). A cornucopia awaited Malmö, if only its inhabitants would leave the ideology of the People's Home behind and drink of the new possibilities provided by the EU.

The entire point of the Øresund Region, in direct contrast to the currency rings, was to increase production and trade circulation rather than limit it. Regional advocates hoped to competitively position their new transnational city within a broader field of capitalist relations rather than withdraw from them. Given the proper infrastructure and regulation, they believed, it could easily become a new, exuberant hub—in fact, a hub of virtually everything, according to them. They argued that it would be a new transportation hub, biotech hub, education hub, tourist hub, and production hub. Consider, for example, this proclamation, found at the offices of the planned (and much debated) CityTunneln, a new subway system for Malmö that would connect local traffic routes with the bridge route. It proleptically claimed:

> Home is best: Malmö sits where it always has. Just the same for Copenhagen. But not for much longer. When the fixed link over the Øresund is inaugurated in 2000, we will be facing a new reality. The changes might not happen overnight, but afterwards we Skåningar [people from Skåne, the southernmost province of Sweden] will understand and learn how to take advantage of the new grand region that we have become a part of. . . . At the turn of year 2006–2007 Malmö finds itself in an intensive phase with a new self confidence. Copenhagen and Sjælland have become part of the immediate surroundings. . . . Distance shrinks and new doors open. Quite simply we gain more to choose from—and *presumably an entirely new opinion about what we call "home."* (emphasis mine)[21]

Countless advertisements from the year prior to the bridge opening echoed these overly ambitious sentiments. So did many editorials in the leading daily newspaper. For example, in an editorial entitled "Take Away Obstacles to Regional Identity," the leaders of the Danish and southern Swedish chambers of commerce specifically posited the need for a train link between the region's two airports: one in Copenhagen and one outside of Malmö (Holst-Nielsen and Larsen 1999: A2). The authors coupled this need for increased transportation fluidity with the need for the euro, asserting that "a common currency is therefore an important prerequisite for integration, both in economic and psychological respects." Increased mobility of goods, people, and money, according to them, would bring about a new regional identity that would create additional opportunities, thereby increasing the movement of these factors further still.

At a conference I attended that was sponsored by the primary Danish financial daily, speakers continually asserted that they wanted the region to become a hive of activity and movement. It was pointed out, for example, that 50 million people lived around the Baltic, and the region would be the center for this population that had previously been separated (the thinking went) by water and war. The idea was to increase mobility and to be the desired stable center around which all the transgressive flows would circulate. One speaker went so far as to say that, in ten years, once the Baltic countries had joined the EU, "the Øresund Region will be the strongest in Europe," and therefore, "Americans will start placing businesses here."

Who else was part of this emerging market and what might the boundaries to this zone be? In fact, one of the primary foci of debates about the EU in southern Sweden regarded its impact on the movement and sale of goods. For example, for many years, the EU was derided as a suprastate organization that only concerned itself with the size and shape of cucumbers and strawberries.[22] This laughable commitment was only matched by the eurocrats' alleged lack of concern with Swedish health: it was claimed that they forced dangerous products into the Swedish marketplace (e.g., salmonella-laced eggs) or challenged the state liquor monopoly. The euro easily fit into this older discourse about the movement of goods, but was elevated—even by some of those opposed to it—for bringing about a cheapening and simplifying of commodity exchange. Directly after stating that the "EU can be so ridiculous [for worrying about such things as the shape of cucumbers]," a woman told me that she liked the idea of the euro "only because it'll be so damn easy. I haven't thought much more about it." In this analysis, matched by the analysis of Øresund proponents, the euro would deliver transparency of pricing and greater movement of goods and people, via ease rather than sacrifice.

The euro had already started channeling certain funds outside Sweden.[23] For example, its arrival in nearby countries was slowly promoting a shift in investment strategies. Banks had started issuing sleek pamphlets pushing their new "euro-funds," and even had salespeople standing on corners pitching them. The Stockholm and Copenhagen stock markets merged in 1999. I was told by one interviewee, a member of the national stock owners association, that this would make it easier for individual investors to buy and sell in Copenhagen; up until that date, he explained, it had been very hard for people to trade stocks across the sound, though it had been easier for large funds and institutional investors. At a conference I attended entitled Giant Stock Day, a speaker informed the audience that his company—Electrolux, one of the largest in Sweden—had decided to register its stock value in euros instead of kronor. It was, he said, a way to "produce trust [in the company] on the market." Such shifts represented the sorts of harmonizations that were slowly altering the flows in Øresund, regardless of whether the two nation-states ever joined the EMU.

One proponent of the euro spoke at a conference sponsored by the Danish financial daily. Immediately after insisting that the euro would eliminate the "traditional arbitrage" that occurred across the sound, i.e., the market in decadent goods that I described above, this speaker explained that the euro would spur a new wave of people in search of "little arbitrage." The euro, by revealing price differences that were previously hidden in the exchange rate, would cause people to search out deals in legitimate, non-decadent goods across the sound. With the aid of the euro, the region would bring about entirely new patterns of shopping, entertainment, culture, research, and education. The legal "black market" in contraband that Swedes and Danes had created across the sound would be replaced by a new, legitimate market that encouraged his newly coined notion of "little arbitrage," but destroyed the traditional arbitrage that had resulted from separate national currencies and regulatory regimes. According to this rhetoric, the euro was a powerful tool indeed.

This man was not merely speaking speculatively. The EU had already begun to rationalize the space within its confines. There was much discussion of how the EU was planning to close down all the tax-free business occurring across Europe, such as Sweden's beloved ferries and the famous tax-free shops at all the airports. These airport shops remain, of course, but travelers from within EU countries are no longer permitted to purchase many of the classic tax-free goods there. Likewise with all the ferries plying the (previously international) waters of Western Europe. If traveling between two EU countries, these ferries no longer have the right to sell tax-free goods. In fact, one particularly popular ferry, the one that traverses from Stockholm to Finland, nowadays must stop at a small set of quasi-independent islands called Åland in order to preserve its raison d'être. The remaining boats running between Sweden and Denmark's other ports have all lost their right to sell goods tax-free.

Previously, European borders were marked by the border-poaching arbitrage provided by tax-free sales of decadent goods that I described above, which mimicked the black market in many ways. Thus, by undertaking such transnational journeys, citizens were slipping outside the gaze of their respective nation-states, just as they did in black market transactions. This new inability to do so within the EU suggests that the EU has overtaken important elements that contribute to producing "legitimate" versus "illegitimate" social spaces. The ships will have to embark for new territory, for these practices now must slip outside the gaze of the EU itself rather than the nation-state.

The EU government, as it struggled toward "state-ness," was quite clearly trying to bring transparency to the economic transactions that used to mark trips "abroad" within Europe. It was also elevating mobility as a moral good—both for people and for commodities. All should be flowing, and flowing transgressively and endlessly. From this perspective, harvesting potatoes in Germany, peeling them in Italy, and selling them in Sweden represented a major success, despite the complaints of the local-currency advocates. Such a configuration of production is an incarnation of the efficient market par excellence, unencumbered by the anachronistic boundaries that marked communities in previous times. Finally, the EU government endeavored to make "foreign" space for all Europeans a space of labor, rather than the space of leisure that it had been for so many decades. The euro would aid in the deliverance of all these goals, and this was openly stated whenever its benefits were touted by its proponents.

It is only a matter of time before people start retaining their receipts from labor-related trips across the sound; should these receipts become common, their presence will index a fresh faith in a new regulatory regime. One woman whose job it was to educate businesspeople on how to cross the sound informed me that businesses could now deduct expenses related to crossing it. Likewise, the customs house that used to regulate the ferry trade in decadent goods has been replaced by rare scouts on the train and a ridiculed mailbox based on the honesty principle at the train station.

Social legitimacy and labor will still get mapped onto home, while the foreign will retain the air of illegitimacy and decadence. The grand point, of course, is that people's sense of community boundaries—what is "home" and what is "foreign"—can change. Copenhagen will become less foreign, St. Petersburg will remain so.

The Greenhouse Effect

Saint-Simon foretold that the modern world would shift "from the government of men to the administration of things" (Rabinow 1995: 1). In Øresund, we can see who is winning the debate.

On October 9, 1999, I feared that I needed a team of ethnographers, for two important events conflicted with each other, and I wouldn't be able to attend both. The local currencies' supra-Scandinavian organization was supposed to have its third annual meeting outside of Copenhagen; at the conference, members would explore how to reinsert human relations into everyday commodity exchange. Meanwhile, in Malmö, all Swedes were being invited to Giant Stock Day; there, Swedes would be told how to stop trusting the communal organization of wealth by the nation-state and start trusting a more anonymous market.

As it happened, the local-currency conference was canceled. When I called the organizer to ask what had happened, he said it had been canceled "because of a lack of interest." Not enough people subscribed to their vision of a small currency promoting autarky and minimizing needs. I proceeded without guilt to Giant Stock Day, which was packed with locals scribbling down the wisdom of the day onto notepads. Plenty of people were interested, apparently, in the world of increased trade represented by the euro.

Notwithstanding this blatant testimony to the ascendance of the euro, in at least one way the proponents of the local currencies were not so different. Both groups were trying to circumscribe—via the tracing of otherwise anonymous money with such things as receipts—a new space of legitimate transactions after the last one had failed. There are, for example, still an abundance of trade protections at the borders of the EU that aim to channel the flows of production and consumption in specific directions, just as the local currencies try to do. Receipts represent one important way in which these regulating regimes try to document and thereby control these flows.

One leader of a local-currency ring said he believed that governments should serve as a "greenhouse" for the market: it required this protection to grow and thrive. He was unconsciously echoing the claims of Childs, who asserted in 1947 that the Swedish People's Home had created an admirable model of "hothouse" capitalism (Childs 1947: 160–161; see chapter 1). I think that advocates of the EU were striving for something very similar. The two camps just radically disagreed about where the greenhouse's walls should be built.

FOUR

The Mark of Money

Regulating the Flow of Subjects

You can't read away development. It has its pace. And we
vagrants will disappear, and all people will work in the
service of society for the sake of all, and life will receive
its inspiration through the hands of labor.

—*Martinson 1949*

[E]very prodigal appears to be a public enemy, and
every frugal man a public benefactor.

—*Smith 1976 [1776]*

While walking toward the Copenhagen harbor one day, I spotted a man
who appeared to be dead, lying face down in the middle of a well-trafficked
street. I did not quite know what to do, but noticed that everyone else
did. The Swedes who were all hurrying to catch the next boat just kept
walking right by him. This seemed an odd display for citizens famed for
their solidarity with their fellow humans. I hesitated. Thankfully, so did
one Swedish woman. We consulted each other and then stooped to investi-
gate whether the man was breathing or not, for he was completely motion-
less. Indeed, he was alive and appeared to have recently exited one of
the bars in the local party zone. He was, in short, merely in need of a

long, alcohol-induced sleep. He had just chosen a particularly perilous spot to collapse.

As we hovered near him and contemplated what to do, a Dane yelled at us in Danish, "Take him back to Sweden!" Of course, there was nothing about this particular human that made him look particularly Swedish or Danish. Rather, his location and behavior (or lack of behavior) identified him to this Dane as a Swede. Presumably, all the Swedes who neglected his dire circumstances also had hazarded a guess as to his background and reason for being there, and this was why they chose to bypass him and his sordid predicament. Copenhagen was well known as a place to escape the moral regulations of the Swedish nation-state, so people expected to see misbehaving Swedes in the Danish capital. But it was not only the man's excessive drunkenness that reminded me that many Swedes escape moral regulations by leaving the nation-state. The general lack of sympathy for someone in need was also notably out of keeping with standard Swedish moral codes: Sweden was a place filled with people who prided themselves on their kindheartedness toward anonymous others, especially fellow citizens.

The Øresund Region was, ironically, quite well integrated prior to the gigantic push to integrate it. But as this episode of the unknown-yet-widely-recognized drunken Swede in the middle of the street shows, it was a region integrated via leisure and individual decadence, not via labor and communal care. Swedes and Danes alike kept several ferry companies afloat with their continual back and forth over the sound. Somehow, however, all this human mobility was not enough for regional boosters. They wanted more; or rather, they wanted to increase a certain type of mobility, not mobility per se. They wanted the region to be a flowing market of regulated goods, labor, and capital, not a flowing market of unregulated black market goods, nonproductive leisure activities, and hidden hoards.

Considering all this, I started to wonder if, somehow, future-oriented activity stood as a central underpinning of the regionalist ideology. In the opinion of regional proponents, were labor and productivity the only path to a unified moral community—to a new conceptualization of the boundaries of home? Such questions led me to think about the manner in which the modernist Swedish welfare state gradually eradicated unregulated, "decadent" behavior from its midst over the course of the nineteenth and twentieth centuries as it built the People's Home. Quite famously, the social "parasite"—the present-oriented and overly mobile vagrant who allegedly wanted to live happily off the labor of others—had disappeared from within the bounds of Sweden. Riding the ferries of Øresund, however, suggested that this alleged parasite had not so much disappeared as just been shipped abroad—to unregulated foreign spaces such as Denmark and Finland.

In an accident of history, the Øresund Region and its bridge were trying to subsume the locus classicus of Swedish extraterritorial leisure: Copenhagen, Denmark. Just as Swedish vagrants of yore were considered non-laboring, spendthrift, and decadent "foreign" intruders into the bounds of a properly state-regulated zone, I will show how Swedes, when abroad in pre-bridge Copenhagen, often assumed a similar role as leisure-oriented and uncontrolled foreigners. Just like the vagrants of the previous era, they too were banished to their "home" (in the historical annals of vagrancy, this was often a disputed locale) on the soonest possible embarking vessel.[1]

In the Øresund Region, the EU and its proponents were pushing to eradicate this practice. The new bridge and the new currency represented intimate parts of this effort. In short, the EU was working to "reterritorialize" (Gupta and Ferguson 1992: 20) Copenhagen *for Swedes*. It planned to transform the regional space from a zone of extraterritorial leisure into a zone of humdrum labor, from an unregulated exterior space into a regulated interior space. The goal was to create an entirely new, transnational sense of social belonging. Regional advocates and the EU, if successful in this endeavor, would eliminate banishment as a punishment for the sins of vagrancy by enlarging the bounds of the home, just as the Swedish state had done. In order to ensure that Swedes would be treated as new Øresundians (instead of as foreigners) when in Copenhagen, regulated labor would be promoted.

Conversely, unregulated leisure that relies on economic and regulatory asymmetry should, ideally, be exported to a new extraterritorial region outside of EU regulatory space, just as the decadent goods discussed in the previous chapter were. Advocates of the region held that adopting the euro was part and parcel of such an effort to promote regulated labor. The evidence will show, therefore, that builders of both the Swedish modern welfare state and the EU aimed for full citizens to be granted the right to "move without money," whereas this used to be the precise "crime" that marked an individual's status as both a vagrant and, more often than not, a foreigner. Social action would work to build a new society wherein a citizen's right to movement cannot be circumscribed by access to money. In other words, there is a relationship between the regulation of labor and the construction of a sentiment of nativeness in the Social Democratic state. As I will show below, the aimless wandering of vagrants was associated with the foreign, and prior to the harmonization of space under the Swedish People's Home, they were always sent "home," that is, to their home village. Because certain types of approved labor were compensated with money, currency often became the material residue that demarcated proper movement.

As I will also show, the currency ring advocates shared the vagrants' distaste for this power of money to categorize individuals, and I believe that this explains why both groups sought to step outside the governing currency nexus. Local-currency advocates sought to find ways to organize a society that focused on spending rather than saving—a society that did not allow savings to be hoarded and fetishized as capital. They wanted to be judged by non-economic standards, and they did not want their conception of freedom to be determined by an object outside themselves and their immediate social group.

If this sounds strange, consider Sahlins' argument in "The Original Affluent Society" (part of his *Stone Age Economics,* 1972). He argues that ideas about what constitutes "wealth" can be contested, and different societies can have different teleological paths for their economic production. The original affluent society was rich because of its members' lack of interest in attaining an infinite variety of goods; they were satisfied with little and therefore could afford much free time. Vagrants and currency ring members often wished to pursue this type of freedom, minimizing their needs and thereby increasing a certain type of freedom that they preferred over other types of freedom.[2] Both groups showed that one of the paths toward achieving this was to reject the power of the dominant currency and the suspicious ease with which it could build a community organized around the division of labor and increased efficiency. Instead, community could be achieved by sacrificing individual ease for the benefit of the group.

Approaching the Diverse Forms of Vagrancy, Analytically

In order to proceed with this argument, it is essential to first turn to the illuminating work of Day, Papataxiarchis, and Stewart (1999). Turning to their work allows me to isolate at least one reason that many states seem to discriminate between the flows of labor and leisure in the manner that I am concerned with here. Day, Papataxiarchis, Stewart, and their contributors show that often states are predisposed to criminalize and banish people with a "present orientation," whereas they valorize and support people with a "future orientation." In their book, *Lilies of the Field: Marginal People Who Live for the Moment*, they bring together a compelling and diverse set of ethnographic examples of marginalized peoples, and suggest that they all share a common ethos: the ethos of living for the present, of living an "anti-economic" life where the world is structured around abundance rather than scarcity. The authors argue that sharing, autonomy, intense mobility, freedom, and a disdain for hierarchy often form vital components of this present-oriented ethos (3–4, 7).[3]

In living a present-oriented life, these people delve into a ritualized space in "non-durational time" that creates an alternative to the burdens forced upon them by dominant society. Politically speaking, living for the present is not a passive but an active stance, for "timelessness constitutes a powerful tool of resistance and opposition to surrounding neighbors and institutions" (Day, Papataxiarchis, and Stewart 1999: 3).[4] In this ritual space, people value today over tomorrow, finding the present full of "joy and satisfaction." Contrariwise, many dominant societies await better days from the ever-distant future and find that the present is filled with "suffering and deprivation" (ibid.: 2). This is a key insight; I rely on it in order to argue that Copenhagen and its boats served as this ritualized time and space for many Swedes.

As their book details, people with present-oriented lifestyles are often targeted by states for "reform" and singled out as suspicious and potentially nefarious by dominant groups. As Stewart explains, they are often accused of being decadent and of "harvesting without sowing" (1999: 29). States have often tried to "settle" them and train them to integrate more fully into the state's harmonized and regulated economic space. What is additionally striking about this is the fact that the phenomenon is so widespread, found in such diverse places as Amazonia and industrial Japan.

The vagrants of nineteenth- and early twentieth-century Sweden could be added to this list. By doing so, I would like to build upon their point that the "ritual construction of a present is not just an escape from the real world but also changes the world. However, in the existing literature, the implications of this sort of [present-oriented] action have not been adequately delineated because political anthropology has focused on instrumental action oriented to the long term" (Day, Papataxiarchis, and Stewart 1999: 18). In other words, we can learn a great deal about states and emergent states by witnessing the interplay between dominant societies and people who are alleged to live with no thought for the morrow. By looking at groups of people whom dominant society perceives as present-oriented (whether it is true or not), we can see how mutual pressures between these social actors bring forth a new world, something as radical, for example, as a functioning and integrated transnational city.

In nineteenth- and early twentieth-century Sweden, the vagrant's present-oriented attitude toward money—his alleged spendthrift ways— often raised the hackles of state bureaucrats and other reformers (see Gill 1999; Papataxiarchis 1999; Stallybrass and White 1986: 125–148 for similar examples). According to the nineteenth-century Swedish state's logic, spending money "carelessly" announced a commitment to the present and to gratifying consumption, whereas saving money clarified one's dedication to the future and to laborious production. Not carrying enough money for tomorrow, therefore, was considered to be evidence of a lack of interest in laboring or, at the very least, evidence of not laboring *enough*.[5] It also served as evidence that one might well be planning (or be forced by exigency) to sponge off the community's hard work. In light of this, proof of regulated laboring (i.e., gainful and reliable employment) served as a vital method for being accepted into the community in the customary Swedish welfare system that preceded the state welfare system.[6]

But, as the history and practice of vagrancy will show, in the marketplace one could enter into a different sort of covenant: one was granted rights according to the amount of money one had in one's pocket. Thus, the vagrant was welcomed into market space despite her ceaseless mobility so long as she had money. Once the money was gone, she was sent packing, back to an alleged home that would care for her regardless of how well she had planned for tomorrow.[7] Often, vagrants were laborers, in fact, essential and hard-working laborers. Among other things, they were busy taming the northern forests or undertaking unwanted work on the farmstead. Swedish police archives document in endless detail the manner in which hard workers were classed as vagrants and cast out of town simply because of their lack of money for tomorrow. Classically, for example, when harvesting work on a farmstead dried up, the workers were dismissed. If caught without money while migrating to the next iteration of unregulated labor, they were classed as vagrants.

This mobile mass was seen as dangerous, threatening society with its alleged prodigality and threats to dominant social mores. In other words, prostitutes and peddlers, orphans and widows, drunks and journeymen, insane people and migrant laborers, could all be classed—bizarrely to our eyes—under the same legal category. They were not necessarily prodigal nor did they necessarily move around too much. Rather, they had the audacity (or mere misfortune) to move into market space without enough money for tomorrow.[8] In short, for one reason or another, these people were all marked as non-savers, and thus received special treatment by the state: banishment, jail, the workhouse, rehabilitation, etc.[9]

It is this different teleological orientation of time, money, and people that proponents of the Øresund Region were trying to change. The EU *qua* state in formation was attempting to colonize an old space of vagrancy—a space that was oriented, for Swedes, around spending and leisure—and convert it into a space of Swedish investment (i.e., saving) and labor.

Beier relates a similar situation from the era of the consolidation of the English state.[10] He utilizes the history of vagrancy reforms in order to contest the claim that the English state was weak at the time. Just like the EU today, it had no standing army or national police force, and its jurisdiction thus relied frequently on uncooperative officials at the local level. In a further similarity, the interests of these local officials often stood opposed to those of the national state, and thus it was hard to ensure any sort of village-level enforcement of national legislation. (In the case of the EU, this jumps to the opposing interests of national and European Union levels.) Beier asserts that vagrancy legislation was the first to dovetail the interests of the local with those of the national, and thus the English state "developed a number of institutions to control vagrants that were novel and greatly extended state authority" (Beier 1985: 12; see also 146).[11]

Taking this as a suggestive parallel to the situation in the EU today, I am arguing that the attempts of the EU government to eradicate forms of vagrancy (both by stopping the flow of leisure-seeking Swedes to Copenhagen and by instituting a vast "unified refugee policy") may be creating a classic instantiation of an unintended consequence. In this case, the extension of EU powers and the commensurate growth of its state could result, since immigration policy stands as one of the vital spheres in which national and EU interests dovetail. As is well documented, most of the nation-states, if not all, that comprise the EU have expressed a profound interest in seeking EU-wide measures with which to cope with their seemingly more localized immigration "problem."

By noting such parallels, I am by no means implying that there are no actual differences between, say, migrant laborers and tourists. I am saying, instead, that certain states in certain historical epochs may have chosen to neglect these differences, and instead lumped these varied social actors together by marking them all as present-oriented non-savers.[12] Non-savers had to be banished or reformed because of the bad example they set and because of their apparent lack of contribution to the future social reproduction of the state.[13]

Following Gal and Kligman (2000), Herzfeld (1997), and Maurer (2005), we should therefore trace this state logic as an ethnographic object (however offensive it may be) and see where it takes us, rather than merely revealing it to be unenlightened. Though it is now denigrated within the nation-state itself, I intend to show that this state logic, which dictated who could and could not move without money, still reigns without question in emergent legal spaces. If we search it out, we might then see something new about the treatment of people who move without money, of people who—for whatever reason and for whatever duration—share an orientation toward the present instead of the future and thereby gain Smith's label of "public enemy" for their alleged prodigality (see the epigraph, above). The EU and Sweden both tried to stop the mobility of alleged non-savers in order to delineate zones of future-oriented production and present-oriented consumption, thereby reconfiguring the geographies of vagrancy. By examining these choices, we can discern connections between types of time and money use (labor versus leisure, saving versus spending) and the shifting borders of belonging and exclusion.

Historical Vagrancy, Ever So Briefly

We could almost complete the task of studying the Swedish government's lengthy endeavor to eliminate vagrancy by merely noting the shifts in the practices of naming the vagrant. An array of governmental reports, laws, parliamentary discussions, and police reports attest to Sweden's long engagement with vagrancy. The titles alone grant a sense of the slow change in attitudes. Beginning their historical career as "wanderers" (*kring-strykande*), by the nineteenth century we start seeing the term "defenseless" (*försvarslösa*; referring to the lack of money on their person).[14] At the end of that century, the term "unattached drifter" (*lösdrivare*) enters the lexicon. Finally, the most telling assemblage from the twentieth century: "societally harmful asociality" (*samhällsfarlig asocialitet*) and the more straightforward "junkie" or "drug abuser" (*missbrukare*). This arc traces a slow shift from a resigned attitude toward the wanderers (who often provided essential services on the farmstead), to the laissez-faire indictment of being defenseless in the daily economic war of man against man, to the scientized danger facing the social collectivity.

Briefly, the Swedish state evidenced a widespread hatred of mobile populations during the building of the People's Home. Vagrants (*luffare*) were a storied and fairly common group of people who wandered the country roads of Sweden. Myriad government reports, newspaper articles, propaganda pieces, and fictional literature attest to their presence and centrality in the Swedish imagination. (One of the most famous Swedish novels of the twentieth century relates the story of Bolle, the vagrant.) Here is a succinct illustration of the prevalent attitudes, taken from a government commission's report:

> Aside from the fact that vagrants can be called parasites upon society, who are far from living in a socially useful manner, [and also] are a burden for society and cause it much expense, this [social] element constitutes a large portion of those who have made themselves guilty of criminal activity or could be feared to surrender themselves to crime, even if they haven't always been won over to this. . . . Vagrancy therefore constitutes a danger for law and order's preservation, and if it is allowed to freely flourish without setting [regulatory] measures from the general public, this danger will without question increase at a high rate. ("Betänkande" 1929: 82)

Here, we see the claim that, without social action, vagrants could readily overrun the country. Furthermore, other reports attest to governmental concerns that children need to be protected from the ways of vagrants, lest they succumb to the tempting lifestyle. Simply put, there was a fear that the life of the road might exert a pull on citizens and draw them into unproductive lives or "unregulated lifestyle[s]" (Koch 1926: 75, 78).[15] One begins to wonder if the builders of the People's Home were scared that the population in general might find it more fun to *not* accept their ideology of parsimony and regulated labor.[16]

In a series of reforms beginning in 1885 and continuing until 1981, vagrants were decidedly eradicated as a shame on the public conscience that needed to be washed away by the establishment of the orderly Social Democratic state.[17] Other groups were also famously settled during the same era: the "travelers," or "tinkers" (as they are sometimes called in the British Isles), the Roma, and the Saami (the transhumant reindeer herders of the Arctic region). The People's Home—composed as it was of countless smaller middle-class homes—quite clearly could not tolerate anyone refusing to hold down a fixed address (see Scott 1998).

Instead of delving more deeply into this cultural history, all that needs to be established here is the vagrant's relationship to the governing morals concerning work, money, and travel. These, in turn, contributed to ideas about foreignness. Vagrants found themselves breaking the law simply because it was illegal to be found abroad with no cash (and, significantly, "abroad" meant anywhere outside the home village, even if they were Swedish vagrants in a Swedish city).[18] They found themselves abhorred because people often believed that they did not want to work and instead wanted to live off other people's hard-earned material wealth. Such people, often referred to as "parasites," had allegedly adopted a lifestyle where movement was the end, not the means: a constant life of wandering with no purpose.[19] In short, vagrants were accused of being wandering, lazy, and drunken spendthrifts. Consider, for example, the following from a government document:

> Unpracticed with the ownership of a large amount of money, he is subjected to, and in most cases, falls victim to the temptation of squandering the money on strong drinks or an excess of clothes or some such, and old buddies or new friends from the bar aid him in quickly finishing off the resource. While in possession of the money he has decided that he has no need of work, and when it is finished he's already back again on the vagrancy trail. (*Underdånigt* 1882: 55)

These sorts of accusations were leveled despite the fact that the labor of the wanderers contributed greatly to building the nation in numerous ways. By and large, vagrants performed all the *unregulated* labor that no one else wanted to do. Indeed, even this didactic quote reveals a certainty that the person will return to some form of work once he runs out of money. The problem, as Weber noted in his famous Protestant ethic essay, was how to make this desire for money more steady, reliable, and continuous, rather than mercurial.

As alleged spendthrifts, they rarely had any money on them and were not managing to save any money either. Such wandering, unlike the sanctioned movement of the businessperson, was illegal not in and of itself, but because it was movement without the legitimizing mark of regulated work and the money that results from it. Carrying money stood as a guarantee against "non-parasitical" behavior in the future; it testified to a legitimate plan for tomorrow, and this was important for the burgeoning and increasingly anonymous towns of the industrializing era.[20] Herein lies one of the keys: as someone who was removed by choice or circumstance from the system of future-oriented money savings, vagrants claimed that they lived "on their own time" (Day, Papataxiarchis, and Stewart 1999; Gmelch 1977). Instead of relying on money, they were constantly proposing barter transactions (mostly food and lodging in exchange for work or a song). Alternatively, as we saw above, they were spending it with panache and vigor as soon as it came into their hands, not worrying about tomorrow at the expense of enjoying an abundant today.

For centuries, such brazen people who moved without money were dealt with under the "law of the home village" (Widen 1906). It dictated that vagrants be returned to some alleged home, thereby demarcating home and abroad, membership and exclusion, depending upon access to money. Thus, just as Harrington (1999) has pointed out, the welfare policies of small villages created new zones of inclusion and exclusion, often defining membership by birth or work (see Wimmer 2002 for a similar story at the national level).

However, there was another sort of belonging that was outside the confines of the village: belonging in the marketplace. Evidencing a proper level of social personhood in this community depended upon having money. Otherwise, one was deemed, legally speaking, a foreigner who was unable to take part in this other community's daily rituals. Such a foreigner was always sent home. The strongest testimony to this foreign status within a market community—not, for example, a typically "imagined one" of blood or soil (Anderson 1983)—is surely the fact that, prior to the vagrancy reforms of the twentieth century, non-Swedish and Swedish vagrants were treated exactly alike: all were sent to their various and scattered homes, regardless of the state in which such a home might be located.[21]

As I traced the governmental reports through the years, I found a slow erosion of the category "unattached drifter." Through modern science, the category was continually fine-tuned, precisely because modernist reformers insisted on the obvious differences between, for example, drunks and migrant laborers. It was simply not rational or fair to have a catchall law for these diverse types merely because they all shared a potentially moneyless tomorrow. First, the age barrier for all laws protecting children was raised to twenty-one, so that a broader swath of people came under this new, protective ambit. Soon after, an "alcoholics law" was passed that called for new treatments of this group. In 1918, a law was passed that addressed the problem of prostitution. By 1929, a law specifically dealt with the mentally ill. A new "care of the poor" law dealt with beggars. New homes were built for the care of the elderly. A 1980 parliamentary report finalized the process, insisting that, from then on, every county should take care of any Swedish citizen, mobile or immobile, found inside its borders. The vagrancy laws of the nineteenth century were finally taken off the books in 1981, and it was no longer illegal to move without money (as long as one was classed as Swedish).

Home was now everywhere, and there was no home county to be shipped back to: the foreignness attached to poverty had allegedly been eradicated. The People's Home and its vast welfare state had colonized market space, previously marked as foreign and outside the community. The entire country became communal, tamed, and regulated toward future-oriented productivity, and the vagrant could not be left behind in this development, as the epigraph above from Martinson presaged. The village and its communal control over labor practices and welfare within its confines had moved to a national level. This is at least one reason that Sweden was widely celebrated as an achieved utopia during the second half of the twentieth century. Aptly, almost 500 years prior to this, Sir Thomas More had envisioned the guaranteed care of migrants as one of the touchstones of utopia. He wrote, "Wherever they go, though they take nothing with them, they never lack for anything because they are at home everywhere" (More 1993 [1516]: 60).

Costly Connectivity

Many people in Sweden saw the state's job as providing for a sort of money-losing connectivity of goods, labor, and capital. As one businessman told me, "You can't grow all by yourself."[22] Many of the reforms to eliminate vagrancy can be seen in this light—as techniques for homogenizing national space in an effort to make the labor flow more readily within the bounds of the nation-state. In the form of harmonized regulations, toll-free highways, subsidized labor migration, and other methods, the Swedish state built supports for the mobility of labor and capital that would otherwise have been too costly for any one individual or company to undertake. At the same time, this regulatory apparatus and infrastructure, as I argued above, was intimately related to the building of a sense of moral community, wherein all are cared for within its specific boundaries.

Proponents of the EU were trying to alter this state-channeled flow in places like the Øresund Region by making it cheaper (in time and money) to move *outside* the nation-state in search of labor. In other words, the entire concept of building the region involved governmental expenditures that sought to facilitate the flows of labor into new territories. The policy carried an implicit belief that labor builds cohesive communities in ways that leisure never can. In so doing, it mimicked the same regulatory developments that gradually eliminated the practice of vagrancy and that simultaneously helped to create a sense of a national People's Home.

The people arguing in favor of the adoption of the euro saw the currency in precisely these terms. The primary lobbying group promoting the euro, the Association for the Monetary Union of Europe, was funded by major industries and businesses of the continent. Its literature explained, tirelessly, that the euro would allow businesses to more fluidly work with an international labor force. Impressively, though many economists and pundits pointed out how expensive it would be to convert to the euro, it was still pushed through as part of a more general idea that states should pay for the fluid connectivity of their citizens.

The proponents of the region picked up on the same theme, constantly informing the public of the need to adopt the euro so that Swedish businesses could survive and even expand into other regulatory spaces, such as Copenhagen. The euro was the mark of an alleged newfound freedom: the freedom to move in a wider social space without being encumbered by currency conversions. Freedom of choice was also advertised as a great boon. By joining the EMU, Swedes would have the freedom to choose where to live, with whom to bank, and where to invest in profound new ways.

It appears that this rhetoric failed with the Swedish population. As we know, Sweden voted against joining the EMU. As evidence of my claim that senses of nativeness were linked with regulated labor, whenever I asked whether joining the euro was "good" or "smart," Swedes would invariably say that its main benefit was that it would make *leisure* travel easier. The EU's governing bodies had failed to convince Swedes that traveling abroad *for work* was worth their while; converting to an entirely new currency just to make a few weeks of vacation each year easier did not seem like a risk worth taking.

In any event, what is clear is that both Sweden and the EU, as state apparatuses, valorized labor and tried to coddle it with both hidden and overt subsidies. Leisure, on the other hand, was largely left to its own devices, and, at worst, the state tried to ship it out of its regulatory space altogether with sumptuary laws and the like.[23] By attending to these different efforts at channeling labor and leisure, we can see the subtle activities of a new state—the EU—as it battled for the hearts and minds of the citizens of old ones.

The following section will clarify this discussion by elaborating on the nature of typical past Swedish leisure practices in the market space of Copenhagen, just outside the nation-state, and the sumptuary laws that dramatically reduced leisure practices within Swedish space. Swedes mimicked the vagrants of yesteryear, in that practicing vagrancy was similar in effect to refusing to contribute to the national welfare via regulated labor; as a momentary vagrant, one refused (or did not have the means to accept, in the case of migrant laborers classed as vagrants) the power of these rules. One escaped, however briefly, into an orientation toward the present. Consequently, even the cash that one might have had as a vagrant or a migrant laborer did not have the same teleological orientation as that of the businessperson: it was not destined to become future-oriented capital, it was only a present-oriented means of consumption. And this was unacceptable if the Øresund Region was to be built, as planned, as a zone of fluid and charged capitalism.

Ship of Fools, Hourly

Comparing the two different modes of transport over the sound speaks volumes about the transformations that were under way in Øresund. When I first arrived in Malmö, one could only cross the sound by boat. There were three ferries in or near Malmö. Two competing companies (Pilen and Scandlines) departed from the city center and landed in a tourist district in Copenhagen, and the other (also owned by Scandlines) connected Limhamn, Sweden, with Dragør, Denmark (this one was not only a passenger ferry, but also transported trucks, buses, and cars). Since the bridge was built, all of these routes have shut down.

What is intriguing about the use of the ferries was their association with leisure travel. The Pilen boat connecting the two cities was openly considered a "party boat." It was much cheaper to ride than its Scandlines competitor, and people thought of it as more "trashy." The level of service was also different: on the Scandlines boat, there were waitresses while the Pilen boat only had a kiosk where one had to wait in line for beverages and food. Though the Scandlines ferry was assuredly the choice for business travelers over the sound, it was also utilized by a great many tourists.[24]

The ferry connecting Dragør and Limhamn also survived off its connection with festivities. The operating company openly proclaimed this during the debate over its closing. The company explained that it had to close many months prior to the bridge opening because the boat subsidized its movement of freight during the slow winter months with its movement of revelers during the summer months. Since the bridge was opening the following summer, it would lose a great deal of money. There were few commuters who were impacted by this shutdown. Despite their protests in the media, the state decided against subsidizing the Dragør ferry, and instead let it die, leaving people to travel to Malmö in order to catch a boat. In other words, if the boat had been a more vital means of transporting laborers instead of, if the neologism be permitted, "leisurers," it would perhaps have continued its service at least until the bridge was functional. By way of comparison, the Swedish state, tellingly, subsidizes every train ticket over the bridge into Copenhagen.[25]

Boats such as these had enabled the creation of a national tradition, called "to tour" (att tura), wherein people hopped on ferries that left Sweden for other lands in order to get wild, or at least to initiate a consumption-oriented splurge on decadent goods. I was endlessly informed (and witnessed) that this was not only a rite of passage for Swedish youth, but was continued by other generations, albeit in more civilized doses.

This is not least related to the cheaper costs of drinking on these boats. Because they were in international waters, they provided tax-free imbibing. The boats were thus organized around festive consumption: the Dragør ferry even had draft beer and tax-free stores on board (tax-free stores, it should briefly be noted, sell mostly "luxury"—decadent—items, including perfume, cigarettes, liquor, and candy). Much beer and Gammel Dansk (a Danish hard liquor) was tossed back, at all hours of the day. Significantly, all of these boats landed in locales that were not associated with Swedish or Danish work; they landed in tourist centers, especially a strip of bars and restaurants that in the evenings was always filled with Swedish revelers. Dragør is a quaint village with typically Danish architecture. Many of its stores survived by selling products (especially decadent ones) to visiting Swedes, who found them cheaper there than at home. The citizens of Dragør were even more worried about the shutting down of the ferry than were those of Limhamn, knowing how much their town depended upon Swedish extraterritorial consumption practices.

The new bridge and its trains caused the quick shutdown of the two ferries most associated with leisure (the nominally more business-oriented Scandlines ferry shut down a little while later). Despite heading into some sort of international space, there were no tax-free products for sale and certainly no beer or Gammel Dansk; instead, only coffee, that singular drink associated more with labor than leisure, was for sale. The trains delivered one to completely different parts of Copenhagen: its airport, its central train station, and other local commuter stops. In fact, they ran along the same commuter rails upon which working Danes depended, stopping in parts of town that were not considered touristy in the least.

Also, the bridge traffic was not policed by the Swedish border patrol nearly as well as the ferries were. When disembarking from the ferries, one had to walk through a customs zone and was often subject at least to a brief scan from the police (people of color invariably had to show identification). Occasionally, one spotted a drug dog sniffing passersby for contraband. The police were looking for illegal immigrants as well as any attempts to carry home too many festive objects from the trip to Denmark (as described in chapter 3, there were specific per capita allotments of alcohol allowed into the country). These trappings were largely absent when crossing via the bridge, replaced by such weak epigones of nation-state power as a voluntary customs-declaration box at the first train stop in Sweden. The shift in all of these practices, I argue, revealed a belief that Copenhagen used to be a zone of potentially dangerous, present-oriented consumption and was becoming a more mundane and orderly space of future-oriented production.

The bridge, in short, was designed to harmonize Copenhagen's and Malmö's labor practices, not their leisure ones. I heard a witty and perhaps unintended encapsulation of this fact when I attended a business conference about the exciting possibilities promised by the new bridge. A Danish speaker at the conference quipped, "The nice thing about the bridge is that it will get the Swedes home at night." Clearly, Swedes had a bad reputation for their disorderly behavior. Indeed, their reputation was so bad that one might hazard the hypothesis that Swedes on festive journeys to Copenhagen shared some of the same behavior, and suffered some of the same stereotypes, as the vagrants of previous eras.

Consider this short poem, published in Malmö's main daily newspaper (it is not uncommon for poetry to be produced for the newspapers, and amateur poetry is a national pastime in Sweden). Unfortunately, my translation does no justice to the rhyme scheme or the rhythm, but it is nonetheless worthwhile to read (the original is reproduced in the notes).[26]

During the 17th and 18th century two brother peoples were seen to fight
Both Swedes and Danes got to suffer heavily
Scania [the southernmost province of Sweden] eventually switched sides
For a long time the people had to wait for the brightening future
Øresund was a dividing sea

During the 19th and 20th century it was mostly relaxing
Swedes and Danes were seen to visit each other
A tour over the sound was a new way to party
And the memory of the trip remained with most people
Øresund was a uniting sea

Toward the border of the 21st century one can see how time flies
On a bridge one will ride the train and drive risk-free
Its pillars were seen to be very stable
But on it no beer nor aquavit nor relaxation is proffered
Øresund won't only be a sea for boats

So we hope that the boats continue to dash
Even though they can occasionally be unstable
They nonetheless invite time for beer, aquavit and relaxation
For young and old and somewhat senile
Øresund will be a sea with a bridge as a hub.

By Nils Gunnar Toremalm of Lund (Sydsvenskan 1999: C1)

This rich poem succinctly summarizes several of my points about changes in the region. The boats facilitated festive visiting between Swedes and Danes. Notably, such festivity depended upon alcohol consumption. With the development of the bridge, the world had become more humdrum, risk-free. Its pillars are sturdy. There is none of the alcohol that was consumed on the boat, which contributed to its sensibility as a zone that specifically conferred a sense of relaxation and leisure. In short, the bridge seems utterly serious, with no room for youngsters or older folk (two classes of nonworkers, in Nordic welfare states at least). The author hopes that the festive boats continue to ply the waters. He even hints that perhaps their festive nature resulted from their unstable movement. Foucault's cryptic assertion that "water and madness have long been linked in the dreams of European man" could easily serve as a theoretical undergirding for this suggestion by the poet (Foucault 1988 [1961]: 12).

The author was not so much worried as nostalgic, hoping that a zone of festivity would not completely lose out to the new stable world that considered the bridge its vital center. It strikes me that this poem marks the distinction between a space of decadence and consumption and a Saint-Simonian space of ceaseless productivity and security: schematically speaking, a space of present-oriented debauchery versus a space of future-oriented productivity. Both zones are zones of connectivity, but their raisons d'être are wholly different.[27]

The general culture of leisure travel should be briefly explored as corollary evidence that many Swedes embraced the attitude of the vagrant when they traveled outside the nation-state. A newspaper article states that, in the early 1990s, Swedes traveled abroad more than any other population in the world (Olsson 1999). The organized group tours (*charterresa*) placed ubiquitous ads in the local papers and had many offices around the country. Even a popular film by one of Sweden's most famous comics (entitled *Charterresa*) satirized Swedish travel abroad. I was told on more than one occasion the seeming urban legend that there was a specific ski town in Austria that had banned Swedes. They always caused too much of a ruckus, fighting and vomiting throughout the town.[28]

Even more suggestively, another rite of passage for virtually all Swedish youth was "to go train hobo-ing" (*att tågluffa*): riding the rails (*tåg*) and exploring Europe on a shoestring. Am I drawing too many conclusions from the use of the term *luffa,* the verb form of the word "vagrant"? Upon leaving the country, they mimicked the practice of true vagrancy that was abhorred and repressed when it occurred within the country during the building of the People's Home.[29] They even slept and hung out on the streets outside train stations (the classic abode of the vagrants of old in Sweden), and they were generally short on cash. This rite of passage was celebrated as a moment of freedom and happy-go-lucky childishness. And it was certainly an extended period of no labor.

A trademark of being a *tågluffare* (an individual who rides the rails in this manner) was that one would come home as soon as one ran out of money; thus, the money that people brought with them at the outset often delimited the length of their trip. In other words, the trip was not defined by an itinerary that needed to be fulfilled, but rather by a resolute wandering that needed to come to an end at a random point in time, when the money ran out. This was also the trademark of vagrants, who traveled with only enough money to get them to the next town or the next meal. (There is also a similarity with the law of the home village: as soon as someone was found penniless abroad, they were sent back home.)[30] This calls to mind Zelizer's (1997) main argument that money gets earmarked for specific purposes; for the *tågluffare,* a specific amount of money was put away for travel and, thus, not for savings and incorporation into the system of Swedish welfare and production. Tellingly, these earmarked bills were transferred into other currencies (for it was much less common to *tågluffa* within Sweden itself) and never made it into the socialized wealth of Sweden.

Noting the manner in which such national rites were played out abroad, one is reminded of Foucault's (1988 [1961]) discussion of the old "ships of fools" that plied the rivers of Europe prior to the incarceration of madmen. Cities would place their insane residents on merchant and pilgrimage boats that would come through town, thereby cleansing their spaces of urban chaos. When these ships did land in cities, the streets were filled with scores of roving lunatics, but only temporarily. With only slight exaggeration (for certainly not all Swedes on the boats were drunk), one can posit that this was a nearly exact parallel to the plight of pre-bridge Copenhagen. Pushed out of southern Sweden by sumptuary laws that discouraged the consumption of alcohol, Swedes in search of altering their minds would inundate Copenhagen hourly. These Swedes had temporarily abandoned their reason, conveniently leaving it at home, so to speak.

This reference to Foucault does not preclude critiques of his work that have instead emphasized the relationship among the eradication of vagrancy, the growth of the welfare state, and evolving notions of nationals versus aliens (e.g., Harrington 1999; see also Wimmer 2002). I agree with Harrington's argument that vagrancy as a bureaucratic "problem" gave rise to new boundaries of exclusion and inclusion. Governments believed that they had to carefully separate out workers and (alleged) nonworkers in order to discern who was contributing to the general welfare and who was not (see also Agamben 2000 on "denizens").[31] I am only relying on Foucault here in order to point out that a present-orientation gets labeled as a sort of unreason that needs to be reformed or banished.

In Copenhagen and other locales abroad, Swedes were natives of market space, encouraged to stay as long as they had money, but exiled as foreigners back to their home villages to sober up as soon as it ran out. As consumption-oriented missions, these Swedish trips abroad allowed for a brief foray into the pleasures of living in the present.[32] They could blissfully forget about tomorrow and spend their money today, without any guilt that they were not saving for the good of themselves and their community. I know a mother who returned home penniless from a leisure trip abroad (a journey she made without her child). Now that the spending frenzy was over, she had to start "being responsible again with [her] money." In classic vagrant fashion, when her flight was canceled and she had to wait until the next day to get home, she slept at the airport because she had no more earmarked money left to spend.[33]

It is as if the ritualized space of present-orientation discussed by Day, Papataxiarchis, and Stewart (1999) could only be recreated outside the Swedish nation-state. Outside the country, Swedes were often in danger of committing all the asocial practices that they attributed to the vagrant: spendthrift ways, mobility, drunkenness, embracing leisure, shunning work, and a general freedom from dominant social mores. Recall, for example, that when I spotted the passed-out reveler on the streets of Copenhagen, most of the Swedes just kept walking right by him. This was a sort of thoughtlessness toward one's fellow man that was considered crude (often colored as a peculiarity blighting only America) and unacceptable *within* the nation-state.

This belief that one must be thoughtful toward one's compatriot argu- ably stood as the moral grounding for the entire welfare state apparatus. That vagrants did not care about anyone but themselves—that they were pathological individualists—was a frequent critique from the era of their desired eradication. In Copenhagen, most of the Swedes—at least on the day when I saw the man sleeping on the street—just wanted to make sure they caught the next boat. Thus, we are no longer talking exclusively about the stereotype of the drunken Swede abroad, but about a more general phenomenon of solipsistic consumption that tended to present itself in foreign spaces instead of the cooperative production that organized itself within the home.[34]

As described above, the advent of the bridge altered the conditions of possibility for this sort of extraterritorial debauchery in Copenhagen. Meanwhile, the boats that traveled to Finland remained famous for their festive nature (though this story is also interesting vis-à-vis new EU laws; see chapter 3). This stands as evidence that states can manipulate the flows of labor and leisure and, in so doing, impact conceptualizations of space.[35] A heavy tax on decadent goods can indeed be seen as a different incarnation of the ship-of-fools policy of early modern Europe, for it successfully ex- ported Swedish (temporary) madness and nonproductivity abroad.[36] Tax- free partying financially rewarded the reveler for "taking it outside," and thus created the utterly economically rational desire to devote oneself to tantalizing consumption (in all its non-alcohol and alcohol-related forms) in front of foreigners instead of one's compatriots.

Thus, with the Øresund Bridge and the EU-sponsored regionalization project, a new state is greasing the wheels of future-oriented labor, just as was documented earlier for the Swedish state. Meanwhile, it appears that leisure needed to support itself (attested to by the closing of the boats, discussed above) or even be shipped abroad by latter-day sumptuary laws. In seeking an answer for why this recurs in many capitalist states and the EU, I am suggesting that the state conceives—rightly or wrongly—of lei- sure as present-oriented action and labor as future-oriented action. Follow- ing Day, Papataxiarchis, and Stewart again, we must ask why states so frequently favor future-oriented action, while they simultaneously insist on the elimination of present-oriented actors, such as alleged vagrants.

Beier gives an answer for early modern England. As he shows, vagrants there were seen as a sort of anti-society and considered fundamentally dangerous to the structures of dominant society. He even claims that the English translation of a 1509 book entitled *The Ship of Fools* marked the beginning of a general fear of a vast group of lawless wanderers threatening the values and pillars of "good" society (Beier 1985: 7). In the case of twentieth-century Sweden, the perils and contaminations of vagrancy could not be altogether eliminated. Thankfully, though, they could be exported on contemporary incarnations of the ships of fools.

Local Currencies and Human Mobility

Having surveyed much of the movement that was related to the use of national currencies in Øresund, I would like to touch upon the relationship between movement and the local-currency rings. As I have mentioned elsewhere (and as is implied by the name), the local currencies "forced" one to stay local.[37] In this sense, the new bridge was anathema to the local-currency project. Indeed, the majority of currency ring advocates whom I interviewed were largely uninterested or even strongly critical of the Øresund Region.

In order to understand this, recall the monetary theories behind the local currencies. The local currencies hoped to encourage (rather than liquidate) a sense of indebtedness among members of the community. Buying and selling should be a humanistic relation, not an economic one. Currency ring members wanted the currency reserve to be comprised and sustained by humans (by real human bodies rather than by abstract institutions or objects) and by the trust between members (rather than by trust in an external material object). Thus, we should not be surprised that an aspiring currency ring member (he had yet to find or establish one close enough to his home) critiqued Øresund as a "megalomaniac project." It was, he asserted, "a lot of stone, glass, metal and concrete. . . . it doesn't grab me at all. . . . [I]t's this giant-scale [trend], it loses the individual." There was no human element to the Øresund project's embrace of a market community, a community of constantly liquidated debts using regular currency, with all of its inherent faults.

Another currency ring member made the relationship between money and mobility even more clear. He told me that "all people are in debt," and the reason that "money doesn't correlate with reality is because it makes it possible for you to be *kvitts* [out of debt, square]" (see previous chapter). But when I asked him how one might travel if the world was filled with only local currencies, he described how there were already plans to address this issue. People involved in the movement, he told me, were talking about issuing circulating credits for travelers. For example, local-currency members across the globe could assume the role of "hosts," allowing members of other local-currency rings to stay at their houses when they traveled abroad. The host would then receive some "global" credits to stay in another location. In theory, if the system became general enough, one could eat and lodge anywhere one wanted to travel by creating relations of indebtedness with foreign others, rather than relying upon the liquidation-of-debt model represented by dominant currencies. Instead of producing a perfect exchange of money for service, as with a hotel, one would be in debt to the person with whom one stayed. Participants would, therefore, be actively engaged in producing human relations between individuals rather than economic ones. This interviewee expressly claimed that the interest in local currencies was a "reaction to EMU. People no longer believe in the political system. . . . it lost its power with the deregulation of currency." The advocates of local currencies saw a solution to economic crises in grander social regulation rather than simply in depending upon a new currency's increased sphere of circulation (i.e., the euro).

Further, the currency ring members' governing theory was self-reliance. "Since when have we become dependent upon a global market?" they often demanded to know. One middle-aged supporter of currency rings complained that Sweden was no longer self-reliant, proclaiming, "We used to grow oranges in Sweden!"[38] With any number of products close at hand in the more self-reliant world they were trying to build, why would one ever need to move across the sound in search of products? In other words, aside from the structural constraints upon moving outside the currency circle (technically, due to the lack of reserves), there were also ethical constraints. One currency ring member insisted that the point of the rings was "to create a society that doesn't parasitize itself upon the rest of the world." In their view, the vast majority of capitalist-generated products were the result of parasitism (usually, a parasitism that relied on false accounting, such as a factory not paying for the damage it did to the local environment, a cost that should have been incorporated into a proper price).

Such a claim was a common mode of denigrating the market system in general—the same market system that the Øresund Region explicitly embraced (see also Kennedy 1995). We can therefore see that the arguments about the potential and desire to move within physical space were directly related to a more overarching argument about the building of the Øresund Region. The local-currency ring members were, in short, dissidents who insisted that an entirely different picture of societal development would be more preferable. They stand as examples of how the rhetoric of the "inevitability" of the region's coming market zone was actually deeply contested, and certainly not enthusiastically accepted by all. They also stand as excellent examples of how beliefs about monetary policy can easily correlate with beliefs about other public policies that would appear to be far removed, such as whether or not a state should spend money building a bridge.

Aside from the ways in which the advocates of local currencies desired to institute new practices that would govern human mobility, another central tenet of local-currency monetary policy relates to the concerns I am elucidating here. All local-currency advocates abhorred the fact that standard money was interest-bearing. They saw this as a central problem with dominant currency, for they believed it created currency's pathological demand to unnaturally make more of itself. This demand then in turn forced a future-orientation upon the individuals who used the money, for they were lashed to a system that only values certain types of labor, labor that produces *more* economic value than the amount that was loaned. Such a system forces the economy at large to constantly be striving to produce more and more—more things and thus more environmental destruction—than was necessary for average humans to survive. Currency ring members preferred to minimize their needs rather than be enthralled to an interest-bearing currency that forced them to produce a specific future, one of increased (and, as they saw, irrational) production and consumption. Thus, refusing to be bound to a particular future dictated by the nation-state and its currency was something that the local-currency advocates shared, oddly, with the alleged vagrants and partying tourists studied above. All of these diverse groups sought, by denying the power of money in their daily lives, to escape a particular national future, even if only momentarily.

Vagrancy Eliminated?

Given all of this, we should look once again at the arrival of the new regime that was attempting to turn Øresund into a grand zone of future-oriented labor. I have argued here that the region's proponents were concerned with regulating labor across the sound. Interestingly, there was never a drive to harmonize leisure practices across the sound. In fact, the geography of debauchery outlined above specifically depended upon the *disharmony* of the leisure regimes governing Denmark and Sweden. Copenhagen, a space of unregulated leisure for Swedes during the twentieth century, was being sold and pushed as a new space of promising and life-enhancing regulated labor in the twenty-first century. These efforts were being supported by an emerging state that wanted to spend money on labor connectivity in the new area: out with the present-orientation and in with the future-orientation.

The EU was making extensive contributions to the realization of the region, and it hoped that this transnational region would become a model space of the borderless Europe, with the national border losing its everyday meaning. People would cross without a thought to the fact that they were leaving one nation-state and entering another. Instead, they would embrace a new regional identity. The people leading the charge shared a belief that future-oriented labor could promote a shared sense of belonging to a community. According to their logic, present-oriented leisure just did not work as a communal glue, nor had it throughout the twentieth century.

The region's proponents were attempting to incorporate a subset of people previously treated as vagrants in Denmark (Swedish citizens) and convert them to the region's new ethic of socially binding and fluid labor. In short, they sought to convince these mobile leisurers that the region, as a newly delineated unit, was a regulated home and not an unregulated abroad. If Copenhagen as a space of vagrancy *for Swedes* was successfully conquered, Swedes would no longer be considered foreign there. Instead of being shipped back on a boat when they ran out of money, they would be cared for in Copenhagen itself, or they might even live there permanently.[39] The EU *qua* state would have produced a new, more expansive home, while the notion of foreignness would shift to countries farther afield.

But for all this talk of the region as a zone of inclusive, future-oriented labor, there were still groups that were labeled present-oriented vagrants, and they were not targeted for any of the EU-led reform policies directed toward Swedes. For them, the region remained a market space. Prior to the completion of the bridge, one always had to pass through a customs control room upon arriving in Sweden. The basic criterion for getting through this zone without having to show papers was skin color. With rare exceptions, people of color had to stop and show passports or ID, even if they were born in Sweden (see Löfgren 1999). As a result, one often spotted a family being denied entry. They were the new globalized era's migrant labor force. In a repetition of history, they too were constantly sent home. But the meaning of "home" had altered. Instead of being sent back to their villages in Sweden, these people were sent home to some other country: Pakistan, Iraq, Turkey, Romania.[40] The determination of foreignness by assessing the amount of cash one carried seemed to have returned, merely attaching itself to new—and equally diverse—populations.

Interestingly, the critiques that were cast at today's immigrants were virtually identical to those voiced against the asocial and unattached roamers of an earlier era, the people caught abroad with no money. I was told numerous urban legends about immigrants' abuse of the so-called everyman's right, the rule in Sweden that guaranteed traditional gathering and usufruct rights on other people's private property. Vagrants had depended upon this law for their enhanced mobility, and people complained that they used it for purposes for which it had not been intended.

Further, I was told many variants of the claim that "it's hard to integrate someone who doesn't want to be [integrated]." This was voiced as part of the immigrant "problem," just as it was the focus of decades of government reports and policies relating to the asocial roamers. Likewise, there was a constant refrain about the relationship among immigrants, criminality, and work: Sweden needed to learn how to integrate these people in order to put a stop to their criminal behavior. Honest work was the solution, just as it was for the vagrant. (There is today a strong belief that most black market goods are transported and sold within the country by various immigrant populations, as documented in chapter 3.) A related complaint circulated that immigrants were lazy and only came to Sweden to live off others: they were the latest incarnation of the alleged parasite.

Finally, countless people voiced the concern that these foreigners would "overrun" the country if the situation were not "controlled." This fear was also one of the central impetuses behind the drive to address the vagrancy problem in early twentieth-century Sweden. As a businessman in his fifties attempted to convince me over a cup of coffee, "Previously, people came here because they were smart at something. The Finns and the Walloons have contributed a lot to Sweden's advancement. But now people only come here to live for free."[41] Such people, scandalously, attempt to move into foreign space without enough money for tomorrow. If they garner a regulated living, however, they become less suspect. Regulated laborers were incorporated laborers, well on their way to becoming "native," at least within a socialist ethos, where joining the system of regulated production stood as the premier mark of social inclusion and proof that one had joined the system of future-oriented social welfare.[42] One immigrant proclaimed in a magazine, "If you succeed in Sweden, you become Swedish; if you don't succeed, you remain an immigrant" (ETC 1999: 46).

I am reminded of a point made long ago by Raymond Williams in his book *The Country and the City* (1973). In the penultimate chapter of that remarkable work, Williams points out that the migration from country to city had not ceased, it had only moved to a grander scale. The "corrupting influence of foreigners" in the metropole now hailed from the West Indies or India rather than from the rural zones of the British Isles. Despite the fact that these workers constantly provide labor that redounds to the glory of the nation, the credit for this glory, except in a few scattered folk songs, always bypasses the workers who helped to build it.

Furthermore, if Beier is correct, forms of vagrancy—at least in the cases presented here—also provide a reactive impetus in the building of the state, forcing it to increase its policing powers in a continuing effort to control them; it must spend money and effort to channel flows of labor and to colonize the flows of leisure. The ritualized spaces directed toward the present must be eradicated (or exiled) in favor of homogenized spaces dedicated to the future. Some of the political implications for present-oriented action brought up by Day, Papataxiarchis, and Stewart thereby become manifest, for boundaries are made anew in this process. As the European Union continues to strive to create a unified refugee policy to be applied within its harmonized market, we should avoid the hatred often leveled upon mobile populations, who are frequently labeled "foreigners," yet who are always greatly aiding in the construction of a new state and, thus, of a new definition of "home."

FIVE

Indebted Communities

Exiling Economic Hierarchy to the Margins

One who is in debt is not free.

—*Title of Swedish prime minister Göran Persson's memoirs*

On June 9, 1999, the citizens of Malmö awoke to a shocking front-page news scandal. Just on the heels of saving the town's ice hockey team from millions of kronor of tax debt owed to the state (an event that had been covered extensively by the media), the wealthy and popular financier who resuscitated the beleaguered team was seized by the police for questioning. As he was driving down the highway from where he had slept the night before, undercover police officers picked up Percy Nilsson for a day of questioning regarding potential tax fraud; his office was searched for potential evidence. By the time they let him go, his passports had been taken from him and his movements were confined to the southern province of Skåne. (This is a common practice in Sweden—a grand extrapolation of "house arrest" to the borders of the national home.)

It is significant that his passports were referred to in the plural. Percy Nilsson was a rags-to-riches phenomenon, a native of his beloved Malmö. He began his career as a carpenter and now presided over a massive construction empire. Yet for all his love of home, he had moved to Belgium years before. The Swedish tax authorities were fearful that Percy—as the press readily referred to him—might perform one of the oldest tricks in the

Swedish book: he might disappear without a trace in the face of mounting debts to the state. By claiming that he lived elsewhere, Nilsson was avoiding untold kronor in taxes and was thereby a Swede who was failing to "do right by himself." His decampment outside the country was the classic antisocial maneuver in the socialist state. It allowed for his alleged debts to the nation-state to go unpaid.

Despite such allegedly shifty maneuvers, many people in Nilsson's camp voiced disgust with the authorities for picking him up with undercover police officers, as though he were a common criminal. Nilsson announced that he felt humiliated by the treatment he received. He even claimed to be thankful that his mother had recently died, so that she did not have to witness the debacle. One man cited in the newspaper said that the behavior of the tax authorities was "nasty," that "Percy Nilsson isn't any bandit or murderer" (Johansson and Wierup 1999b: A7). No indeed. As we will see, he was more pirate than bandit, an important distinction.

Manipulating one's spatial location as a means to avoid debt has a long and storied history in Øresund—and in Europe in general—as do the measures that have traditionally been employed to combat such behavior (see also Roitman 2003). Significantly, Copenhagen was one of the most common places to which Swedes disappeared in the past, and the attitudes toward this sort of behavior shed light on the efforts to unify the region.

This chapter begins by briefly studying the history of the debtors' prison. Because relying on a prison system as a method for addressing everyday bankruptcy seems so foreign to people in the twenty-first century, it is helpful to look at the debtors' prison as a contrast to today's system. I then work my way forward to the Øresund Region and the EU in order to examine the dominant credit and debt moralities and the practices of debt forgiveness today. These moralities, I argue, promote a sense of community boundedness (and the occasional need or desire to escape it). The local currencies also starkly reveal the way in which debt socialization practices are related to community boundaries, for the currency rings show a deep dislike of individualistic accumulation, and they have successfully built a system where debts within the circle can be easily socialized. Finally, I argue that the euro and Øresund may be gradually changing the boundaries of debt forgiveness and individual wealth accumulation that previously operated in southern Sweden and eastern Denmark, not least by forcing a new monetary hierarchy to prevail over previously separate cities. In the process, it will become clear that there is no economic distinction that delineates the debt-forgiveness practices that occur within the community from those that are invoked (or not) outside of it; deciding who receives forgiveness and who does not has nothing to do with the profit motive and everything to do with cultural boundaries of inclusion and exclusion.

In the twenty-first century in much of Europe and America, debtors are forgiven every day. When their debt is forgiven, it is socialized, meaning that other people besides the debtor lose money. We all agree (whether we know it or not) to pay in order to preserve the human dignity of the debtor and, probably more significant, in order to preserve the risk-seeking, entre-preneurial spirit that drives the Western economy. (For example, it is said that credit card companies assume that $2.50 of every $100 charged should be written off as unrecoverable; this cost is built into the rates that we all pay to these companies.) Yet, outside our community boundaries we view debt forgiveness with deep skepticism.[1] Much of the developing world is mired in infamous debt, yet there is only the weakest of fringe movements that strive to have it forgiven—to consider all people, radically, as part of the same global community. In fact, the movement is so fringe that it is often dubbed anarchist, and the riots these "troublemakers" cause at IMF meet-ings are well known.

In short, there is an entire ethos regarding the idea of accumulation and its inverse, indebtedness, that is rarely discussed but clearly evident, espe-cially when one attends to the ethnographic data presented by the compet-ing currencies of Øresund. This ethos is intimately related to the pragmat-ics of movement through time and space, for legitimate monetary relations entail a specific set of borders, as Nilsson's plight illustrated. If one wants to escape these monetary borders, one has to leave the community altogether and become a pirate by stashing one's treasure in a remote and hidden locale. Dominant beliefs concerning degrees of freedom to move through time and space are tied straightforwardly to the notion of indebtedness.[2] Indeed, the Swedish prime minister published a book while I was living in Øresund. Its title, he explained, came from the norms and values of his upbringing: "One who is in debt is not free." We must carefully delve into this individualist dictum that paradoxically lies at the heart of Scandinavia's social democracies, to see how a new ethos is insisting that community can be built without this sort of rigorous disavowal of debt.

A Brief History of the Debtors' Prison and Its Demise[3]

The widespread historiographic neglect of the phenomenon of the debtors' prison is particularly odd when one considers Foucault's famous thesis from *Discipline and Punish* (1995 [1977]).[4] Foucault traced a trend throughout the Western world during the nineteenth century: a pan-Western reform movement that shifted the system of punishment from one that vengefully tortured the body to one that sought to reform the soul. One of the significant effects of this reform effort was a new interest in building prisons. New types of prison technologies were theorized and introduced (e.g., the well-known panopticon), and do-gooders roamed the planet on missions to gather data on often deplorable prison conditions.

But this is only half the story, for just as these new prisons were proliferating, the debtors' prison was falling into abeyance and slowly losing its legitimacy. The debtors' prisons that had littered Europe were all shuttering their doors for the last time. Given this fact, it seems important to think seriously about why bankruptcy and indebtedness have been neglected as part of the history of criminality.

As many have documented, prior to the prison-building movements described by Foucault, many punishments involved a simple payment. Simmel (1978 [1907]) discussed the *wergild* system, in which human bodies and body parts had precise monetary values attached to them for the purpose of determining punishment and compensation. Nietzsche pointed out that "quite detailed legal assessments of the value of individual parts of the body" existed with which crimes and punishments could be calculated and adjudicated (1956: 196). Franzen gives a concrete example from Sweden: a man who had committed a crime could choose between paying a fine of forty marks or "losing his nose" (1998: 182).[5] Perhaps the simple reason for the long existence of the debtors' prison[6] is that an unpaid debt is clearly the only crime for which one cannot demand monetary compensation, so there is no choice except to punish the body.

Perhaps, however, immobilization for not having money might naturally suggest itself as a means to convince debtors to do right by themselves and to remind any future debtors of the value of keeping up payments. Just as the vagrants discussed earlier offended the sensibilities of their era by scandalously moving without money, perhaps debtors awakened anger and vengeance because they too managed to move (retain their freedom) in spite of their lack of credit. All the way until the time of our protagonist, Percy Nilsson, we have been scared that the debtor would turn vagrant and abandon his society, his social ties, and his monetary debts.[7]

Parliamentary debates of the early to mid-nineteenth century attest to this fear, clearly giving evidence that indebtedness can often be equated with thievery. Agitating for the alteration of extradition treaties so that debtors could be brought back to Sweden from Denmark and other foreign zones, one report from 1840–1841 pointed out:

> [S]windling debtors, who take themselves out of the Kingdom with the intention of not returning, become unmolestable with that treasure [*skatt*] that they have tricked away from the honest man and converted into mobile means. This makes a mockery of the law, that a swindler could be free from the demands of the law because he luckily managed to make it *across the Øresund* or the Torneå River [which forms the border with Finland and Russia]. (Riksdagen 1840–1841: 12:6–7; emphasis mine)

After explaining that such practices will increase in frequency once people understand that they can thusly avoid their debts, the parliamentarian suggested that "the conventions regarding criminals that [we] have with foreign powers should be broadened to include swindling debtors" (ibid.). Since one of the state's premier duties was to ensure the smooth traffic in goods and money, any tactics that undermined this public system would necessitate state action. Thus, this author asserted the need to include unpaid debt within the scope of other criminal legislation. Unpaid debt was the equivalent of thievery, appropriating someone else's hard-earned economic treasure[8] without compensation, and hiding abroad with it to boot.

But with the newfound ability to police borders by revoking passports instead of using imprisonment, the state was enacting reforms along the lines suggested by Foucault, but perhaps in a more dramatic fashion than even he could have imagined. The entire confines of the nation-state had become the new reforming prison, replacing the vengeful debtors' prison. Released from his cell, the debtor could now do right by himself and attempt to return to society's money relations, but only because the state could now forcefully keep him within the confines of the circle of debt while overseeing his daily reform.

In further keeping with Foucault's theories, debtors' bodies, it was surmised, should not be punished; rather, society should discover a means to better reform and aid them in returning to solvency. A rash of bankruptcy legislation reforms and studies occurred across Europe at the same time as the prison reforms that Foucault discussed, and the arguments that promoted such legislation were grounded in morality rather than economic rationalism.

Here, I can only provide brief examples of the debate in order to illuminate my argument. One nobleman, an earl named Sparre, who had been inspired by reforms in other countries, spoke in the parliament in 1859 and tried to convince his compatriots to abandon the debtors' prison. He stated that "incarceration as punishment for every debtor, regardless of what caused his insolvency, remains a survival from those times when, with a not yet fully educated concept about humanity, *the creditor's right to the debtor's property was conflated with a right over his person,* even though higher laws than society's forbid this" (Riksdagen 1859–1860: 41:1, emphases mine; see also Simmel 1978 [1907]: 362).

Earl Sparre did not win the argument that time around, but by 1868 the Swedish government had delimited sentences in the debtors' prison to six weeks. Society, the report argued, had decided that other "measures of force" could now be used instead of the restriction of mobility. From now on, the newly developed bankruptcy laws would take care of any debtors who swore to "do right by themselves" (Riksdagen 1877: 2:59–60). Just as the vagrancy laws sought to do, the modern state hoped to separate the value of humans from the value of money: they would be judged by moral criteria rather than economic ones. Bankrupt citizens were now categorized as either those who wished to repay their debts or those who refused to do so.

During this period of debate, creditors also had their say in trying to keep the prisons open. Interestingly, they critiqued a spendthrift bent on the part of the debtor that calls to mind the virtually identical critique of the vagrant. One of the characters in a pamphlet, when asked for a bottle of wine, responded, "Damn brother, can you even ask such a question? You know that I have never held anything away from my friends, and that's why I'm sitting there [in prison; they had taken a stroll away from the jail]" (Anonymous 1829: 4–5).[9] These people were portrayed as shiftless spendthrifts by their creditors, valuing leisure over labor. At the same time, they were viewed by the opposing camp as people who had merely failed to value money properly, choosing the importance of maintaining human relations over the tight following of a budget.

Indeed, some people in favor of celebrating non-monetary human qualities came to view the prison, paradoxically, as a space of freedom. As a zone that oddly protected them from their creditors, it provided them with the first time in their lives when they were free of the cares of money. One satirical play by a famous Swedish dramatist of the era had its protagonist, a debtor, proclaiming: "Eventually I became desperate and swore that I would never pay a single farthing more; I held to my word like a gentleman, and now I'm sitting here. God bless my creditors! I am now an independent man and see myself surrounded by well-meaning people. I only hope that we are permitted to live here together until we die!" (Blanche 1847: 5). Akin to a well-known character from Dickens' *Little Dorrit* (1998 [1857]: 73), this person announced his epiphany that money relations were the *true* prison within which people suffered. Clearly, these were the sorts of people who drove creditors mad, as they revealed the same desire to remove themselves from money relations that we witnessed with the vagrant. The system needed to be reformed. Perhaps the costs of retrieving private debts could somehow be foisted onto the modern state.

Somewhat speculatively, I would argue that the elimination of the debtors' prison paralleled the nationalizing of other practices that were previously private. For example, in taking on the building of a national road or railway network, or even in agreeing to clean streets in newly burgeoning cities, the government was agreeing to take on as a public cost things that would be prohibitively expensive for private parties. Likewise with the cost of credit and debt relations. There were enormous private costs in navigating such agreements. The creditor often had to absorb the full cost of losing his money; worse still, in an effort to not lose all his money, he had to spend additional money to incarcerate his debtors in the often hopeless effort of trying to cajole more money out of them. The debtor feared the cost of landing in jail if he fell on hard times, which must have provided a powerful disincentive to borrowing much-needed capital.

By setting up bankruptcy legislation that cared better for both parties (by transforming the private costs into public costs), the emerging socialist state massively improved conditions for the flow of capital, not unlike its support for the flow of goods by building and maintaining roads. The state, in this instance, was providing that "money-losing connectivity" so admired by the Saint-Simonians. Consequently, we can surmise that the substantial increase in the efficient movement of capital between parties (i.e., an increase in borrowing and lending) that Europe witnessed in the second half of the nineteenth century had more to do with the era's bankruptcy reforms than is typically acknowledged. Having eradicated the threat of the debtors' prison and the private costs attendant upon lending and borrowing, the movement of capital flourished.

Interestingly, the international debt treaties that were proposed during this same era were to be signed with the same foreign powers—e.g., Denmark and Russia (which then owned Finland)—with which Sweden signed vagrancy treaties. Both groups were somehow refusing to acknowledge the power that money represented in their lives. By moving to a new country, they were contesting that power, openly flaunting their ability to survive without these monetary calculations. Both groups were straining toward an unalienated existence, refusing to allow an external authority to govern their movements and daily decisions. But, legislatively speaking, vagrants and inveterate debtors were inversely related. In the vagrancy treaties, each state was hoping to return vagrants to their home, so that the state would not have to take care of foreign "parasites," people who were not going to do right by themselves in their *new* locality. In the debt treaties, the states feared that the parasites might have unjustly escaped their clutches; they wanted debtors to return from their attempted status of vagrancy in order to do right by themselves in their *old* locality. Hence, Swedish law saw the problems of vagrancy and indebtedness in similar ways, fearing the use of foreign space as a means to manipulate or completely evade one's social and monetary debts.

Monetary Morality: Credit

In 1868, the use of the debtors' prison was severely constricted as a penal technique in Sweden; in 1879, it was virtually nullified and Sweden became one of the last European states to do away with the "barbaric" practice.[10] The era when debt and bodily punishment were intricately intertwined had passed, left behind as a relic of a less civilized age. Hence, we arrive at the "more civilized" credit and debt morality and legislation that governed daily life as the Øresund Region was being conceptualized and built.

In order to grasp the changes that were afoot in Øresund and the EU more generally, we must first understand what was being challenged by these trends.

As is well documented, there had been, during the era of the People's Home, an almost hegemonic commitment to the idea of equality. As a result of this commitment, excess wealth was never to be shown; as soon as it was, people were often accused of gaining it through shifty or, at least, unfair measures. Even the members of the highest economic class, the "overclass" (as it is referred to in Sweden), were largely hidden from daily life and conversation. They were the few who managed to attend one of a handful of private high schools in Sweden, along with the remaining members of the noble class. Many of my informants told me that these people were *osynliga* (invisible), and no one knew them personally. They represented the remnants of the inbred noble class hailing from the days of feudalism.

This group's power was hidden as well. People in Sweden adamantly trusted their government to be democratic, but people also informed me of the "secret" deal in 1938 that sealed the long-standing agreement between labor and capital that built the People's Home. This secrecy had resulted in such anachronisms as one family's company owning 40 percent of the wealth on Stockholm's stock market through the 1990s. Though virtually everyone knew this statistic, it did not seem to bother people. So long as such power remained *hidden,* it did not cloud the commitment to equality shining over the Social Democratic state.[11]

There was an ethical imperative in both Sweden and Denmark which dictated that "you should not think that you are someone." This rule, referred to as the Law of Jante, was the most famed incarnation of the commitment to egalitarianism. It lay at the heart of the popular belief that all labor hours should be valued more or less equally. The variant market rates of labor were fallacious indices, for all people were working hard; thus, the state should redistribute resources. I heard countless versions of what one person told me, "In Sweden, one is ashamed to be rich." One letter to the Malmö newspaper asserted quite seriously that it should be illegal to make more than 500,000 kronor per year; anything beyond this could not possibly reflect special talents but must be the result of a faulty market index (Isaksson 2000: B7).

As a result of these sorts of beliefs, extraordinary amounts of wealth were hidden—abroad or in the black market—in order to escape this moral critique. An author of an investment guidebook explained that "the family economy is the most taboo-laden subject" in all of Swedish discourse (Wilke 1999: 16). For years, there was a debate about the rate of CEO compensation. Most people thought their salaries were positively outlandish, while the CEOs themselves were driving a campaign to bring them up to par with the rest of the world's CEO salaries, claiming that Sweden was suffering a brain drain as a result of its egalitarian ethos.

Furthermore, this egalitarian ethos against excessive accumulation called into question the very nature of owning the labor of other people via money. In a letter to a magazine that was edited by a well-known defender of the People's Home, a person complained of the magical and hidden ways in which a stock fund account grew. His aunt had given him some money and this man was shocked that, without any labor on his part, the money magically increased: "No reasonable person can claim that this is a sound increase in value [7 percent]." Indignant, he explained, "I did the only right thing, took the money out [of the investment account] and placed it in my regular salary account. Here there will be consumption" was how he triumphantly ended his epistle (ETC 2000: 6).[12] Despite Sweden's enormous successes in the capitalist world, letters such as these reveal that, for many, the country still remained very much in the socialist camp, and shifts afoot in Øresund and the EU more broadly were a direct threat to this sort of belief system.

One of the most intriguing aspects of this attitude toward wealth was displayed in the widespread popularity of the lottery and horse racing. Lottery outlets and horse-racing betting parlors were everywhere in Sweden: on every street corner, at every gas station.[13] Just like the tax system, proceeds from the lottery went to the general social welfare, specifically benefiting all athletic enterprises. Thus, the lottery was similar to the value-added tax discussed in chapter 3: it represented a form of everyday consumption that redounded to the investment strategies of the state as a whole. The stock market, on the other hand, was seen as a chancy way to undertake a purely private investment; as a private endeavor, it further entailed owning the labor of others. The stock market was viewed with so much skepticism that one mutual fund ran ads in the paper that depicted a devil speaking about the wonderful horrors of his investments. (The fund being promoted only invested in "ethical stocks" whose companies claimed to not exploit anyone.)[14]

In the desire to play the lottery, one could discern a popular interest in wealth, but it was magical wealth (Comaroff and Comaroff 2000). Indeed, one person told me, "One shouldn't be able to work up [*arbeta ihop*] a million [kronor], but one could win [*vinna ihop*] a million [kronor]." Expressing a similar ideology regarding success in general, a friend told me, "It's true. In Sweden, success has to be the result of chance, not hard work." In other words, chance allowed one to escape the rigors of the Law of Jante, which dictated that one could not be better than anyone else. Instead of one's wealth being the result of being better than one's fellow citizens, it turned out that it was the result of pure and random chance.

The once-popular *vinnarkonto* (winner's accounts) represented the perfect combination of socialist ideology speaking against investment with the ideology insisting that mere chance causes financial success. These types of bank accounts, popular in the 1970s and 1980s, invited the holder to forgo the monthly interest that would have been paid in favor of entering a lottery with all the other holders of winner's accounts. At specific intervals, all the interest from the accounts was pooled and handed out to one person by lottery. In the twenty-first century, the Swedish Debt Office began a similar campaign with state debt issuance. With techniques such as these, a suspicion of the fecund nature of money (displayed openly in interest rates) has been transformed into an embrace of the vagaries of chance.

All of this suspicion of money brings me to the concept of a non-monetary hierarchy, which prevailed in both Sweden and Denmark and which will prove important when I discuss the changes being wrought by the Øresund Region. Because both countries redistributed wealth so effectively, I often heard that "most people have essentially the same amount of money." But though economic egalitarianism was manifest, a social hierarchy remained unmentioned. There was an elaborate race toward fame and success in both societies, so long as one was not trying to achieve success by means of crude money making.[15] Many Swedes and Danes adhered to this belief, striving to increase their social rather than their monetary credit and seeing the world of monetary accumulation as hollow and crude (Bourdieu 1984).

For example, many commentators in Sweden lamented that the youth today all want to become famous. No one, the pundits said, wanted to do anything "regular" any more, the sort of regular labor that built the famous welfare state. I can report that there did seem to be an inordinate number of people who thought they would become famous musicians, artists, or movie stars. (Sweden had been much in the global music press, because there had been an astonishing amount of musical ferment there.) There was also a fierce commitment to fashion: I was told several times that Stockholm was the most fashion-conscious city in the world and that, as a result, the fashion industry always tried out new products there first. It is additionally intriguing that, unlike many other countries, this commitment to urbane style extended to the countryside. Even the most remote villages of northern Sweden and western Denmark had almost absurdly fashionable youth. There was also a spatial element to this sort of fame seeking: one needed to be attuned to the right neighborhoods, cafes, and bars; one needed to know which international cuisine had lately become popular. Of course, this sort of hierarchizing occurs in many countries; I am only suggesting that it assumed more significance in Sweden and Denmark because of the demand that the monetary hierarchy be hidden.

As testimony to this relative disdain for the seeking of wealth via financial efforts, it is worth noting the way in which, when one person became wealthy and famous for a specific non-financial practice, an astounding number of people followed in his footsteps. Björn Borg was an internationally renowned tennis player of the 1970s and 1980s. As a result, a tennis craze swept the nation, and about ten years after his string of victories, the world saw an almost terrifying number of top-notch tennis players hailing from Sweden. At one point, four of the world's top ten players came from tiny Sweden, which only has a population totaling about 9 million; other tennis-crazy lands could not come close to this level of competitiveness despite having vastly larger populations.

These statistics are no aberration. The same saga repeated itself in the world of golf (to the extent that tennis is not even that popular any more in Sweden). In 2002, I read an article in the *New York Times* reporting that a similar phenomenon had arisen in the world of high-end cooking. The reporter cited a person saying, "We're seeing a kind of Björn Borg effect. When he won at Wimbledon, young Swedes saw tennis as the road to fame and fortune. Today they all want to cook. Chefs are treated like rock stars in Sweden now" (Apple 2002: F1). These are all means to achieve legitimate fame (i.e., non-monetary credit) through pursuing a unique craft, rather than through the mysterious machinations of money.

Monetary Morality: Debt

I interviewed a debt collections lawyer and asked him why there were so many different laws relating to bankruptcy. I thought it was all a bit confusing. He laughed and said, "There's a German proverb: 'Why should one do something easily if one can do it with difficulty?'" This gives one a sense of the difficulties of delving into the legal mechanisms of bankruptcy and economic criminality. Trying to understand economic criminality and indebtedness tosses the ethnographer into the realm of legalese and arcana, but it is worth sifting through in order to understand how bankruptcy law relates to the story I am telling here.

As described in chapter 3, there was a standard moral preference in Sweden toward immediately liquidating credit and debt relations so that one would not be in thrall to another person. Indebtedness was feared, and even considered shameful.[16] A line from a play by the famed Swedish dramatist August Strindberg puts it succinctly: "I began to feel that you were driven by a secret longing to be rid of your creditor, the only witness of your degradation. . . . Because you are weak and can never shoulder a debt yourself" (Strindberg 1993: 159). It is surely significant that the term for "debt" (*skuld*) is the same term used for "guilt" in Swedish (Nietzsche 1956).

At the same time, attitudes depended on who the creditor was, and it is therefore interesting to compare the different attitudes toward different creditors. I was told that debts to friends and family were "holy" and must be paid back—as soon as possible, if one even managed to fall into debt with them in the first place. Debts to the state, however, were widely regarded as entrenched and often assumed to be unpayable. The most mentioned example of this belief was the way that the state used to loan money for education.[17] Once one graduated, one paid a small sum—4 percent—of all future salary payments. Countless people told me that they would never manage to repay the entire student loan over the course of their working lives. And it seems that the state structured the system with this in mind: all debts were forgiven when the worker achieved the age of sixty-five. Again, this is a crucial element of credit and debt relations: who paid for the forgiven debt? However they felt about these matters, it is vital to note that the *general populace* of Sweden collectively agreed to pay for everyone's educational debts, for the forgiven debt did not merely disappear. The state had to find some way to shuffle resources in order to write off these bad loans.[18]

Because of generous practices such as this, the state was viewed, I was told, as a "fellow being" (*medmänniska*). This practice was also cited as a reason that Swedes were more free to pursue any career they chose: they did not need to make money in order to pay back their education loans. The rate of payback was 4 percent no matter what the salary and no matter what the amount of the loan. Here, then, is a techno-bureaucratic instantiation of the belief that freedom resides in somehow escaping the monetary valuation of daily living: one should be able to choose forms of labor for "truly human" reasons rather than for their compensation.[19]

Straightforward bankruptcy, it turns out, was another method of trying to escape the monetary valuation of daily living. In the years leading up to the opening of the bridge, numerous bankruptcies were discussed in the daily press. Occasionally, they were discussed as criminal indictments. In order to start grasping the differences, I attended bankruptcy court. Hearings were announced in the newspapers and open to the public, though it was uncommon for anyone to show up merely to watch; instead, they were announced in the papers so that creditors might know of them, arrive in court, and demand their just due. The debtor often failed to show up at the hearing; this was confirmed in several interviews. The people who worked at the court, presumably more so in a smaller town like Malmö, all knew each other. These court workers seemed to have a resigned air about their rote activity (each hearing followed the same procedures and they all sounded very similar to one another); it was as if they thought, "Here we go, another bankruptcy."

I was shocked to hear jokes being hurled about (at the expense of the debtor), because officialdom in Sweden was famed for its decorum and by-the-books attitude. The jokes appeared when the debtor was considered to be (but not yet indicted as) a criminal. Once, for example, the Swedish state collections officer introduced the case against a man by saying, in a sarcastic tone, "I want to know what he does and where he does it," since this debtor had refused to tell her anything about his business practices. She was implicitly accusing this man of black market transactions, and said that a search of his house had found important accounting materials that proved that he was engaged in some sort of business despite his denials. Other debtors were similarly indicted for hiding their assets behind "shell companies."[20] All of these people were indebted to the state running businesses —not unlike Percy Nilsson—that were using various techniques to avoid Swedish taxes.

Each session at the court cost 500 kronor, and this tab was added to what the debtor owed to the state. To me, this often seemed laughable, given the exorbitant amounts of the debts. One debt to the state, for example, tallied 848,000 kronor. In this case, the state did not even know who stood behind the company that was going into bankruptcy. Did the state workers really think that they would get the additional 500 kronor? Clearly, this was a rote technicality that had little to do with reality. Some of these debtors had already left the country and had no intention of paying any of the debt; it would perforce be socialized by the state. Some of those whom were found denied any knowledge of the company in question. The frequency of the sessions gave me the sense that bankruptcy laws provided some of the fundamental oil that allowed the wheels of commerce to spin. People were going into bankruptcy all the time in Sweden, and the state maintained a highly developed bureaucracy in order to deal with it.

I went to the Kronofogdemyndigheterna (Debt Enforcement Agency)[21] in order to meet two debt officers for an interview. Over the main door to the offices hung a sign declaring, "Everyone should do right by themselves." Here it was again, emblazoned at a state office for all debtors to see, the nationwide motto that told everyone to be sure to liquidate their debts. One reason I had asked for these interviews was to better understand the new "debt-cleansing law" (skuldsaneringslagen), which would seemingly allow someone to escape doing right by themselves.[22] Under the new law, the state walked one through a lengthy and tedious process (so lengthy that it was the subject of parliamentary debate in order to fix it), and one emerged cleansed of one's debts. In various ways, the state could pick up some of the tab for these debts, though not always. After providing oaths about one's assets, a formula was used in order to figure out how much one could pay each month to one's creditors.

Previously, creditors could refuse to accept these often minimal payments, but with the changes in the law they no longer had a choice, even if the payments were so small that the debt would not be paid off for decades. In other words, creditors still assumed a risk in loaning money, and not all debt was socialized. It would perhaps be more proper to say that the state forced the socialization of debt; rather than allowing a debtor to fester in prison, the state forced all creditors to come to new terms with the debtor. The state had socialized the costs of the machinery that dealt with bankrupts, but the state often also lost its own money to debtors, as in the examples of accused tax dodgers. This was clearly a socialization of actual debt: money that technically should have been redistributed to the social body had instead been appropriated by one person or company. Sweden's taxpayers as a unit paid for these sorts of debts.

Perhaps more intriguingly, the debt-cleansing law fell within the Foucaultian formula of prison reform. It brought debtors back into the fold, no matter how bad their situation (in fact, I was told that the debt-cleansing law only was used in the worst-case scenarios). It convinced them to reform their ways and submitted them to a regime of surveillance, dependent upon a new control of their spending habits revolving around a so-called existence minimum, which was equal for all people. In the debt collections office, one woman told of a debtor who insisted that, because he had gotten used to a certain style of life, he would be incapable of living on the usual existence minimum. He had requested a minimum of 30,000 kronor per month. She told me that she laughed at him and said no. In other words, here was a system of reformation that proudly followed the Law of Jante and brought people back into the sphere of normal monetary relations: people would pay their debts, and they would not be special.

On the other hand, businesses that went bankrupt never had to go through the rigors of the debt-cleansing law, and their debts were simply socialized after the bankruptcy passed through court. Because companies just disappeared after they went bankrupt, there was no way to gain additional money out of them via a continued regime of surveillance; their assets were liquidated and distributed to creditors, but they "escaped their debts" ("Konkurs" 2002). In other words, this was similar to the logic of the disappeared debtor: just like a debtor who vanished across the Danish border, the company that vanished into thin air had escaped future surveillance and therefore future payments. Often, such unpaid debts were owed directly to the state, but sometimes also to other creditors. No matter what, this debt could be considered a dubious appropriation of another's assets by the debtor. In the era of the debtors' prison, such circumstances were bluntly referred to as "thievery" and "swindling," whereas in the era of the building of the Øresund Region, they were part of a "debt-cleansing" regime.

In 2000, there was a much-discussed bankruptcy filing by Sweden's most famous socialist newspaper, *Work* (*Arbetet*), which had been published throughout its history in Malmö. In a response that echoed the complaints heard during the era of the debtors' prison, I heard the accusation that the Social Democrats were using state funds to keep the paper running. Specifically, the critique claimed that the umbrella union organization (Landsorganisationen) had myriad resources that it was not releasing in order to save the paper, while the state paid the salaries of the employees instead.

Other people told me similar things about attitudes toward indebtedness. Commenting on the apparently common bankruptcy practice of one well-known Swedish media magnate, a friend of mine said, "He's supposed to be a real devil [*verklig djävel*]." "Why?" I asked. "He's put a whole line of companies into bankruptcy, and that isn't so proper [*fint*] here in Sweden." Another person told me, "It's an enormously big sin to not pay one's debts in Sweden." It was such a big sin that the state workers with whom I spoke about bankruptcy laws insisted that things had not changed that much since the era of the debtors' prison. They pointed out that there was still an automatic "travel restriction," and that one could actually still land in jail for certain economic crimes. However, one interviewee at the state collections agency was careful to point out, when talking about various ways to land in jail, "That is a punishment [for a crime, e.g., contempt of court]; one doesn't go to jail because of debt." Her co-worker quickly retorted that, for today's imprisoned debtor, these "fine legal terms don't make a difference. They don't have any reason to be happy that the debtors' prison no longer exists."

Aside from refusing to give an oath about the extent of one's assets, the major crime that landed one in jail was owing money to the state itself, rather than owing it to private individuals. All of the exiles famed for their indebtedness were in debt to the state, mostly for unpaid taxes. Technically, this was often labeled as "economic criminality," but the description of the crime always mentioned a debt to the state. Aside from Nilsson, there were numerous famous debtors. Paul Klimfors, who started a wildly successful taxi service in Malmö (because it drastically undercut the prices of its competitors), was one such criminal. In a variety of ways, he kept much of the money from his company in cash and thereby evaded taxes: in short, each cab fare was treated as a black market transaction. I spent a day at the courthouse looking through the records on his case. At one point, he had carried two suitcases filled with cash to Spain. He had also laundered money in Switzerland, where he had a numbered account. The Swedish government, perhaps revealing a naive desire to grant its citizens credit (honor), lifted his travel restriction for a four-day trip to Poland. Klimfors and his debt to the state went into hiding in the Canary Islands; many years later, the state decided that, given the time that had elapsed, it no longer had enough evidence to convict him.

Similarly, a countess named Ulla Bielke has been "hiding" in South America for close to two decades. She selected a country that had no extradition treaty with Sweden (Paraguay) and walked off with a whopping 76 million kronor "tax debt," as it has been called. She was placed in bankruptcy court in absentia, even though everyone knows she has money abroad (TT 1999b). Another infamous debtor disappeared right after he registered for bankruptcy for debts of up to 1.4 billion kronor. His wife was quoted in the newspaper as saying that she knew he had money hidden abroad. When he disappeared, his passport, bag, and clothes were all missing. After searching for him all over the globe, Swedish police concluded that he was dead (Tagesson 1999: A8). Forgive my skepticism.

If one follows the state's logic that these people were "stealing" from the state by not paying their tax debts, it might be worth thinking of them as modern-day pirates. Unlike prototypical bandits, pirates, as depicted in lore, were more individualistic. Bandits' behavior was even labeled "social banditry" by Hobsbawm, because they had to redistribute resources throughout the community in which they operated (Hobsbawm 1969; but see Roitman 2005). Because their own gains were gleaned from the community in which they lived, they had to pay that community back or risk being turned in to the authorities. Pirates, on the other hand, specifically left the places they plundered and sought to place their wealth outside that zone, preferably in a hidden chest in some distant locale, to be dug up at a later date when the need arose. Or in some numbered account in Switzerland when the need arose. Interestingly, the things tax debtors in Sweden steal from the state are called *skatt*: taxes. Treasures are also called *skatt*. The pirates of Sweden turned taxes into treasures, displacing homegrown *skatt* into foreign-buried *skatt*.[23]

Once one notes the similarity of their practices to piracy, it becomes clear why the state still tried to imprison these people. Nilsson only received a travel restriction, but Klimfors was ordered imprisoned in absentia. Countess Bielke would surely be locked up if she ever returned to Sweden, but since 1989 she has been a naturalized citizen of Paraguay, a sort of latter-day Port Royal. Other debtors similarly evaded their monetary obligations, and the fears of foreign hiding places that plagued the Swedish parliament in the nineteenth century remained at the turn of the twenty-first. I was told by a collections lawyer that the authorities worry a lot about people leaving the country. These pirates behave in an antisocial manner, manipulating national borders in order to escape monetary promises made at home.

One fascinating thing about the legislation and legal practices directed toward debtors in Øresund was the way that community boundaries were revealed by them. First, the escaping debtor illuminated the extent of community powers. He had escaped outside the circle of debt and evaded his responsibilities. The boundaries also involved a question of which institutions addressed the problems of insolvency. Though individual Swedish creditors could lose money by extending credit abroad, it was not the state's responsibility to attempt to regain such foreign debt. Such a creditor had to appeal to the local institutions of debt forgiveness wherever she had loaned her money.[24] In other words, Sweden would not pick up the tab for foreign debtors, only local ones. Boundaries of credit and debt such as this, and their relationship to currency, become even more obvious when we take a look at the local currencies.

Credit and Debt in the Local Currencies

Before moving on to the way that the Øresund Region was impacting all of these nationalized practices, I must again turn briefly to the idiosyncratic beliefs surrounding accumulation and indebtedness that prevailed in the local-currency rings. The first thing that should be mentioned is the disapproval of accumulation and, by implication, loaning at interest. I was repeatedly told that the special thing about a local currency was precisely its lack of interest in interest. As a result, there was no demand—internal to the system itself—for economic expansion. One member explained it by saying, "The national currency is capitalistic, and attached to the dollar. It demands expansion [because of interest]. The local currency is not conditioned upon expansion. Enterprise can increase [here] but it doesn't *have* to increase. Regular money gives you growth even if you don't want it."[25]

This distrust of interest was so strong in Sweden—beyond even the confines of the currency rings—that there was even a bank that refused to pay interest. Often mentioned to me, the Jord, Arbete, Kapital (JAK) bank was named after "land, work and capital, the three cornerstones of classic political economy" (JAK 1998: 14). JAK hoped to "work toward building an economy that does not exploit people or nature, by [providing] our savings loans [their special type of loan] and by illuminating the [detrimental] effects of interest" (ibid.: 3). The leader of JAK in Skåne refused a request to be interviewed, but I gathered a fair amount of material on it. It followed banking practices in the Arab world, where interest was illegal, as followers of JAK and the currency rings constantly informed me (see Maurer 2005). As an interest-free bank, JAK promised in its brochure that its loans "give you greater possibilities to control your economy and to be debt-free" (JAK 1998: 3). With this promise of freedom from debt, JAK promised greater freedom from social bonds than a standard capitalist bank. Considering that JAK was a solidaristic bank founded to produce a more just society, such a promise to be free of social bonds is quite ironic.

Instead of interest payments, one received "savings points" when banking at JAK, and these were utilized in a formula that determined how much one was allowed to borrow at some future date (JAK 1998: 7). JAK's program was admired by most currency ring members as a model (although one person complained that there remained hidden interest in the form of fees). However, one leader of a currency ring, I was told by someone else, thought that *all* banks should be boycotted, although he did not admit this to me when I spoke with him directly.[26] Others spoke approvingly of Gesell's monetary theory (see chapter 2), which dictated that currency should lose value if it remained stationary. This policy represented the extreme consequence of a disapproval of the economic practice of lending at interest. Instead of money producing more of itself because it was stationary (from the perspective of the individual), it should *lose* value as a result of any immobilization.

This was an ideology about money that favored consumption over savings. Many currency ring advocates were concerned with interest precisely because they saw it as encouraging the immobilization of money; money needed to be circulated so that it would be as egalitarian as possible

and no one could save up more than anyone else. In the pithy definition they frequently provided, "Money should only be a means of exchange, not a good in itself." Such a belief protected against accumulation, for money that was itself a commodity could be accumulated and hoarded, but money that was a pure means of exchange—i.e., a mere symbol and not valued in and of itself—could not (see Langholm 1983; Meikle 1995).

As a final piece of evidence on this matter of accumulation, I cite here some stanzas from a poem that was scripted by a currency ring member and circulated in a Scandinavia-wide newsletter.[27]

How can one build
an entire house
When one only has lumber
and nails
Spires as they are called too
and tools
and available hands
But is lacking inches
or centimeters
For those one must borrow
From one of the collectors [savers]
who has saved many
inches or centimeters
hidden them in the cellar
with an eye toward lending
to those people who only have a few
or simply no
inches or centimeters.

The others have to agreeably borrow
But that's not free
They have to pay back
with more
inches and centimeters
Interest, they call it
And it's no good
if one can't afford
to borrow inches and centimeters.
. . .
He who has the biggest debt

the biggest minus
in the red
is the richest
Because he,
regardless if it's a he or a she
has gotten something
but still has only given
Numbers
black numbers [as in "ink," not the black market, and idiomatically
    referencing the concept of "in the black"]
as repayment
upon further notice.

(LETS-Link Norden 1999)

This was a quite fascinating piece, for it equated, as did Simmel, money with pure quantity. Zelizer has countered that money also carries qualities, but clearly this person disagreed. For him, money was only a measurement (inches or centimeters)[28] that was socially created and thus not as real as the timber, nails, tools, and hands that one really needed to build a house. Since money is merely fictitious, he suggested, why not just convert it to another sort of measurement—local money—and start building that damn house? More important, note his aversion to "those collectors" who hid their fictitious measurements in a dark cellar only to gain at other people's cost: people, we are led to believe, who were only trying to build a simple, yet solid and real, house.[29]

Such collectors were examples of "parasites," and as I have shown in other chapters, currency ring members shared a general desire to, as one person told me, "build a society that doesn't parasitize itself on others." The goal was to increase self-sufficiency by simultaneously increasing debt at the local community level while reducing debt with outside communities and anonymous others. This belief revealed itself beyond the level of strictly local practices with the local currency, for currency ring members often asserted a dislike of the World Bank and the IMF. They were often prepared to agitate for the wholesale forgiveness of developing countries' debt; JAK's newsletter (entitled *Interest-Free*) provided regular installments complaining about this global issue. In other words, people committed to the rings, generally speaking, saw a commitment to the local as a way to build a better global society.[30]

Though their trade and monetary policies followed a sort of cameralist doctrine (as outlined in chapter 2), they followed such theories only in the service of solidarity with *all* peoples, rather than, like the cameralists themselves, as a method of merely improving their own lot. The cameralists had their motives wrong, but their strategy was right: turn inward so as not to be a parasite and to build a sustainable planet, not to build an insuperable global hegemon.

Significantly for my arguments, this was merely a transfer to a group level of the doctrine in Sweden that "one who is in debt is not free." It was the same ethos that convinced many Swedes to pay their exact tab at the restaurant, rather than splitting it equally among all the friends at dinner (see chapter 3). This did not come from any hatred of specific groups, which is typically associated with claims of parasitism.[31] Rather, it was part of a logic that asserted that debts created bonds that kept the individual from being completely free.[32]

I found that general Swedish cultural norms and ideas about indebtedness impacted the constitution and success of the rings. Knowing the general fears of indebtedness in Sweden, I always asked if this caused a problem with the movement of goods in the circles. Invariably, the answer was yes, because all transactions in a local currency intentionally placed one in debt to someone else. It worked like this: when one decided to buy something within a currency ring, one was spending money that only existed within the ring; one did not go into debt with one individual, but with the ring in general. Thus, whoever "sold" one the good could only receive his just due if he managed to find something he needed or wanted within the currency ring. The transaction was not an immediate liquidation of debts, as in a normal cash transaction, but rather the creation of a debt, as the poem above also explained.[33]

This problem was particularly apparent in the currency rings right when they were starting out, because they chose to start with everyone's account balance at zero. Thus, the first transactions blatantly placed the purchaser in the abhorred state of indebtedness, with her account showing a negative balance. One currency ring member discussed this in more detail, telling me that "it can be hard to get a ring started because no one wants to be in debt. One should do right by oneself." As a result, he said, there were some rings that had chosen to start everyone's account at a specific number, say 3,000 units, so that people would not feel like they were going into debt. He laughed slightly, explaining, "It's psychological. This is just a way to place the zero boundary in a different manner. You're tricking each other and yourself."

The rings, as I have stated elsewhere, depended upon mutual trust and knowledge among all the exchange partners. In this regard, excessive indebtedness needed to be checked with the governing board. There were limits to how much one could trade prior to giving anything back. This limit was negotiable: one could request a further "loan" or "credit" to one's account in order to keep trading. In discussing this matter with one ring board member, his sanguine manner about the issue suggested to me that he was not at all worried about the danger of swindling debtors in the currency rings as nation-state regulators of credit and debt relations must always be. It was as though the currency rings had managed to defuse the traditional proverb that a retired banker had told me: "Money is safe when it's coming in, unsafe when it's going out." Currency ring members, with their combined trust and vigilance, astonishingly believed that "money is safe when it's coming in, and remains safe when it's going out." Unlike the banker, who felt a certain surety in unflowing money, currency ring members hoped for the continual circulation of money—so long as they could, as humans interacting with the economy, channel the flows in the directions they desired.

One currency ring member even told me that the idea of fraudulence seemed impossible to him. "Fraudulence, I have trouble imagining. It shows immediately if someone joins and wants to exploit it [the currency ring]. It shows directly, if people don't fit in." Such a comment, while proving that the currency rings were a place where trust was engendered, built, and preserved, also revealed the potential for boundary building. Exactly how was it determined that someone was behaving fraudulently? Given that many Swedes had already mentioned their stereotype that Danes "will trick the shirt right off your back," perhaps one should not be too surprised if some rings manage to build themselves around ethnic groupings as their model spreads around the globe.[34]

On this topic of fraudulence, I always specifically asked ring members what happened when people wanted to move. Some people cannot be as committed to local society as currency ring members would hope. This could potentially create a circumstance where someone joined a ring, bought up everything available within it, and then left town prior to anyone trading with the departed member. A person leaving a ring in this manner would essentially be the same as the debtor who left the nation-state to escape his debts.

Without hesitation, people told me that this would not be a problem, and the reason why is quite interesting for the purposes of this chapter. Because the money in the ring was communally delimited, any debts accumulated were dispersed throughout the ring. In other words, the entire ring would stand as creditor to this one debtor, having lost real capital to him in the form of goods or services. Thus, without too much pain, it could socialize the debt. As one person told me, "The total sum is always zero. All the money that one person gets will match money that someone else has lost. Our balance is always zero, communally [*gemensamt*]." Whoever had "lost" real assets to the departing debtor would actually still retain an excess of cash that she could use with the other remaining ring members. Unlike a standard case of a swindling debtor, the entire community handled the loss together, rather than any onerous burden being carried by one creditor. In short, the debt of the currency rings was a broad social relationship rather than a dyadic one between specific individuals.

Because flows were specifically delimited and the monetary "reserves" were merely in an abstract notion of trust rather than any material resources, the damages that resulted from transgressions of the system were minimal. Additionally, the power of interest and its alleged ability to control people had been eliminated; currency ring members consciously saw themselves as part of a global movement, and many of them would be happy to see the demise of interest everywhere. Most of them would celebrate if they one day found that the entire globe had taken up the practice of local currencies as a superior model to that of national currencies and the credit and debt relations that are built into them. A world without interest would be a world without cancerous, unnecessary growth—a world without power and parasites.[35]

Thus, the local currencies revealed in extreme fashion the power of currency to create borders. Here was a system that disapproved of depending on labor from outside the group, for one should know one's exchange partner. Trading within a ring entailed a commitment to self-sufficiency over buying goods in a broader market that cheapened commodities via the practices of comparative advantage and competition. The system also relied heavily on the movement of objects, but would be immensely threatened as an institution if subjects (people) moved too much. By maintaining a close eye on all of the transactions of their members, wealth in the rings could never be secretly hoarded (hence a general sense of egalitarianism prevailed; purchasing too many items could even be cause for a discussion by the board), and all debt could be successfully socialized in the case of default. But this commitment to self-sufficiency and to the lack of human mobility placed the local-currency advocates in direct conflict with the plans for the transgressive flows of the Øresund Region. Embracing the region, with its highly fluid market, love of interest, and distaste for local boundaries, would be tantamount to disavowing an interest in local-currency rings.

Back to the Euro and the Øresund Region

Just as the Øresund Region had been sold as a sort of Saint-Simonian utopia of abundance and production, the euro also had been sold this way to the citizens of Sweden and Denmark. The euro would bring forth all the same transparencies and rationalities that the region hoped to deliver. Proponents often believed that the Øresund Region had been deprived of its natural market for centuries due to the administrative fetters of the two nation-states of Denmark and Sweden. So, too, with the euro: it would reveal to Europeans that there was a broader "home" market than they had ever realized. Just as the region promised to eliminate the arbitrage relating to the trade in decadent goods (see chapter 3), so the euro promised that prices would equal out over European space. One bank brochure used the example of Danish beer, explaining, " [M]eanwhile, EMU will probably speed up a development where it is hard to maintain big differences between countries' VAT taxes, other taxes on goods, and capital taxes. . . . There can be a risk that the state's total tax income diminishes, which in turn can result in a reduction in public spending. Indirectly, the maneuvering room for financial politics will be trimmed" (Sparbanken 1997: 8).

Even the labor market would face this leveling process, for unsolidaristic devaluations of national currencies were no longer an option for eurozone countries.[36] One avid proponent of the euro, a politician running for the European parliament, voiced a common indictment of the devaluations of the Swedish national currency. They were a means to boost Swedish labor at the expense of foreign labor; by making Swedish labor cheaper, capital was encouraged to stay (or flow back into) the nation-state (see also chapter 2). The euro would no longer allow for such nationalistic tendencies enabled by currency. It would force Swedish politicians to deal with the "real, underlying" problems of labor surfeits, rather than resorting to these alleged quick fixes.

The euro would also eliminate exchange risk, according to the Swedish Employers Federation, thus pushing more investments in more economically rational directions after currency was freed from the constraints of national borders. The region planned to provide the exact same sort of redirection of capital flows. Finally, many advocates promised that the euro would usher in a cornucopia of consumptive possibilities for European consumers. They would be able to compare prices more easily, more goods would enter home markets to compete with local ones, and all travel within the euro zone would escape the evils of currency exchange fees. The region, as I have shown in other chapters, was presented as a place of new and exciting exchange possibilities as Swedes and Danes would be introduced to new products and governmental regulations would become more harmonized. In short, both the region and the euro would bring forth a world of increased transparency, one no longer obscured by the tinted glasses of the nation-state.

In this regard, it is interesting to return to the non-monetary hierarchy that I described above. As I argued in chapter 4, the citizens of each country were valued by their money whenever they traveled across the sound in the years prior to the completion of the bridge, and the regionalists are hoping to gradually alter this practice. Swedes and Danes alike departed for the other edge of the sound in order to escape the rigors of their home communities. Danes famously sought the cheaper taxes on the Swedish side, while Swedes arrived in Denmark in order to binge on products that were much more expensive at home. In short, each group was, at least temporarily, resisting or rebelling against the redistribution network provided by their home political communities.

There was, however, a subtlety to these transnational movements. Neither group of transnationals ended up engaging in the non-monetary hierarchy of the other side. In Copenhagen, for example, there were only specific parts of town that were truly appropriate for Swedish consumption. The Swedes who traveled over the sound generally made little or no effort to learn the rules of the non-monetary hierarchy prevailing in Denmark. For example, one friend told me that she knew that there existed all sorts of great cafes, restaurants, and music halls in Copenhagen, but she only went over the sound to shop; at the time, Swedes and Danes were not apt to socialize with one another. Likewise, the Danes who traveled to Sweden rarely integrated into what they often considered to be a "country of forbiddance" (*förbudsland*) or even, as Malmö was sometimes called, "where Asia begins."[37]

Thus, cultures were not integrating as much across the sound as the regional organizers had hoped. Danes knew that if they were in Malmö, it was for monetary reasons, just as the Swedes knew the same was true for their trips to Copenhagen. The other side, for each group, was always a place where the Law of Jante could be evaded. It was always a foreign space, and they became anonymous, market-based foreigners when they stepped into it. In utilizing the other currency, one could embrace one's love of individual monetary resources, one's desire to keep one's money from linking up with the redistributive network of the home. This scenario recalls the situation presented in the discussion about vagrancy: people were leaving their homes in order to escape the rigors of the credit and debt morality reigning there, whether they refused money altogether (the archetypal vagrant) or embraced it so much that they hoped to keep more of it to themselves (the archetypal miser).

This is a fascinating state of affairs, for one of the clarion calls by advocates of both the euro and the region was that the Law of Jante needed to be revoked. At a conference I attended in Malmö that was sponsored by Denmark's main business daily, a Swedish speaker announced while discussing the future of the region: "We can't let the Law of Jante hold us down. That's an important question for Sweden." Immediately prior to this, he had mentioned that there is an English proverb that proclaims, "The average never wins."

As I ambled along the streets of Copenhagen in the year prior to the bridge opening, a bank had begun plastering its walls with a sticker that read: "You shall ~~not~~ think that you are someone." This open dismissal of the Law of Jante attested to the desire to free citizens into a realm of individualistic accumulation; egalitarianism would have to start taking a back seat as a result. If Øresund were to succeed, it would appear that Danes and Swedes needed to both abandon the Law of Jante and embrace a monetary hierarchy throughout the Øresund Region (rather than just on their respective foreign shores), since their respective cultural and non-monetary hierarchies were impenetrable to outsiders (see Peebles 2002). The region, according to this vision, was to be built on a market, where people would be marked by their money, no matter what side of the sound they might find themselves on. Before the region could feel like a new home, it needed first to raze the previous national homes.

In order to embrace this new ethos of individual accumulation, the proponents of the euro were teaching Swedes new things. One ad displayed a well-known Swedish millionaire sitting on a sunny balcony beside a bottle of mineral water, its label written in Greek. Greece was the paradigmatic escape for the charter tours, the place where Swedes were allowed to escape the rigors of the People's Home and play the vagrant. In the ad, the millionaire argued, "My theory is that the Swedish government is wise and will want to join EMU with a low [-valued] krona. . . . If my theory is right, it's better for you and me to save money now in euros instead of kronor" (Akelius Fund Management n.d.: 2). He further pointed out that his company never reported anything to the Swedish government, so reporting income was the responsibility of the investor (ibid.: 3). Banks in Sweden also began pushing "Euro-land" funds on their customers as the millennium came to a close. Not only was the interest in investing itself a new phenomenon for Swedes, but it would appear that there was a growing distrust of the state's ability to care for the future value of money, and thus more people had begun to consider moving it outside the state's grasp.

In a similar vein, a man who wrote an investment strategy book entitled *Put Your Money in Motion!* was interviewed on the radio. The interviewer asked if he thought it was good that more money was now saved in stocks than in state debt. He responded, "It's certainly better that we private people have money instead of the state. Individuals have to build up their own buffer because we can't count on the state pension" ("Björn Wilke Intervju" 1999).

When I spoke with a business consultant who similarly claimed that the state's new pension plan was "no different than an Albanian chain letter [Ponzi scheme]," he also was concerned with keeping money out of the hands of the state. He offered some advice for any coming catastrophe: "it's important to keep a little sum of money out of the country so that when everything goes wrong you can just take off." While this was not the mindset of everyone in Sweden, it was not uncommon either. This attitude emerged when one no longer trusted the state with one's money. In such a situation, one withdrew it from the state's redistributive network and re-attached it directly to oneself as a sort of hoard—a pirate's treasure.

Not only was this theory of placing money abroad common, but the state itself had recently encouraged the massive transfer of wealth outside its shores. By changing the pension scheme in 1999 so that 2.5 percent of everyone's pension would be invested in the stock market, billions of kronor began seeping out of the country. In short, the state was following the same logic as the people cited above; not trusting any longer in its ability to provide a reasonable pension, the Swedish state began educating its citizenry to move their money outside the country in search of higher returns.

The euro, as many a proponent and ad campaign averred, would greatly facilitate this transfer, allowing money to evade the constraint of the national currency (exchange risk provides a legitimate disincentive to investing abroad) in favor of a pan-European one. In their new, massively widened network, money flows would find the most efficient investments for the individual rather than supporting the national industries of the home community. At the same time, it is important to note that the same transaction costs that cajoled (instead of forced) investments to stay within nation-state borders would apply to the euro's borders, thereby cajoling many investments to stay in euro-zone countries.[38]

In the past, individual money had often moved abroad in order to evade taxes. Tax flight (treasure flight) was a major problem for Sweden, so much so that it had been actively campaigning to eradicate the tax havens that remained within the EU. Luxembourg was one of this campaign's primary targets; it was well known that large sums of individual money often ended up there. One ad in the newspaper announced the opening of a new Swedish bank in Luxembourg; it was only seeking twenty-seven customers: twenty seven millionaires whose money it would promise to take care of in this hoard-friendly and secretive land (Ekström 1999: A16).

Though some people were asserting that the EU as a whole should become a "tax paradise" (Finne 2000: 9) in order to stop tax evasion, it was more likely that the EU would seek to shut down all such paradises that existed within its borders, just as it insisted upon doing with regard to the flow of goods, as shown in chapter 3. In order to properly regulate the borders of a new home, money inside the EU at large would be hunted in all of its hidden spots and would be made transparent, drawn out of its hoards and into the redistributive network of circulation (see Peebles 2008). If money were going to keep favoring Luxembourg, it would be a result of its brilliant future as a zone of regulation, work, and investment, not because of its popularity as a place for hidden treasures.

Øresund as the New Pirate's Cove

On April 1, 1999, the main local newspaper satirized the euphoric building of the region. In its traditional April Fools Day edition, readers were told of all the big plans for the artificial island being built for the bridge in the middle of the sound. The article was titled "Live the Good Life on Pepper Island," and it provided a detailed sketch of the beautiful and stunning plans, revealing the location of the beaches, the enormous soccer and concert arena, the luxury hotel, the casino, the tax-free warehouse, and the housing for the new citizens of this neutral zone. The newspaper proclaimed that the island was intended to be the "power center" of the new Øresund Region. Since the island was new and not yet on any maps, the EU had yet to discover it. It could therefore remain hidden from EU laws and escape EU regulations. It would provide a utopian abundance of individual accumulation and consumption with its casino and tax-free luxury cars and liquor. Even good old Percy Nilsson was mentioned as being a prime mover in the project.

The idea of creating Pepper Island as a tax-free paradise was supposedly born at an EU meeting in Ireland of all the member states' prime ministers. When the Swedish and Danish ones met for a press conference to promote the Øresund Region, apparently only one journalist arrived. Thus, Denmark's prime minister stated, "It was too boring. We were forced to come up with something fun." The Swedish prime minister was initially skeptical, but when they discussed the matter over a beer in Dublin, he was horrified by the high price of his beer (reported at five pounds, the same as a Swedish beer). He wanted to know if there wasn't "one damn island" in all of Europe that had reasonable beer prices. Øresund's Pepper Island was the answer.

The newspaper quoted one Inge Kruth as saying, "It'll be like living in a tax-free boutique." It was also reported that the island would compete for all the "mailbox companies" that ordinarily exist on remote tax-free islands.

These often hollow companies are famous for not producing anything real, just providing a venue for laundering money. But the project leaders remained concerned that the EU would rescind its drive to eliminate tax-free shopping for intra-EU travelers. A Danish government source was reported as stating that this would cause the project at Pepper Island to collapse because, "after all, you have to have a tax hell in order to have a tax heaven [*paradis*]."

This satire, in short, was announcing the menacing internalization of all the things that the People's Home had tried to send elsewhere. The money that the Percy Nilssons of Sweden were hiding abroad would now come home to roost in full view; pirates no longer needed to rely on distant shores, they could continue to thieve and store their value right next door. The dominant idea that the People's Home elevated labor and material production as the true sources of wealth would also disintegrate, as Pepper Island's residents would learn to live off the world's desire to throw money aimlessly into games of chance while attending to their immaterial mailbox companies. Likewise, beaches and golf courses would produce value via leisure, not labor. The selling of luxury and decadent goods announced the end of the non-monetary hierarchy in favor of the superficial flash of conspicuous consumption.

On Pepper Island, oriented almost entirely around money and its magical fecundity, people would not be valued for any other reason than the size of their wallet and their ability to throw away cash at the roulette wheel or on a new Mercedes. Individual wealth, unlike in the People's Home, would surely be visible rather than hidden. There would be no redistributive taxation network: the workers of Pepper Island would be individually wealthy because they would never have to contribute their individual resources to the community. Pepper Island would be a utopia / dystopia of minimal government and extreme capitalist individualism, the inverse of the People's Home.

Though this scenario remained purely fictitious (Pepper Island, I can report, is a barren artificial wasteland), it spoke to the radical shifts afoot in Øresund by satirizing the visions of the sort of society that some were trying to conjure forth on both sides of the sound, if not on its new man-made island. It was no accident that the satirists reported that the idea was spawned at an EU meeting. Pepper Island, as the inverse of the People's

Home, was also in many ways the vision of the neutral, market-oriented local places that the EU was helping to form.

What would happen to the socialization of debt in such a society? The Swedish state collections agency, while not prioritizing native creditors over foreign ones, only announced its bankruptcy hearings in Swedish newspapers. But since the advocates of the euro insisted that one of its main benefits would reside in the exponential increase in its capital market, surely more transnational lending and borrowing would come in its wake. Øresund, the EU, and the euro all represent, I would argue, the new lines being drawn to delineate debt socialization in Europe today.

It remains unclear what will happen, in the long run, to bankrupts with the advent of the euro. However, if the historical shift from the debtors' prison to the seizure of passports is at all informative, it should not be surprising to hear that, in the future, Percy Nilsson and his ilk will have to find a new place to hide; Swedes who leave the nation-state for an EU member state will no longer be considered thieves or pirates. They will be readmitted back into the fold of monetary relations by the surveillance of newly extended debt-forgiveness laws. The EU may eventually have the right to revoke passports, and the size of the debtors' prison will increase yet again. Sweden has been agitating the EU for precisely these sorts of reforms.

As this chapter has shown, when a debtor is within a community, she is not assumed to be a criminal so long as she has the intention of repaying. Outside the community, the debtor becomes a pirate, accruing monetary resources to her own person. The spatial configuration of communal debt forgiveness and socialization is ever changing, but it maps onto the same community of credit and debt relations mediated by specific currencies.

Conclusion

Scientific Money for Scientific States

One or another kind of artful tinkering with money is then
supposed to overcome the contradictions of which
money is merely the perceptible appearance.

—*Marx 1973*

Throughout the world, numerous conurbations straddle international borders. El Paso, Texas, and Juárez, Mexico; N'Djamena, Chad, and Kousseri,
Cameroon; Frankfurt (Oder), Germany, and Slubice, Poland; Singapore
and Johor Bahru, Malaysia. Typically, such binational spaces have never
been considered part of a particularly august group that other cities have
hoped to join. Indeed, the "border town" has a long and storied status—
arguably, a global stereotype—as a space of shady dealings and a vast *lump-
enproletariat*. Such urban spaces are often thriving precisely because of the
bifurcation of regulatory space that occurs within the urban space itself,
which provides for much poaching, underground trade, arbitrage, illegal
migration, and human trafficking.

Prior to the building of the bridge, Malmö and Copenhagen shared
elements of this global stereotype about border towns. The twentieth-
century welfare state made the transnational proletariat (seemingly) obso-
lete, but in the nineteenth century, Swedish migrant workers crossed to
Copenhagen with great frequency in search of work. And as I have shown

throughout this text, the reasons that Swedes traveled to Copenhagen over the years since then have mimicked the black market dealings of typical border towns in significant ways.

All this trade in goods, labor, and capital was facilitated by the ferries that used to ply the sound's waters. Yet it was never facilitated by one dominant currency. In many instances, one currency comes to dominate in the world's binational urban spaces, even though two currencies supposedly prevail in these areas. The domination by one particular currency indexes domination that prevails in other spheres as well. In other words, a disharmony of regulation creates the conditions for a thriving trade that then organically adopts one harmonized currency, regardless of potential governmental dictates to the contrary.

Such a unified currency space never emerged in Malmö or Copenhagen, which stands as an index of the general lack of domination between the nation-states of Sweden and Denmark. It also, however, stands as an index of the great success of internal regulation within each nation-state. The success of each regulatory regime dampened the need of workers to traverse the border, which is typical of binational urban spaces marked by a significant power imbalance. Each state took extraordinary care of its citizens and built excellent regulatory frameworks for business to thrive without crossing borders. In twentieth-century Denmark and Sweden, there was no native proletariat itching to get to either side. Consequently, unlike many other binational urban spaces, one side (Copenhagen) became marked as a space for escaping work, rather than a space to seek it out. The mobility and flow of people were thereby circumscribed, and the lesser mobility partly explains why a unified currency never emerged from the daily exchange practices of Swedes and Danes in the Øresund Region.

Somehow, many believed that a mere bridge might magically change all of this. But many people more intimately involved knew that something else needed to come in the bridge's wake: a unified regulatory space coupled with a unified currency. In the new regulatory space, poaching, underground trade, arbitrage, and their taints of foreignness would be banished to new shores.

In this sense, the proponents of the Øresund Region were trying to achieve something truly novel. They were attempting to deliver a binational space that would no longer be marked by a difference in currency or a substantive difference in regulation, but which would retain cultural difference. The Øresund Region would stand as a living example of the EU's dream that economies and cultures can be treated as separate entities: a pan-national government can make a pan-national market fully integrated and harmoniously regulated without altering the cultures of the people who constitute it. Tens of thousands of Swedes could commute to work forty-hour weeks in Copenhagen without gradually changing the Swedishness of the Malmö that they call home or the Danishness of the Copenhagen in which they work. This odd constellation of harmonized regulations, a common currency, and safely stable national cultures might well make this area unique among the world's border towns at some future date.

Seeking a Perfect Money

Similarly unique compared to the rest of the world's border towns, if the euro as the unified currency ever arrives, it will be by governmental fiat, rather than by way of daily economic practice. This is an ironic fact for a binational urban space promoting itself as a glistening and fertile market. Instead of relying on millions of independent users to pick the best currency with which to achieve their daily aims, the euro would arrive only after legally rendering its competition defunct.

In this sense, the promoters of the euro were like many utopians of past eras: they had achieved a conception of what was best, and they wanted to implement it on their own terms. They saw the euro as essential to building the Øresund Region. In their analysis of what ailed Sweden and Denmark, the respective currencies of each country stood in the way of their own salvation. The national currencies were unnaturally insulating Swedes and Danes from each other, and they needed to better integrate into a combined region of capitalist production and reduced transaction costs. In short, according to regional proponents, the euro would be the perfect form of money for building a new and better world in the wake of the failures of the old one.

This drive to find a perfect money that would aid in the more perfect organization of society is the story I have traced, using the shifts in the Øresund Region as the backdrop. There were not only euro proponents who thought their currency could solve a host of societal problems, but also proponents of local currencies and political figures who continued to tinker with national currency policy as a method of insulating the nation-state from the anarchic throes of the market.

In each case, people had a belief that a better currency could help solve many of the problems confronting their world. In this sense, the drive to find a perfect money is part and parcel of the more general utopian thrust of modernity itself. Throughout recent history, national and EU monetary reformers have both tried to create and sustain a zone called "the economy" that could be separated from morality, i.e., they sought to delineate clearly the borders between homes and markets. Creating a perfect money necessarily involved scientizing money by analyzing its properties and tabulating its movements. This project was tied up with the desire to use measurement to conquer the natural world, to bring human order to natural chaos. The project to bring the world a perfect form of money has thus always been related to the projects to bring it universal standards in weight, volume, and length as well.

Part of this scientizing project involved separating monetary value from human value, for otherwise money was mixed up with tough moral questions. For example, bankruptcy previously was viewed as an immoral state for the individual; the bankrupt individual had failed to do right by himself. He had reneged on his loans and thereby stolen economic value from some other human; just like a thief, such bankrupts were jailed. The bankruptcy reforms that I have detailed indicated a desire to remove the immoral stain of monetary indebtedness and replace it with scientific reasons for indebtedness. While there remained a strong compunction to settle one's debt in the Øresund Region, it was no longer criminal to fail to do so. Failure to make good on debts was instead separated out as a specific problem of economics, which was concerned with the location of the individual in a web of events and networks over which he might not always have had full control. Bankruptcy became a scientific problem rather than a moral one. As such, the state and its bureaucrats could deal with the problem, so long as it was defined properly.

So, too, has the status of vagrancy been scientized. Previously, it was considered criminal to be found abroad without money. Gradually, reformers began to claim that the problems lay elsewhere—alcoholism, the business cycle, insanity, a loose family structure, ethnic origin, inveterate criminality, etc.—and not with the lack of money per se. Lacking money was no longer a moral failure, and thus the fixation on punishing it as a crime disappeared. The classic, stereotypical vagrant could still be arrested, but not for a lack of money and only if his behavior could be shown to be related to other moral failings (e.g., the desire to drink too much). But as I showed, people from outside the EU arriving in the region were not offered the same sympathetic assessments and were instead directly probed by the authorities about the amount of money they carried for tomorrow.

Likewise, my focus on taxation policies and their spatial application has illuminated the governing morals that attempted to distinguish homes from markets. But further, even in the moral arena, the state produced a regulated sphere of exchange so that receipts announced that one had no moral commitments to direct partners in commodity exchange. Personal relationships constituted solely around money were forbidden, and the only place one found them was in the black market, the local currencies, and abroad. These were, in short, the only transactions that the state perceived as clandestine.

As a result of reforms such as these, money filtrated out of the sphere of morality and become a scientific problem. Why were people losing it? Why were people spending too much of it? Why were people failing to save it? In short, the problem became one of questioning the underlying categories and causes that could explain people's inability to control their money supply. None of these questions were asked of the vagrant or the bankrupt prior to the drive to separate monetary value (quantity) and human value (quality) during the modern age. Their inability to control money was itself the problem.

I have made frequent reference to the Swedish moral injunction to do right by oneself. To do so essentially involved proving that one could indeed control one's money, that one could approach it with all the rigor of a scientific accountant, which explains the importance in Sweden of the receipt and the refusal to accept minor everyday gifts. The successful control of money announced one's status as a modern and independent individual. Yet, with the national border in Øresund as a backdrop, this moral injunction has been shown to be spatially bounded; at various times, people slipped outside its scientific rigors and embraced the distinctly unscientific attitude of vagrancy and receiptless, spendthrift ways.

There still remains a bedrock moral structure underneath all these scientific claims and projects. As my ethnographic data revealed, many people in the Øresund Region believed that parasitical vagrants still roamed the land, smugglers still evaded taxes, and duplicitous bankrupts still threatened the wheels of commerce. They just traveled under new names, and boundaries played an important role in these historical changes.

As Sahlins writes: "The appropriation of another man's goods . . . which is a sin . . . in the bosom of one's community, may be not merely condoned but positively rewarded with the admiration of one's fellows—if it is perpetrated *on an outsider*" (1972: 199; emphasis mine). I have noted this sort of logic running through the discourses on the movement of goods, people, and capital. Practices that came under the gaze of the scientific state in the modern home were abandoned to the whims of monetary valuation in the external sphere of the neoliberal market. Once one notes the congruence in moral critiques against illegal immigrants and hoarders of money abroad with the past indictments of vagrants and bankrupts, one sees clearly the continual ability to delimit borders of inclusion and exclusion via daily monetary practices and exchange regulations.

State practices have always played a vital role in this process. First of all, the state consolidated these boundaries by classifying one person as a victim of the business cycle in need of help and another as an illegal immigrant. If one held a Swedish passport, one was in the former category, while if one hailed from a foreign locale, one fell into the latter category, despite the fact that a similar business cycle downturn may have been precisely what cast one onto the same road as the Swedish vagrant. In other words, the problem of vagrancy never disappeared; it merely was shoved outside of the cleansed People's Home.

Likewise, an entire industry and bureaucracy became devoted to navigating the troubled waters of bankruptcy. Debt forgiveness was gradually built into the daily routine of the loaning and borrowing of capital, so long as one came from Sweden. People or states that fell outside of this category were not extended the same charitable benefit of the doubt, and thus received no debt forgiveness except in very special circumstances. This was so much the case that the best way to evade the heavy surveillance entailed in debt forgiveness (because the charity comes at the cost of a loss of personal control) was to flee outside the nation-state. One needed to cut one's ties to the community and embrace one's newfound status as a pirate. Hoarding money abroad in a private stash, the scientized debtor was suddenly labeled as the thieving (immoral) bankrupt who had allegedly disappeared with the passage of the nineteenth century.

By focusing on these boundaries of inclusion and exclusion via money, I have followed Helleiner and others in believing that the project to create a perfect money was intimately related to the project to build the nation. By promising (though not necessarily delivering) to better represent economic value, governments were newly encouraging their citizens to place their faith in the government (a national standard), not in some odd bits of metal (an international standard). Not being clipped by a tyrannical regent or lost by bungling, competing private banks over-issuing paper, scientific money no longer needed to be secured in an individual hoard; its value was now protected by the home nation (fiat money), not by the foreign market (commodity money). Tying a citizen's economic value to the stability of the national currency was a way to force the citizen's independent wealth to hinge upon the wealth of the state (Bensel 1990; Peebles 2008). Their interests thus dovetailed, as both now had an interest in the stability of the national currency.

Viewing the regional proponents' advocacy of the euro through this lens has clarified that the EU is attempting to convert European space into regulated labor space, into a new home. Previously, European boundary zones relied on a disharmony of regulatory regimes in order to secure leisure mobility. But today, the EU aims to harmonize these regulatory regimes in an effort to guarantee labor mobility. It is hoped that the cross-border leisure seekers of the twentieth century will give way to the transnational labor seekers of the twenty-first century.

By expanding the sphere of market relations in Europe today, the EU is thereby challenging Sweden's (and those of other nation-states with similar, but less emblematic histories) long battle to scientize money relations. So far, most Europeans are not biting, as most choose to stay in the relatively placid spheres of their respective national homes, where dangerous practices such as bankruptcy and vagrancy are judged by non-monetary criteria, that is, by human qualities. In short, these represent the criteria of belonging, placing community over markets. But when they do venture into the EU's market space, they are abroad, and I have shown that their rights and actions become associated with the extent of their monetary value.

Of course, the ultimate question remains: Can the euro contribute to a shared sense of European community, just as the Swedish krona has in the past? Consequently, can the Øresund Region successfully fuse two separate homes into one transnational city? The answer, I believe, lies in a twofold approach. First, one must trace the organizational structure of currencies in the ways that I have done here. Second, one should attempt to discern the extent to which the EU is trying to follow the economic reforms that many European states undertook during the twentieth century. In other words, while the EU's market regime is conquering entities like the People's Home, it will need to build up its own distinctive home. But the euro cannot do this alone, it requires social effort. The EU will need, for example, to start socializing debt and caring for vagrants. Until that time, Swedish bankrupts will still be safely abroad in Brussels, and Swedish "vagrants" will still be drinking too much on the streets of Copenhagen.

In order to achieve this (if this is the goal), the EU may also need to prove that it, too, can deliver an economic sphere tamed by the home. The people who try to escape—or are forced out of—monetary relations need to be brought into the fold, to be seen as members of the same community. This would mitigate the foreignness of the market and replace it with the nativeness of the home. Such were the general hopes of the proponents of the Øresund Region, just as the local-currency advocates were also trying to bring monetary relations into a native home on a much smaller scale. Today in Sweden and Denmark, the jury is still out as to whether the projects to build the region or a thriving local currency remain purely utopian.

In any event, such utopian projects are always exclusionary in some manner. It should be clear that no matter how far society goes in scientizing and regulating money relations, there are always people who will fall outside the system, either by choice or by force. The community—the home— that strives to value people for non-monetary reasons always manages to exclude someone from these charitable criteria. Furthermore, whether one approves or not, often people *want* to fall outside the home's monetary morality and embrace the foreign space of the market. Thus, the only thing that seems assured about the impact of the euro is that it will continue to provoke the age-old argument between homes and markets. As a result of this endless tension, people will probably keep trying to perfect the social order and its monetary lubricant for as long as we think of ourselves as modern.

NOTES

INTRODUCTION

1. With their rich tradition in social democracy, such a division was particularly visible in Sweden and Denmark, but it is a division that one can find in countless historical examples.

2. See http://www.malmo.se/Kommun-politik/Om-oss/Statistik-om-Malmo/01.-Befolkning/Folkmangd-Oresundsregionen.html; http://www.scb.se/Pages/Table AndChart_287608.aspx (accessed June 21, 2010).

3. Calculated from http://www.malmo.se/Kommun-politik/Om-oss/Statistik-om-Malmo/01.-Befolkning/Folkmangd-Oresundsregionen.html, http://www.scb.se/Pages/TableAndChart_287608.aspx, and http://www.statistikbanken.dk (accessed June 21, 2010).

4. See http://www.tendensoresund.org/sv/flyttstrommar/flyttarns-aldersstruktur and http://www.tendensoresund.org/sv/pendlingen-over-oresund (both accessed June 21, 2010).

5. Many social scientists have been expertly documenting the growth and development of the Øresund Region. See, e.g., Berg, Linde-Laursen, and Löfgren 2000 and 2002; Linde-Laursen 1995 and 2010; Idvall 1997 and 2000; Nilsson 1999 and 2000; O'Dell 2003.

6. This argument was tied to a centuries-old political movement known as Scandinavismen, which sought to bring together Norway, Denmark, and Sweden. Fredrik Nilsson (2000), among others, traces this movement admirably.

7. This is similar to other nationalist and subnationalist movements that have emerged more forcefully as the EU has gained power; see, e.g., Holmes 2000.

8. It is important to note that even this tone of economic competition with other Swedish cities is emblematic of changes under way. The People's Home was solidaristic as a unit: a whole redistributive net ensured (theoretical) equality among all corners of the state. For the Øresund Region to hope to best Stockholm in a competition for human and global capital is distinctly unsolidaristic.

9. In the copious literature from political science and economics, "regionalization" refers to the notion that entire countries are banding together in the face of changes in the global economy (see Perkmann and Sum 2002; Frankel 1998; Hammarlund 2005). For example, the EU and the North American Free Trade Agreement (NAFTA) are twentieth-century examples of regionalization. Sweden and Denmark have a long tradition of this sort of regionalization, having banded together with the rest of the Nordic countries as a trade-cultural-legal-monetary bloc on the world stage several times in the past.

10. See Kockel 2002; Narotzky and Smith 2006 for other discussions of European region-alization efforts.

11. Borneman and Fowler (1997) have helpfully christened this process "Europeanization."

12. For more on Europeanization, see Balibar 2004; Bellier and Wilson 2000; Corbett 2005; Harmsen and Wilson 2000; Kaelberer 2004; Risse 2010; Shore 2000, 2005; Spohn and Triandafyllidou 2003.

13. There are people who disagree with Shore on this point. See, e.g., Böröcz and Sarkar 2005.

14. See Hart 2001, 2006; Helleiner 2003; Lee 1996; Maurer 2005; North 1999; O'Doherty et al. 1999; Thorne 1996; Williams 1996.

15. There is a technical distinction between LETS exchange rings and local "scrip" money. The former relies on receipts and accounting, whereas the latter relies on cou-pons that behave much like standard currency. Since I am mostly interested in the moral debates underpinning these currencies, I will not worry about the distinction. Both forms of local currency rely on the same monetary theories, and both try—in their own ways—to circumscribe the boundaries of exchange by turning away from national currencies.

16. When I first moved to Malmö, I acquired an apartment that seemed ideal, though it was a bit out of my price range. I boldly claimed it, assuming I could find a roommate with no trouble at all. Instead, I discovered that the ethos of independence was so strong that agreeing to share an apartment was considered almost taboo. When I finally secured someone "bohemian" enough to consider the proposition, he informed me months later that many of his acquaintances assumed we were homosexual partners.

1. IMAGINING UTOPIA, CONSTRUCTING ØRESUND

1. See Foucault 1986.

2. See Buck-Morss 2000; Crapanzano 2003; Miyazaki 2006.

3. Some of these works were alluded to above, others will be studied in particular chapters. For now, suffice it to say that Ambjörnsson's 1981 study is an excellent investiga-tion of the utopian imagination. Strindberg is, of course, one of the rare Swedes who is fre-quently referenced by people outside of Sweden in discussions of modern literature. He was a fond advocate of Quiding's programmatic utopian outline, Slutliqvid med Sveriges Lag (1978 [1886]), and he also produced several utopian short stories himself, e.g., Utopier i Ver-kligheten (1987 [1885]).

4. I am not referring to Engels' (1978) understanding of "utopianism," which sees it as "unreasonable" and "fantastical." Often, one reads specific disclaimers that Sweden was not utopia, e.g., Childs (1947: xiii–xiv); the point that follows upon such claims is always that Swedes are "pragmatic" or "a practical people" and thus they never set unachievable goals for themselves, which would be Engels' derogatory interpretation of utopianism. But the overwhelming implication of books such as Childs' or Tomasson's is that, with their pragmatism, Swedes have approximated "the ideal type of the modern industrial society to a greater extent than any other nation in the world" (Tomasson 1970: 1). Com-pare this with Bell's (1967) critique of the American Communist Party, which he argues was so "utopian" that it never managed to accomplish anything pragmatic and thus was incapable of even gradual efforts toward building a lived utopia.

5. A worker at the American embassy, writing in the '50s, reported, "Thousands of Americans visit[ed] Sweden every summer. Hundreds came to the Embassy. Most of them

had heard that Sweden was far advanced in welfare and provided something of a model for the rest of the world. Successive Congressional committees also visited Sweden to study the co-operatives, housing, the medical program, and labor problems" (Fleisher 1956: 11). Childs (1947: 169) also reported that some government officials were so overwhelmed by the numbers of people coming to view their facilities that it was necessary to organize a "social tour" which took in "the more obvious points in Stockholm."

6. Childs' point about laissez-faire is largely rhetorical, for he proceeds in several chapters to discuss the various controls on market pricing in different fields of the Swedish economy.

7. For example, Fleisher 1956; Tomasson 1970; Tilton 1990; Milner 1989; Burke 1998. Milner and Burke both advocated "Sweden as model" as late as 1989 and 1998, respectively. Because it is easy to forget the era when Sweden was more on the global map, note this comment from Anthony Sampson: "The Soviet Union has finally gone the way of all Utopias; along with China, Cuba, Sweden and Tanzania, denounced and discredited by its own inhabitants" (Sampson quoted in Kumar 1993: 64). Of course, after the credit crisis of 2008, a new Swedish model once again forcefully made its presence known on the global stage.

8. In many ways this is not surprising, since the Swedish Social Democrats were openly following the lead of the German Social Democrats, who experienced a famous split between Karl Kautsky and Rosa Luxemburg, the former winning out and orienting the party toward "reform, not revolution" (see Tingsten 1941: 249; Kautsky 1971: 2; McLellan 1988: 108–124).

9. But not all agreed. For example, Huntford (1972) and Bryar (1992) both held that seeing Sweden as a model society was dangerous, for the country was wildly flawed and even totalitarian.

10. Jenkins, for the record, decides in the affirmative. He states, "Surely no more devastating criticism could be made against the Swedish system than that, in the blind pursuit of economic efficiency, the pleasure has been taken out of life," and he claims that Sweden is permeated by an "excruciating dullness" (Jenkins 1968: 242). Paradoxically, it is precisely Sweden's capacity to produce a potentially dull society that makes it so fascinating to study (see Fajans 1997). It presents one of the potential outcomes of a scientific and pragmatic following of the modernist ethos. For a more philosophical investigation of the impact of modernist ideals on notions of self-fulfillment and self-expression, see Taylor 1989 (chs. 22–25).

11. A mere two years after Hansson's speech, there was a debate over whether to nationalize up to 25 percent of the shoe industry, but the state was only interested in acquiring control over the market in "work" shoes and specifically *not* in "luxury" shoes (Tingsten 1941: 326).

12. The similarity of vision among businesspeople and politicians is so compelling that one wonders whether Jean Monnet, one of the prime movers behind the EU project, was not perhaps a Saint-Simonian. That doctrine may have been passed down to him through the French academy's lineage from Comte and Durkheim, who were influenced by Saint-Simon (Comte was his student).

13. The latter part of this statement needs qualification. It is not that Europeans do not care about the EU and its agenda; on the contrary, the project often evokes strong arguments for and against it. Yet it is remarkable that (1) the EU citizenry is largely unconcerned about the openly documented and irrefutable lack of democracy in the EU gov-

ernment; and (2) there is an enduring lack of comprehension regarding what the EU is actually all about. It is not uncommon to find, for example, Swedes who know exceedingly little about the EMU and its technical operations. The government structure of the EU in general is often not clearly understood by the general public—so much so that a brochure entitled "How the EU Works" attempts to clarify its odd structure. Even basic facts seem unknown: I once was engaged in a conversation with Swedish and British residents who all adamantly believed that Turkey was a member of the EU.

14. For example, in a pamphlet tellingly titled "The European Union: What's in It for Me?" (Pawnell 1996), one can read: "You want to retire to the sunny half of the EU? No problem, you can take up residence and draw your pension wherever you want, be it at a Finnish lakeside or near a Mediterranean beach" (photo caption, 26).

15. *The Raspberry Ice Cream War* is also a basic primer in neoclassical economics.

16. See http://eur-lex.europa.eu/en/treaties/dat/11992M/htm/11992M.html (accessed April 30, 2010).

17. Comparing Article 2 to a parallel clause in the Rome Treaty provides an excellent example of the increased ambitiousness and enhanced scope of the EU as a utopian project. In the Rome Treaty of 1957, only about half of these goals were set out.

18. For a long time, analysts primarily considered the legislation of the EU to be "negative" rather than "positive," that is, it serves to dismantle national regulations rather than seeking to set up its own regulations (see Newman 1996: 74; Bergström et al. 1996: 7–40). This further suggests a commitment to freeing the individual from any onerous regimes that demand sacrifice.

19. See http://eur-lex.europa.eu/en/treaties/dat/11992M/htm/11992M.html (accessed April 30, 2010).

20. The nature of EU citizenship is complex, but unfortunately it cannot be explored further here. Suffice it to say that it still depends upon each member state's rules of citizenship (whether blood, soil, or otherwise). But as Shaw (2010) and many others have pointed out, mobility is still required to attain all the rights promised by the EU.

21. Indeed, the EU incessantly claims the contrary. It has a specific bureau that promotes "culture," and often advertises its commitment to a Europe of diverse "peoples" (emphasis on the plural was intentional in the treaties). It is well known that the EU publishes most of its documents in multiple languages, so as to ensure that no one language comes to mark or dominate the EU project as a whole. But see Dietler 1994 and Shore 2000 for interesting counterclaims.

22. Of course, outside the area of its purported utopia, the EU has been criticized for just the opposite. It has been accused of building a "fortress Europe."

23. The other place where the most obvious groups of transnationals worked was in Sweden's agricultural and silvicultural regions. But these workers were far from the EU's imagined exemplary citizens, despite their extreme mobility. Annual migrant workers were frequently from outside the EU, and as such did not fit into the EU's highly schematized utopian vision of bourgeois fluidity. This mobile flux of workers is considered further in the chapter on vagrancy.

24. One could already detect this program at work on the committee's original website, where paragraphs or articles alternated between Swedish and Danish. After centuries of asserting the distinctions between the two languages, the committee seemed to be openly suggesting that they represent but two dialects of a mutually understood tongue.

25. The translation may be more appropriately "skånskan is its own language with roots in *one* Skåne." The Swedish word *ett* can be translated as either "one" or "a," depending on the context. In this instance, it is hard to say, so I chose the less contentious translation. The translation as "one" makes the statement more subversive and proto-nationalistic. In support of translating *ett* as "one," I might add that the article goes on to discuss the splitting of skånskan into several dialects as a result of Swedish policy, whereas prior to this it had been *one* language, presumably in *one* unified region.

26. Not least, a highly interesting, experimental currency union was pushed through, which is considered to have been one of the most successful in history so far (Cohen 1998). It is explored in the next chapter.

27. I have not undertaken enough research on Deloncle yet to state for certain that he was a Saint-Simonian, but a glance at the parliamentary motions he introduced in France (listed at the Bibliothèque nationale de France) reveals that his *only* concerns were the appropriation of nature and the ceaseless promotion of international commerce in the colonies, in Europe, and in Brazil. He promoted the financing of scientific expeditions to the South Pole, the laying of underwater cables in the Caribbean, and commerce treaties with a lengthy list of colonies and monarchs. These are the classic trappings of a fervent Saint-Simonian.

28. For an admirable and almost hilarious redux of the utopian visions in Øresund between the 1960s and the 1990s, see Wieslander 1997. She writes that, around the same time that the major local newspaper was proclaiming the arrival of "air-cars," a proposal was made to cover the two cities with a giant plastic tent, so that they could experience a "fine and mild temperature year round" (Wieslander 1997: 79).

29. Just as the previous Saint-Simonians focused exclusively on the built environment and the flows of the capitalist market, Øresund may turn out to be another old story: the failed utopia, with speculation and grandeur attempting to ruthlessly materialize a vision that actually has little purchase once it is made manifest. The older Saint-Simonian projects, including blindly building railroads where there was no need, collapsed in a sea of bankruptcy. Øresund has witnessed a similar flood of cross-sound business closures, and the bridge-tunnel so far has carried nowhere near the amount of traffic that had been anticipated. The Chunnel project under the English Channel was mired in a notorious mountain of debt, with debt holders' investments collapsing to near zero. The dot.com bubble was, of course, also similar, and it raises the question of whether these projects focusing on *connection* are almost always overvalued at the outset, as people become feverishly excited about the new possibilities of space-time compression. The underlying premise of these expansions—the theory that "if you build it, they will come"—may be fundamentally flawed, but we nonetheless depend upon it to build important infrastructure that then aids in valorizing capital through time.

30. Virilio (1986), it seems to me, is also unnecessarily committed to the impact of acceleration and speed. Indeed, the level of speed is more significant to him than movement itself, which I believe betrays a romanticist attachment to "slower times."

31. Indeed, socialism as a political project famously entered Sweden through Malmö— via media and local organizations, but also through a famous guerrilla action where a Swedish laborer bombed a ship in Malmö's harbor that had numerous British strikebreakers lodged on it.

32. A letter to the editor in *Sydsvenskan* (Malmö's largest daily) from a Dane named Thomas Aabo responded to Drude Dahlerup's article (February 7, 1999) that complained

about the Swedish tax system, its reliance on *personnummers,* etc. (Dahlerup had moved to Sweden from Denmark). Aabo agreed that it was particularly hard for foreigners to deal with the tax system, because it uses language that he thinks only locals can possibly understand. He wrote sardonically that they use the "language of honor and heroes" that only natives can grasp. He continued, "I can only wonder how the hell Malmö can hope to receive a massive immigration as a result of the bridge when they maintain a tax authority that is worse than Kafka with regard to red tape, unfairness, and bureaucracy. Now you stand warned Drude, Get yourself a native or the like, with some education. Otherwise you run the risk that the 'People's Home' will run over you and your rights."

33. Birger Olofsson, then head of the Øresundskomiteen, went on to say that the name successfully plays upon the word "sound," hinting that the region has a "sound future" (Johansson 1999).

34. I am reminded of Hegel's ludicrous reproach of all of sub-Saharan Africa as not involved in the movements of "world history," that is, the unfolding of the "Absolute Spirit" (Hegel 1985: 99). In other words, Palludan sounds a good deal like a Hegelian, believing that a world spirit will come to know itself better through the materialistic incarnation of the bridge.

2. THE ARTS OF "SCIENTIFIC" MONEY

1. In this manner, my research diverged from the concerns of most people who study this new global movement.

2. See Taussig 1997 for a brief discussion of national hoards.

3. Fiat money is alleged to be detached from any metal or paper reserves and whose value is determined by the state. It is, in my opinion, often a problematic term. Sproul (2003) agrees.

4. The quantity theory of money currently reigns supreme in economics, repopularized by Milton Friedman. But it is an old idea, hailing, argues Davies (1994: 228), at least from the days of the French mathematician Oresme (1320–1382).

5. Though in the twentieth century, as we will see, Sweden did openly utilize its currency to create barriers to the mobility of economic value. Such practices were widespread throughout Europe until the early 1990s. At the time, however, these policies were not considered inhibitors of the flow of value by many economists precisely because they were believed to be vital to establishing stable prices, which were considered facilitators of flows.

6. There are disagreements about the SMU's exact dates, presumably reflecting the paucity of primary document research on the topic. Some authors give 1873 as a starting date, some 1874, some 1875. As a conclusive end date, I have seen 1914 as well as more nebulous datings around 1918–1919. Indeed, one author asserts that, though most people claim that the SMU ended with the beginning of World War I, "That information is not entirely correct. . . . How it finally came to an end remains to be researched" (Lundh 1997: 655).

7. The 1867 conference was scheduled to converge with Paris's 1867 World Exposition.

8. For more data, see Peebles 2003 and Einaudi 2001.

9. Even prior to the 1867 conference, France had led the Latin Monetary Union, which was a successful union of the currencies of Belgium, Italy, Switzerland, and France. Greece joined in 1868 (see Cohen 1998: 70–71).

10. This theory would be entirely plausible had they not blamed "foreigners" for hoarding the Swedish currency. Surely, Swedes were hoarding it as much as were Danes and Norwegians.

11. See Chown 1994: part 3 for a compendium of suspensions.

12. Or, in more straightforward language: "all efforts to secure such stability [of money] would appear vain so long as metals are used as standards of value and free minting of the standard money on private account is permitted" (Wicksell 1935: 58).

13. This sounds exceedingly similar to the 2008 "credit crunch." As I write, this has occurred in Iceland, and may well happen in other countries.

14. Mirowski (1989: 241, 290–291) places the shift to consumption a bit earlier, but only in the theoretical literature rather than in policy.

15. I am aware, following Marx (1973: 160), that of course things like gold are only valuable because of their ability to represent social relations among people. Thus, the faith actually resides in the social bonds and not in the object per se. But this transformation was nonetheless voiced as one that liberated humanity from objects.

16. As one of those illuminating tangential asides of history, the man responsible for crafting this scientific index of consumption, which allowed for the successful stabilization of the Swedish currency, was Dag Hammarskjöld, the second secretary-general of the United Nations. Perhaps he was interested in producing stability not only in the monetary realm (see Fisher 1935: 322).

17. For a far more extensive treatment of the Swedish stabilization program, see Fisher's *Stabilized Money: A History of the Movement* (1935), where he discusses several Swedish economists who published important books on the topic and were much concerned with exporting the Swedish model abroad.

18. Since this era of stabilized money has passed, some economists have pointed out that science and rationality may have had nothing to do with the success of the stabilization project. They assert that the hefty devaluation that preceded it caused Swedish price levels to remain solid when all around was turbulence (Rehn 1984; Lundberg 1996; even Fisher 1935 talks about opponents). This possibility provides nice fodder for one of the standard critiques of the modernist spirit: it was all a myth, and the bold and "precise" science was all tomfoolery and imprecision.

19. See Chapter 1, which explains that the government abandoned concerns with nationalizing production at this point and instead started focusing on distribution.

20. See Rabinow 1995 on the general fascination with healthy circulation that swept Europe at this time.

21. Interestingly, the important Hamburg Giro Bank of the premodern era worked within exactly such a schema, charging the merchants who left their money there a fee for the service of hoarding their money (Wicksell 1935: 74).

22. It is interesting to consider Gesell's ideas in light of Woodburn's (1982) and others' arguments about the hierarchizing tendencies that emerge when economic storage through time becomes more practiced.

23. For a discussion of this topic, see Peebles 2008.

24. Marx also addressed hoarding in an evolutionary light (see Marx 1990: ch. 3). One need not adhere to an evolutionary framework to see that the institution of banking did serve to draw money out of mattresses. In other words, such a historical development need not be viewed as "more civilized" behavior, but the separation between money and the body did occur at certain times in specific places.

25. Writers on money can often be divided into two camps, those who approve of interest and those who do not. This split is related to ideas about labor and leisure; the fact that money can make money for people while they fail to work makes such profit abhorrent to some people. The accusation is leveled that, in such cases, there is no transparent connection between labor and money. Thus, money's fecundity seems both hidden and unnatural. Kennedy elucidates this in the most dramatic way, though she is merely restating similar fears voiced by Gesell years earlier. Relating interest to the lack of work, she writes: "people who work for their money are getting poorer at the same rate at which the investment of those who own money doubles. That is the whole mystery of how money 'works,' which banks do not like to have uncovered" (Kennedy 1995: 59). She then explains that, due to this system, "We are living in World War III already . . . an economic war. It is a non-declared war; a war of usurious interest rates, ruinous prices, and distorted exchange conditions. . . . Remote controlled interest rates and terms of trade have so far killed millions of people on a plundered planet" (ibid.: 74). Note that, under this paradigm, the hidden nature of interest causes additional hidden effects: first, a distortion of prices that produces false profits, and second, a hidden, though global, war.

26. Lest this sound utopian, consider this practice's similarity to a futures contract.

27. There are several examples of Gesell's theories working in practice, including Wörgl, Austria, and the "stamp scrip" movement in the United States. Several currency ring proponents with whom I spoke referred to these fondly and readily. Kennedy claims astonishing levels of success for Wörgl, until the state stepped in and abolished the local currency that was thriving at the expense of the national one. She writes: "At a time [1932–1933] when most countries in Europe had severe problems with decreasing numbers of jobs, Wörgl reduced its unemployment rate by 25% within this one year. The fees collected by the town government which caused the money to change hands so quickly amounted to a total of . . . 3,840 Schillings. This was used for public purposes" (Kennedy 1995: 38–39).

28. Except perhaps in the case of the hegemonic U.S. dollar, and even this has many international standards of value backing it up.

29. The gold standard in the United States evidences the exact same history.

30. See Peebles 2004a for the Swedish currency crisis.

31. See the Basel II agreement for international dicta setting forth such rules for private banks. Basel III increased these minimums. See http://www.bis.org/publ/bcbsca.htm (accessed September 18, 2010).

32. Though it surely does not stand as final evidence in this debate over the difference between hoards and reserves, I would point out that it is highly suggestive that currency ring members railed against the evils of hoarding (one of the prime reasons the rings are founded is to combat hoarding), and currency rings have no central reserves.

33. See http://www.riksbank.se/templates/Page.aspx?id=9139 (accessed September 20, 2010).

34. Nogaro states that currency devaluation became known as a useful tool in trade policy in 1925, when Britain remained on a gold standard that others had abandoned and its exports suffered as a result. He states, "Japan made systematic use of it as a dumping process," and Franklin Roosevelt also devalued the dollar in 1933. Nogaro argues that the potential ills of unilateral currency devaluations spurred the United States to forge a policy that promoted the guaranteed stability of the Bretton Woods agreement (Nogaro 1949: 114–115).

35. As I have shown, many economists do not believe that this is a successful defense mechanism. What is important, however, is that for many years the government believed that it was highly strategic.

36. There have been other moments in history when the currency floated. But, at least during the twentieth century, those times were often considered transitional, whereas now there is a generalized consensus that the currency should float. However, occasionally one hears calls for returns to fixed exchange rates or "currency boards," such as in Argentina in the 1990s.

37. Under Myrdal's and Keynes' theories, the market has substantial distortionary powers that need to be regulated.

38. Douglas Holmes (2009) provides an excellent analysis of the ECB's monetary policy.

39. See also the many books that appeared during the run-up to the referendum, e.g., Carlen and Wibe 1999; Hermele 2003; Jakobsson 2003; Berge 2003; Eklund and Ådahl 1998; Munkhammar 2003; Lundgren 2003.

40. See, e.g., Akin and Robbins 1999; Foster 1998; Guyer 2004; Hart 2001; Lemon 1998; Maurer 2005; Zelizer 1997.

41. These were an abysmal failure due to lack of interest, which further validates my assertion that the euro debate was relatively passionless.

42. That the conference was only intended for particular people's consumption was evident in the comments of the finance minister from Austria, who openly stated that the costs of labor would have to be reduced if the EMU were to be accepted by the public (because only this would create more jobs). If reported widely, this comment would have surely caused favorable opinions toward the euro to falter.

43. Banks stand to gain inordinate sums of money if the state slowly retreats from such activities as pension funding. Merrill Lynch (a bank that is no longer extant) openly admitted this in several papers, as it predicted that workers would begin to place more and more of their money into privately held funds.

44. As an example of the ongoing ebb and flow of monetary policy debate, which is still seeking a stabilized locus of value, I would cite the Nobel Prize–winning economist John Nash (the subject of the film *A Beautiful Mind*). I attended a lecture he gave a few years ago where he attempted to outline a future perfect currency that would be outside the control of governments. He wanted it to be based on an amalgam of important commodity metals (commodity money is, of course, an ancient tradition, so this wasn't new, aside from the amalgam part). More significant, he drew up a chart that distinguished states based on whether or not they controlled their own money. States which placed jurisdiction over money "outside themselves" (either in a metal or in another state's currency) were classed as "states that have not sinned." Hubristic states that had attempted to control money during the twentieth century were grouped together as "states that have sinned." One could hardly hope for a more obvious coupling of monetary policy and governing morals.

3. RECEIPTS AND DECEITS

1. Later, I noticed the same chair at a friend's apartment. He told me it was worth thousands of kronor, one of the more expensive chairs on the market.

2. In focusing on such ethnographic data, I take my cue from anthropological studies of Eastern Europe that bring illegitimate transactions to the fore (e.g., Altshuler 2000;

Ledeneva 1998; Lemon 1998; Sampson 1994; Seabright 2000; Verdery 1996; Woodruff 1999). See Newell 2006 for an insightful article on illegal transactions in Africa.

3. This may seem paradoxical for a country that is a famous welfare state. But I believe that there is a deep misunderstanding of the wellsprings of socialism in Sweden (and additionally of those same wellsprings in Marx). If we follow both Durkheim (1984 [1893]) and Dumont (1977), it becomes clear that one of the main impetuses for building an elaborate social welfare state was precisely so that *individuals* could be as free as possible. Contrary to popular belief, much European socialism was not about creating some amorphous communitas, but rather, it was about elevating the individual's freedom beyond the control of others. One of the premier ways in which to control others, as both Mauss (1990) and many businesspeople know, is to have them in your debt.

4. The focus on alcohol is not the result of my own predilections. Rather, the exchange of beverages in ritual environments is one of the more typical zones where objects are converted from commodities into gifts, though this is rarely the case in Sweden.

5. See Agnew (1986: 28–29) for a discussion of the initial disdain and distrust of written bonds in economic transactions when they were first introduced in the Middle Ages. Instead, people wanted oaths and witnesses; a piece of paper could easily be forged, whereas people were trustworthy. It is interesting to see how much things have changed. In this sense, the receipt and the potential manipulations of it amounted to an ongoing dialogue about the legibility or illegibility of the state (Das 2004).

6. The most notorious black market in Sweden is undoubtedly the black market for living space in Stockholm, where people pay seemingly outlandish prices to a whole network of illegal brokers in order to skip ahead of years-long waiting lists for the cherished housing stock in the center of town.

7. Transactions in some goods and services have lower VAT rates.

8. See Berdahl 1999 on how socialist states rationalized away the existence of such black market processes precisely by calling them "peasant survivals."

9. In Sahlins' (1972) terms, people were questioning its rights as a "pooler" of resources.

10. Because of the bridge, the ferries plying the waters between Malmö and Copenhagen have disappeared, though they still run between Helsingborg and Helsingør.

11. In the case of credit card purchases, the ultimate bill was paid by the buyer in Swedish kronor. However, the shop in Denmark was paid by the credit card company in Danish kroner, which means that any VAT associated with the transaction accrued to the Danish state, not the Swedish one.

12. See Donnan and Wilson 1999 on the subversive economy of borders.

13. This dualism extends to people. There is a common stereotype that "the Danes are good at trade, the Swedes are good at production." Danes are even accused of being "shifty." While Swedes evidence a commitment to transparency and labor, Danes are marked as "middlemen," which has often been associated with "parasitism." That is to say, Danes stereotyped in this way are alleged to be not working as hard as those committed to production and they are thought to be capable of producing money in hidden fashions— magically and dishonestly.

14. But one could find cameralists throughout much of Europe at the time (e.g., Linnaeus was a cameralist; see Koerner 1999).

15. See Koerner's biography of Linnaeus, which has a chapter entitled "Should Coconuts Chance Come into My Hands." See also Heckscher's classic text *Mercantilism*

(1952), which he wrote as a response to the increasing popularity of tariffs in the post–World War I era. And indeed, he has an appendix to volume 2 that points out the reemergence of interest in cameralist doctrines at the beginning of the twentieth century (Heckscher 1952: 2:253).

16. It is, of course, interesting that this currency ring advocate referred to the dollar instead of the krona. I would argue that this is because the currency ring advocates often see themselves as part of a global movement, and the problem lies more with the world that the dollar has wrought rather than the one that the krona has brought forth. The dollar, in other words, is shorthand for "global capitalism."

17. This stance against an ever-increasing alienation is common to all facets of the anti-globalization movement, and it shows special sympathies with the growing "slow food" movement.

18. The lack of interest from the government on this front suggests that Tolstoy (1902) may have been correct. Governments are completely uninterested in accepting something that forces their hand by channeling their expenditures in specific directions. Paying taxes in any currency that one chooses stands as the anti-Tolstoyian moment, and it is surprisingly uncommon (see Gregory 1996; Hegel 1991). I owe thanks to John Kelly for the discovery of the obscure excursus on money by Tolstoy.

19. The fact that this was a common critique reveals how economic criminality is a major concern in Sweden. In other countries, the local currencies are critiqued for a variety of reasons, but rarely is their ability to evade taxes the overriding concern (though see Maurer 2005).

20. This is the era that Marx, Henry Sumner Maine, Georg Simmel, and others claim passed away with the advent of money exchange.

21. Though it appears oddly written, I have translated the tenses correctly in this quotation. This sort of prolepsis was typical of much regional advocacy.

22. A popular urban legend asserted that highly specialized EU rules meant that Swedish cucumbers wouldn't be considered cucumbers. Apparently, they weren't straight enough.

23. Even before the euro arrived in the broader EU, a wave of industry decamped from Sweden for other parts of the EU, and this wave continued with intensity after the currency's introduction. The most famous example of this was the purchasing of Volvo by Ford. One interviewee told me: "all of Sweden's pride . . . fifty-six years of accumulated value sold for 8 billion kronor, when these new data companies are worth the same in five years." At a bankers' conference on the euro at the Plaza Hotel on April 15, 1998, in New York City, one speaker made the important point that "mergers and acquisitions will attain a nationalistic bent in Europe that they have not in the U.S." This was clearly the case with regard to the Volvo sale, which occupied the headlines for several weeks and was the cause of much nostalgia and concern.

4. The Mark of Money

1. Anders Linde-Laursen reports (personal communication) that, in the past, Swedes have been herded en masse onto the Helsingør ferry.

2. Woodburn (1982) helpfully argues that the distinction revolves around ways of envisioning (or fighting against) the ability to store economic value over time.

3. The authors cite Woodburn, among others, as an inspiration, and his work is particularly interesting for those interested in the question of orientation toward the future or the present (see Woodburn 1982).

4. It seems to me that Day, Papataxiarchis, and Stewart's book (1999) should be considered an essential text for anthropologists who are interested in analyzing the effectiveness of various practices of resistance or who are openly calling for a more activist discipline. Though the book does not endorse any particular political stance, it provides food for thought and covers different ground than many other studies within the literature on resistance.

5. It is worth noting that vagrancy legislation was often a thinly disguised method of criminalizing poverty (see Beier 1985).

6. Levander (1974 [1934]) covers this period nicely in his *Fattig Folk och Tiggare,* where he claims that the Swedish attitude toward poor people underwent a sea change when the country adopted Protestantism. (Levander was writing around the time of Weber's seminal publications.) He describes an ancient practice in which the villages of Scandinavia passed a sort of gavel around from house to house. If an impoverished wanderer showed up, he would receive food and lodging at whichever house currently held the gavel. Also, a town's local beggars would receive a "beggar's pass" that meant that they would be given care, while foreign beggars couldn't receive the same (and "foreign," importantly, only meant "from another town," not "from another country"). Levander claims that the beggars even used to unionize, and the union boss would make sure that no foreign beggars or local miscreants who gave the other beggars a bad name would stay in town too long. Such beggar's passes were also common in England (Beier 1985: 111) and Germany (Harrington 1999).

7. Market space and home spaces can, of course, be coextensive. The same city, Copenhagen for example, may be a home space for Danes and a market space for Swedes. There is a layering of space, a layering that states often try to eliminate or at least redefine for new groups of outsiders (see Lefebvre 1991).

8. This isn't as unique of a circumstance as it might sound. Market spaces throughout much of European history have welcomed foreigners so long as they have money. Market space is a zone that Marx critiqued heavily, the zone where money is the supreme value over all other values, e.g., those directed toward love or blood. According to Marx, the reason that foreigners are allowed in market space is because *everyone* is a foreigner in the anonymous market space whose governing value is money. The story told here is a chronicling, then, of the effort to overpower the law of money with the law of the state.

9. This catchall nature of nineteenth-century vagrancy law was not unique to Sweden, which further justifies a search for its organizing principle. Good comparative material exists for the United States, Germany, Holland, France, and England (see, e.g., Allsop 1967; Beaune 1983; Beier 1985; Foucault 1988 [1961]; Hacking 1998; Harrington 1999; Hill 1972; Lucassen and Lucassen 1997; Marx 1990: 877–895; Sassen 1999). It is a well-known fact among scholars of vagrancy that the laws were used to police all sorts of criminal elements and only became rigorously applied to today's definition of a vagrant in the modern era (Beier 1985; Hill 1972). Beier, for example, lists an array of people covered by vagrancy legislation: "pedlars and tinkers, soldiers and mariners, many entertainers, students, unlicensed healers and even fortune-tellers," as well as the Roma and the Irish (Beier 1985: 10). He calls it "the classic crime of status" (ibid.: xxi–xxii), rather than the result of any misdeed. In other words, though people today may be committed to noting the important dif-

ferences between migrant laborers and tourists, the nineteenth-century state was not at all committed to these categorical distinctions, instead lumping them together in the service of both governmental policy and punishment.

10. Many excellent studies of the relationship between mobile groups and states exist. See, for example, Caplan and Torpey 2001; Comaroff and Comaroff 1992; Day, Papataxiarchis, and Stewart 1999; Fontaine 1996; James 2007; Lucassen and Lucassen 1997; Lucassen 1993; Sassen 1999; Torpey 1998.

11. Primary document research suggests that the same may have been true in Sweden. In one report (*Underdånigt* 1882: 60), a police chief in Malmö complained that his department could not successfully control the vagrancy problem on the outskirts of town because he did not have enough officers. Twenty-first-century reports from Europe seem to further confirm my claim. French president Nicolas Sarkozy, when accused of deporting Roma en masse from France despite their EU citizenship rights, "suggested that the [European] commission should come up with some Europe-wide proposals to resolve the migrant issue" (Castle and Bennhold 2010).

12. For another story of a state trying to banish or reform migrant labor within its bounds, see Comaroff and Comaroff 1992.

13. As soon as one combines these points with the well-known findings of macroeconomics that savings rates determine the rate of national investment and thus prosperity, one can see why states interested in guaranteeing *future* prosperity would work hard to eliminate people with an orientation toward the present from within their territory.

14. All qualifications of this term in the primary literature stated that the person was "found without the means to defend himself." We know they were referring to money because of the reports, which always clarified the amount of money or goods that the person had (e.g., the presumed value of a watch), and this amount was deemed insufficient.

15. Hacking (1998) recounts that there was the emergence and wide employment of a new psychological diagnosis throughout Europe around the same time. Evocatively christened as "dromomania," "fugue," "wandertreib," and "automatisme ambulatoire," the men (and they were almost always men) who suffered from this malady could not resist the pull of the road, embarking on cross-continental wanderings without a moment's notice. Hacking explains that the emergence of this new diagnosis relied on the creation of an "ecological niche" appropriate for it. One vital component of this niche was the rise of mass tourism—a burgeoning industry whose goal was to facilitate movement across new boundaries. (He also couples it to the increasing vagrancy problem of the era.) Suggestively, Benjamin also claims that the epoch that Hacking studies witnessed the "apotheosis of the traveler" (Benjamin 1999: 587–588).

16. Harry Martinson (1949) certainly suggested as much, as have many others, albeit for different states, including E. P. Thompson (1993: 373), Rousseau, and Wordsworth (see Langan 1995). Or, one could turn to as old a source as Adam Smith, who feared that an entire system of socially beneficial production could break down if people ever noticed that "[i]n ease of body and peace of mind, all the different ranks of life are nearly upon a level, and the beggar, who suns himself by the side of the highway, possesses that security which kings are fighting for" (Smith 1984 [1790]: 185).

17. There is not space here to give proper due to this fascinating history. The ubiquity and subsequent demise of the vagrant in Swedish society have been largely neglected, but not for lack of primary sources. Wallentin makes an excellent preliminary foray into the

material, agreeing, "The topic has been so little studied, despite the fact that there is abundant primary material" (Wallentin 1989: 2). See Peebles (2003: 209–223) for much more primary document research than can be related here. Other mobile groups have been covered much better. Two excellent books have been written about the Travelers, a mobile group. Birgitta Svensson provides a riveting read in her *Bortom All Ära och Redlighet* (1993), tracing the Travelers' interactions with the state over several centuries in a Foucaultian light. Gunborg Lindholm's *Vägarnas Folk* (1995) provides an excellent description with evocative details of Traveler culture. A smaller literature was spawned in the 1990s on the Roma because of their tendency to be singled out by the Swedish state's sterilization program that reigned from the 1940s to the '70s.

18. Harrington mentions a similar distinction between "native" and "foreign," where the latter includes people from nearby towns (Harrington 1999: 320–321).

19. See Raffles 2007 for an extensive review and analysis of the use of the term "parasite" to impugn social groups, not least "wandering" Jews.

20. See Malmöhusläns Landskansliet DIVa: 2918, March 11, 1879, in the Malmö archives. This is an example of a successful petition from a foreigner (in this case, a Russian merchant) to stay in Malmö after the applicant proved and received testimony from trustworthy people that he had the monetary resources to stay. In fact, he gave the state three years of taxes ahead of time in order to fulfill the requirements; further, one Swedish acquaintance attested that "he can well provide for himself with the business he is running" and that he was a "well-renowned and upstanding person."

21. In Malmö's police archives, I found Germans, Russians, and other Europeans all being served with the identical punishment as the Swedes in the archives: banishment to their "home" (Malmö Stadsarkiv DIIa: 5, Kriminal polisen i Malmö).

22. Though it is not necessary to my argument about Sweden, I would posit that many successful capitalist states rely on the same idea, although they may build their structures of mobility in less obvious, or at least different, ways. For example, the U.S. Constitution's commerce clause has proven essential in allowing for the mobility of labor throughout the union; less obviously, subsidized airports, roads, and even subways stand as other examples. An article in the *New York Observer* (Von Hoffman 2005) pointed out that the airline industry would be defunct were it not for the massive infrastructure commitments made by the U.S. government; this sort of support, in turn, lowers the cost of local goods and makes them more attractive compared to goods from other countries. Orange juice from Florida sold in New York is cheaper for consumers than it would be if the trucking companies had to pay for the roads entirely on their own; orange juice from Brazil, traveling by cargo vessel, is not subsidized in like manner (though it is cheaper nonetheless for other, important, reasons). In other words, often a good way to spot a successful capitalist country is to note how well it has released the factors of production and supported their mobility throughout the territory. One of the things that makes the EU so interesting to study is that it has to openly agitate for things that are often naturalized in other states.

23. There are, of course, special zones of state-sponsored leisure. It is interesting that these zones are virtually always in places where an economy based on production has utterly failed, and so a commitment to leisure manifests as a method of creating new forms of labor. In America, one thinks of casino riverboats in depressed areas; in Sweden, one thinks of eco-tourism in the economically declining north. The point, however, is that Copenhagen is different: its status as a zone of labor for Danes has never faltered in this

manner, and so it need not rely on Swedish debauchery as a vital infusion into its economy. It would thrive more from an infusion of Swedish labor, or so the proponents of Øresund espouse. Löfgren (2002) provides much detail on the creation of new leisure zones and how people behave differently in them than they do in their home spaces. Interestingly, the critique of excessive mobility even cropped up in the instances he cites, since the Swedish and American bourgeoisie were offended by the new vacationers invading their summer zones. These people camped, and moved around too much from week to week (Löfgren 2002: 145).

24. Löfgren (1999) is quick to point out that the ferries were used by many different people for many different reasons. Nonetheless, the overwhelming thrust of his description is on the liminal and festive aspect of the ferry ride, as it transported people away from the everyday.

25. The Swedish state pays the equivalent of each passenger's bridge toll. This amounts to about forty or fifty kronor, which was, during certain hours, the total cost of riding the cheaper boat across the water. The boat company was rightfully enraged that the government was not subsidizing its operations in an equal amount (for this decision aided in driving them out of business). One could, fairly, ask why, since both transport companies were privately owned (see TT 1999a). My conclusion is that the Swedish government is paying for the train toll because the train delivers people to work, while the Pilen ferry delivers people to bars.

26. For the record, the rhyme scheme is AAAAB CCCCB DDDDB DDDDB. Here is the original version:

Under 16-och 1700 tal brödrafolk sågs strida
Både svenskar och danskar fick svårligen lida
Skåneland bytte så småningom sida
Länge fick folken den ljusnande framtiden bida
Øresund var ett skiljande hav

Under 18 och 1900-tal blev det lugnt för det mesta
Svenskar och danskar varandra sågs gästa
En tur över Sundet blev ett nytt sätt att festa
Och minne av färden behöll nog de flesta
Øresund blev ett enande hav

På gränsen mot 2000-tal märks hur tiderna ila
På en bro ska man riskfritt både tåga och bila
Dess pelare sågs ju bli väldigt stabila
Men där vankas ej öl eller snaps eller vila
Øresund blir ej enbart för båtar ett hav

Så vi hoppas att båtarna fortsätter pila
Fastän de stundtals kan vara labila
De bjuder dock tid för öl, snaps och vila
För unga och vuxna och något senila
Øresund blir ett hav med ett bro som ett nav.

27. In this regard, the poem is a radical, if subtle, critique of all the claims of the bridge's proponents. They have endlessly espoused the belief that the bridge will finally unite an otherwise separated group of naturally related people. The poet thinks that the festive boats have done an equally good job at uniting the two countries all along.

28. Other nationals of other countries do this as well (the British in Portugal come to mind), but this only bolsters one of my central points: states grease the wheels of production to such an extent that excessive consumption often takes place in a ritualized time and space. For many groups of people, the nation has become the home to such an extent that departing from its bounds marks the beginning of a ritual moment, a passage into liminality. See Berdahl 1999 and Malkki 1995 for arguments that border crossings can be analyzed by turning to the literature on liminality.

29. Strangely, vagrancy was simultaneously romanticized during this era, a story that, unfortunately, cannot be told here. For example, it surely means something that Martinson's book *Vägen till Klockrike* (The Road to the Kingdom of Bells; 1949) is one of the most famous books of twentieth-century Sweden.

30. Some European vagrants took advantage of state efforts to send them home. When their money ran out, they would announce themselves as vagrants, i.e., get caught, and receive a train ticket and a few coins for the trip home. This was true of Swedish vagrants in Malmö, as attested in the police archives (Malmö Stadsarkiv DIIa). Hacking also relates similar tales in his fascinating book (Hacking 1998). Sometimes, French embassies would entirely subsidize the return trip of extraterritorial vagrants to their homes in France.

31. Harrington takes issue with standard explanations about the new repressions of vagrancy in the early modern period (1999: 312–313). He argues that "bureaucratic momentum" (ibid.: 318), rather than ideological shifts, had a major hand in matters; I heartily agree with him here, as there have been changes in laws that resulted in the gradual (seeming) eradication of vagrancy. He does agree that the standard explanations are traceable in the historic record; he just believes that bureaucratic momentum is the "cause" and these are the "effects" (319). The relevant ideological shifts include (1) Weber's argument that a new Calvinist admiration of labor was becoming dominant, (2) mercantilist concerns about convincing the populace to work, and (3) rising anxiety concerning crime and social order.

32. As detailed in the introduction, others have pointed out this distinction between home space and market space.

33. This sort of predicament is becoming less likely, as more Swedes now carry credit cards. But that is another story altogether.

34. See Daun (1996 [1989]: 44) and Wagner (1977) for similar arguments about moral inversions outside the Swedish nation-state. Bunzl (2000) and Lindquist (2008) have also documented people traversing nearby borders in order to escape the moral strictures of a home community.

35. These practices will not change overnight: Swedes now utilize the new bridge in order to go wild in Copenhagen. But for those who are interested in seeing the region converted into a space of labor, the structures are now in place for the project to proceed.

36. There are acceptable "descents into madness" within the space of the nation-state as well, but they are always temporally delimited (as opposed to spatially delimited, as my case here). The month of July is a famous time of leisure, and much more alcohol is traditionally consumed during this time. Interestingly, many Swedes complain that the tendency to harmonize labor regulations all across Europe will cause these ritual temporalities to slip away too, as the sacred month of July fractures into shorter vacations throughout the summer.

37. But this is true only in the sense that tax-free alcohol "forces" you to break social rules more often outside the nation-state than within it; clearly, agency plays a role,

but we can still note the manner in which currencies can be configured to attempt to channel flows.

38. And they did. But the Ricardian point is that it is significantly cheaper to grow oranges somewhere else rather than in a greenhouse on a south-facing wall in Sweden.

39. Indeed, this precise issue proved to be a sizable problem for early EU jurisprudence. How could a mobile transnational labor force be assured that it would receive the famous welfare benefits of Western European states whenever it crossed a border? Without this assurance, labor mobility was severely hampered. The European Court of Justice worked hard to ensure that local benefits would be provided to newly arrived foreigners from other EU lands (see Peebles 1997).

40. See Hacking 1998: 79 for a similar assessment of the border in Catalonia.

41. Anyone who has followed the debate will recognize that several of these critiques are quite common throughout the EU, not just in Sweden. This suggests that the labeling emerges from the same logic that Harrington pointed out: the "need" of welfare programs to separate natives from foreigners.

42. The old Social Democratic adage that was cited to explain this ethos was "gör din plikt, kräv din rätt" (do your duty, demand your due).

5. INDEBTED COMMUNITIES

1. The 2008 credit crunch evidenced this quite dramatically. Each nation-state involved in the crunch initially only wanted to bail out banks that were considered home banks, even though the problem was legendarily global. When Icelandic banks needed a bailout well beyond what the small country of Iceland could provide, Britain forcefully argued against Iceland's initial practice of only saving Icelandic depositors' money (Forelle 2008). More generally, the EU's initial inability to come to an EU-wide solution to the credit crunch spelled trouble on the stock markets and was fascinating from the perspective being argued throughout this book about the euro and its relationship to a pan-European sense of community. In the United States, many have argued that homeowners who are "underwater" (their house is worth less than their mortgage) should receive some form of debt forgiveness, rather than be viewed as people who made an uninformed investment or behaved in a reckless fashion with someone else's capital.

2. In this regard, Munn's (1986) theory about movement and debt in Gawa also applies to Øresund.

3. For a broader consideration and more data from Swedish history, see Peebles 2003.

4. Secondary sources in many European tongues are rare. Though there are some titles considering this important phenomenon, none have received the attention they deserve in wider academic circles (see, e.g., Duffy 1985; Finn 2003; Lester 1995; Mann 2002).

5. In the Germanic literature, the scholarly research on the Icelandic sagas clearly attests to this relationship between monetary and bodily values. Murders could readily be compensated for with money; it was only on the refusal to pay that blood feuds continued indefinitely (see the debate between Miller 1990 and Posner 1995).

6. Sweden's equivalent of the *Encyclopaedia Britannica* claims that the use of the debtors' prison dates from the fourteenth century in Sweden (*Nordisk Familjebok* 1905: 792–793). Perhaps as a measure of the concept's age, Swedes much later took on the Germanic term for debt, *skuld,* but the debtors' prisons retained the appellation *gäldstuga* (debt cot-

tage), which is based on the old Norse term *gäld,* which means, interestingly, both "money" and "debt." See etymologies in Hellquist 1922.

7. Kowaleski, in her study of credit and debt adjudication in medieval Exeter, England, tells us that imprisonment was one penalty imposed on debtors, but she asserts that "outlawry" represented the ultimate sanction by the courts (Kowaleski 1995: 216). This is an evocative form of punishment, for outlawry—a sort of forced vagrancy—represents one of the fears of the creditor and is one of the reasons, surely, for the existence of the debtors' prison.

8. Later in the chapter, I will discuss the felicitous fact that the word for treasure (*skatt*) in Sweden and Denmark is the same as the word for tax (*skatt*).

9. In Swedish debtors' prison, one could gain special dispensation for a temporary leave. In this case, he had a prescription from a doctor to get some fresh air, but af Segerstad also mentions that actors were allowed to leave the confines of the prison in order to play roles in local theater productions (af Segerstad 1981: 395–400). In Dickens' *Little Dorrit,* some members of the family are allowed to come and go freely from the prison, but the father, William Dorrit, is not permitted to leave.

10. France was apparently the first to banish the debtors' prison, with legislation in 1867. The North German Federation followed in 1868, Austria and Belgium in 1871, Denmark in 1872, Switzerland and Norway in 1874. England limited its use in 1869, but failed to outlaw it completely. Finland joined this clear international trend in 1895 (see *Nordisk Familjebok* 1905: 792–793).

11. The left-wing magazine *ETC,* whose editor is critiqued by one of my informants below, ran an entire issue on the hidden class of wealthy people in Sweden. The magazine satirized them, providing diagrams for how to tie a garbage bag and using survey data to raise awareness about them. Perhaps, the magazine intoned, being wealthy should be considered a social illness (not unlike vagrancy), for there are numerous problems of exclusion from which the wealthy suffer (see *ETC* 1999).

12. What he fails to notice is that the bank is, of course, circulating his money in money-increasing ventures. He forgoes his right to the magical increases in his own capital, but he does not thereby nullify this power in general. It is additionally interesting to note the difference with the beliefs prevailing on Gawa, where Munn (1986) describes a general dislike of all consumption as selfish and thoughtless. Despite Gawans' particular types of value redistribution, which result in a general equaling out of the social welfare, their ethos of nonconsumption is, in a way, very capitalistic, in that they hope to save for the future rather than consume in the present.

13. I was told by many people that the Swedish lottery is not a "poor people's tax" as it is in the United States, for virtually everyone plays it. However, I would again appeal to the hidden nature of class differences; one critic of the People's Home whom I interviewed insisted that there are socioeconomic differences in who plays.

14. In an interesting twist of events, Malmö was approved to open up Sweden's first casino. Right when individuals were beginning to believe that they could assemble non-hidden wealth without resorting to chance (the lottery), the industry of chance itself was becoming a vision of wealth for the entire community. It is as though Malmö had watched so much of its labor depart for foreign shores that it had campaigned to turn leisure itself into a form of labor-creating value. See Comaroff and Comaroff 2000: 295.

15. I am reminded of Adam Smith's equal disdain for financial enterprises: "An augmentation of fortune is the means by which the greater part of men propose and wish to

better their condition. It is the means the most vulgar and the most obvious" (Smith 1976 [1776]: 363).

16. This may explain why it took so long for credit cards to gain a foothold in Sweden.

17. The state has stopped this age-old practice, which is very telling for the arguments being made in this book.

18. Of course, the United States also has a system of government-guaranteed loans, but there is presumably much more defaulting on loans compared to Sweden. In the United States, the repayment schedule is related to the amount borrowed, not to one's ability to pay, so it is easy to imagine defaulting if one's job doesn't pay enough money. In Sweden, there was no need to default so long as one was employed, though of course when one hit the age of sixty-five, one automatically defaulted. The point is that, in the United States, debts are also socialized, just in a different way.

19. One is also tempted to relate this sort of hefty one-way gifting to relations of power between citizen and state. Mauss describes how a transactor during the potlatch tried to place his gift partner in debt so that he would have power over him. In Sweden, the state places many of its citizens into unpayable debt. By the standards of anthropological theory, this would be considered "agonistic" gifting (Mauss 1990: 6–7).

20. As testimony to the pervasiveness of economic criminality in Sweden and the desire to hide wealth, note that shell companies are exceedingly common. They are so common that a parliamentary report was exclusively dedicated to discussing them as a problem (Bulvaner 1998).

21. To clarify: In Sweden, there is a state collections agency, known as the Kronofogde-myndigheterna (a seemingly untranslatable term; my dictionary calls it an "enforcement agency," but this loses its attachment to the word "crown" via the term *krono* and to *fogde,* which means "bailiff"). It is this agency's task to track down and alternately aid or imprison debtors, depending on how much the debtors wish to cooperate with the state. There is also an important branch of the legal profession that deals specifically with debt collections. These people are hired and accredited by the Kronofogdemyndigheterna to seek out all the assets of debtors, and they are hired by other creditors as well.

22. My informants told me that this law was developed because of the enormous amount of lending that occurred in the 1980s. One stated, "These people could never have paid off these debts, even if they had wanted to." In other words, the law was passed in order to socialize the debt and to get these people back into the regular cycle of money relations. The 2008 credit crunch serves, yet again, as another example. The banks were "bailed out" by the governments because they had debts that were beyond anyone's ability to repay. In the news media, this was called "toxic debt." If toxic debt was owned by an entity deemed "too big to fail," then the debt (or, at least, the risk entailed in owning the debt) was socialized in various ways.

23. I do not know of a scholarly equivalent to the literature on social banditry for the practice of piracy, but the question is gaining in popularity. Two separate courses at Columbia University during the 2005–2006 school year and one at The New School during the 2007–2008 school year addressed the question of piracy as a social phenomenon.

24. Lloyd provides us with some amazing examples of these sorts of community boundaries in the Middle Ages. He describes how the ethnicity of foreign traders was essential in determining how a debt would be paid. For example, if a Dutch trader became insolvent, other traders from his same town could have their goods seized, even if they didn't know the man. The point, of course, was that each trading guild was expected to police its own

members. If any given member became insolvent, his debt was socialized among his fellow traders, so they had an interest in making sure he kept to his promises (Lloyd 1982: 15–16).

25. This argument shares much with Marx. As Marx insists, capital takes on a life of its own and, as an object outside of ourselves, continually demands more and more living labor. Its vampiric tendencies are well covered in the Marxist corpus. Herman Daly (1996) and others are leading the charge to promote a "zero-growth" economy.

26. This sentiment was echoed in the successful Swedish movie *Together*, depicting a Swedish utopian commune in the 1970s. A character who is a stringent Maoist explains his theory of revolution to his girlfriend: if all the banks are boycotted by the workers, the entire capitalist system will collapse.

27. I thank Anders Linde-Laursen for helping to translate from Danish. Here is the original:

> Hvordan kan man bygge
> et helt hus
> når man kun har træ
> og søm
> Spir hedder de også
> og verktøj
> og ledige hænder
> Men mangler tommer
> eller centimeter
> For dem må man lane
> af nogle af de samlere
> der har samlet mange
> tommer eller centimeter
> og gemt dem i kældre and
> med henblik på udlån
> til dem der kun har få
> eller slet ingen
> tommer eller centimeter.
>
> De andre må pænt lane
> Men det er ikke gratis
> De må betale tilbage
> med flere
> tommer eller centimeter
> Renter kalder de det
> så det er ikke så godt
> hvis man ikke har råd
> til at låne tommer eller centimeter
> . . .
> Den som har den største gæld
> det største minus
> røde tal
> er den rigeste
> For den
> det være sig en han eller hun
> har fået noget
> men endnu kun givet

Tal
sorte tal
til gengæld
indtil videre.

28. The author seems to be suggesting that all measurements are equally meaningless, for he mentions the historical measurement unit—inches—that is no longer used in Denmark (the poem is written in Danish). He's basically saying, "Call it what you will, kronor, euros, dollars; they're all just false accounting. Just as we eliminated the inch as a unit of measurement, someday we may replace the krone with local currency, for it's a better system."

29. Usually, "saver" would be rendered as *sparer,* which has no negative connotations—a neutral term from the world of banking. Instead, he has chosen *samlere* (collectors), which has overtones of greed, tilting toward the notion of hoarding.

30. See Hart 2001 for more on this belief.

31. See Raffles 2007 for a thorough discussion of this tendency.

32. But see Ezra Pound (Kenner 1973) and Major C. H. Douglas (1920) as examples of people who espouse monetary theories akin to those of the local currencies and *do* end up harboring hatred toward specific groups.

33. Of course, this is the explanation for the evolution of *all* money; we are incessantly told that money was a "solution" to the problems of barter (but see Humphrey and Hugh-Jones 1992). By accepting national paper money, one is assuming that one will be able to trade it at a later date for a good or service other than money from within the community of users. The difference is that sound national currencies are now seen as the paragon of liquidity itself, so no one thinks of them as mere steps in a bartering process, but rather as ends in themselves.

34. Maurer 2005 has an interesting story about this precise desire producing an Islamic currency ring.

35. See the quotes from Gesell cited in chapter 2. He had a similar fear of interest and its potential damage to the world.

36. The Greek debt crisis of 2010 has driven home this point quite thoroughly.

37. This is a common disparagement by Danes against Malmö, since they believe that it is "overrun" with immigrants.

38. Although capital knows no home, as Adam Smith insisted (Smith 1976 [1776]: 444–445), it is typically measured in a currency that concretizes its otherwise abstract nature. Transaction costs can make it less attractive to traverse boundaries and more preferable to stay at home.

REFERENCES

Adler-Karlsson, Gunnar. 1969. *Functional Socialism: A Swedish Theory for Democratic Socialization.* Stockholm: Prisma.

af Segerstad, Nils Hård. 1981. "Om Gäldstugan på Söder i Stockholm." *Släkt och Hävd* 3–4: 395–400.

Agamben, Giorgio. 2000. *Means without Ends: Notes on Politics.* Minneapolis: University of Minnesota Press.

Agnew, Jean-Christophe. 1986. *Worlds Apart: The Market and the Theater in Anglo-American Thought, 1550–1750.* New York: Cambridge University Press.

Akelius Fund Management, Ltd. n.d. *Akelius Bästa.* Dublin, Ireland: Akelius Fund Management.

Akin, David, and Joel Robbins, eds. 1999. *Money and Modernity: State and Local Currencies in Melanesia.* Pittsburgh, Pa.: University of Pittsburgh Press.

Allsop, Kenneth. 1967. *Hard Travellin': The Story of the Migrant Worker.* London: Pimlico.

Altshuler, David. 2000. "Tunneling towards Capitalism in the Czech Republic." *Ethnography* 2(1): 115–138.

Ambjörnsson, Ronny. 1981. *Det Okända Landet: Tre Studier om Svenska Utopister.* Stockholm: Gidlund.

Anderson, Benedict. 1983. *Imagined Communities.* New York: Verso.

Andersson, Åke. n.d.a. "Autonomt Sydsverige med Örestad som köl." *Oresundcity.* http://web.archive.org/web/19991002031301/http://www.oresundcity.se/6/autonom.htm. Accessed September 20, 2010.

——. n.d.b. "Skånskan eget språk med en rad dialekter." *Oresundcity.* http://web.archive.org/web/*/http://www.oresundcity.se/3/skanska.htm. Accessed September 20, 2010.

Anonymous. 1815. *Theoretisk Undersökning och Praktisk Conclusion, jemte Moralisk Tillämpning uti Twiste-ämnet om Penninge-nåd, Mynt, Agio, Cours, Realisation och Dyr Tid, m.m.: Eller en anwändbar Finance-Cateches för Alla Policerade Nationers Regeringar från Norra till Södra Polen.* Stockholm: A. Gadelius.

Anonymous. 1818. *Specie-Riksdalern under Slöjan, eller: Vi Äga ej, Fåfängt eftersträfva vi att i en Hast Äga, men Blott med Tiden Kunna Vi Hoppas att Äga ett Eget Nationalt Klingande Mynt.* Stockholm: Olof Grahn.

Anonymous. 1829. *Gäldstugan, eller Desz Hemligheter, Hemtade ur Desz Uråldriga Arkiver.* Stockholm: M. G. Lundberg.

Appadurai, Arjun. 1986. *The Social Life of Things.* New York: Cambridge University Press.

——. 2006. *Fear of Small Numbers.* Durham, N.C.: Duke University Press.

Apple, R. W., Jr. 2002. "Northern Lights: The New Flavors of Sweden." *New York Times*. October 16, p. F1.

Aretxaga, Begoña. 2005. *States of Terror: Begoña Aretxaga's Essays*. Reno, Nev.: Center for Basque Studies.

Asad, Talal. 2002. "Muslims and European Identity: Can Europe Represent Islam?" In *The Idea of Europe*. Anthony Pagden, ed. Cambridge: Cambridge University Press.

Asher, Andrew D. 2005. "A Paradise on the Oder? Ethnicity, Europeanization, and the EU Referendum in a Polish-German Border City." *City and Society* 17(1): 127–152.

Balibar, Etienne. 2004. *We, the People of Europe? Reflections on Transnational Citizenship*. Princeton, N.J.: Princeton University Press.

Beaune, Jean-Claude. 1983. *Le Vagabond et la Machine: Essai sur L'Automatisme Ambulatoire Médecine, Technique et Société en France 1880–1910*. Seyssel, France: Champ Vallon.

Beier, A. L. 1985. *Masterless Men: The Vagrancy Problem in England 1560–1640*. London: Methuen.

Bell, Daniel. 1967. *Marxian Socialism in the United States*. Princeton, N.J.: Princeton University Press.

Bellier, Irene, and Thomas M. Wilson, eds. 2000. *An Anthropology of the European Union: Building, Imagining and Experiencing the New Europe*. New York: Berg.

Benjamin, Walter. 1999. *The Arcades Project*. Cambridge, Mass.: Harvard University Press.

Bensel, Richard F. 1990. *Yankee Leviathan: The Origins of Central State Authority in America, 1859–1877*. New York: Cambridge University Press.

Berdahl, Daphne. 1999. *Where the World Ended: Re-unification and Identity in the German Borderland*. Berkeley: University of California Press.

Berezin, Mabel, and Martin Schain. 2003. *Europe without Borders: Remapping Territory, Citizenship, and Identity in a Transnational Age*. Baltimore, Md.: Johns Hopkins University Press.

Berg, Per-Olof, Anders Linde-Laursen, and Orvar Löfgren, eds. 2000. *Invoking a Transnational Metropolis: The Making of the Øresund Region*. Lund, Sweden: Studentlitteratur.

———. 2002. *Öresundsbro På Uppmärksamhetens Marknad*. Lund, Sweden: Studentlitteratur.

Berge, Ursula. 2003. *Behåll Kronan! Rösta Nej Till EMU's Tredje Steg*. Avesta, Sweden: Pocky.

Bergström, Axel, et al. 1870. *Betänkande angående Sveriges övergång till ett Nytt Myntsystem med Guld såsom Värdemätare*. Stockholm: P. A. Norstedt and Söner.

Bergström, Villy, et al. 1996. *Skall Sverige Ansluta sig till Valuta-unionen EMU?* Stockholm: Utbildningsförlaget Brevskolan.

"Betänkande med Förslag till Lagstiftning om Åtgärder mot Lösdriveri samt Åtgärder mot Sedeslöst Leverne av Samhällsskadlig Art." 1929. Tillkallade Sakkunniga. *Statens Offentliga Utredningar 1929: 9* (Socialdepartementet). Stockholm: Kungliga Boktryckeriet, P. A. Norstedt and Söner.

"Björn Wilke Intervju." 1999. *Pengar och Rätt*. Sverigesradio P1. September 21.

Blanche, Aug. 1847. *En Födelsedag På Gäldstugan*. Stockholm: Albert Bonniers.

Borneman, John, and Nick Fowler. 1997. "Europeanization." *Annual Review of Anthropology* 26: 487–514.

Böröcz, Jozsef, and Mahua Sarkar. 2005. "What Is the EU?" *International Sociology* 20(2): 153–173.

Bourdieu, Pierre. 1984. *Distinction: A Social Critique of the Judgement of Taste*. Cambridge, Mass.: Harvard University Press.

Bronk, Richard, and David Bowers. 1998. *EMU: A Trojan Horse? Supply-Side Reform and the Continued Importance of Country-Risk Factors in Euro-Land*. New York: Merrill Lynch, Global Securities Research and Economics Group.

Bryar, David. 1992. *How Dumb Can You Get? An Immigrant's View of the Swedish Mentality*. Bombay: Davidinho.

Buck-Morss, Susan. 2000. *Dreamworld and Catastrophe: The Passing of Mass Utopia in East and West*. Cambridge, Mass.: MIT Press.

Bulvaner och annat. 1998. *Betänkande av Bulvanutredningen*. Serie SOU 1998: 047 (researcher: John Munck).

Bunzl, Matti. 2000. "The Prague Experience: Gay Male Sex Tourism and the Neocolonial Invention of an Embodied Border." In *Altering States: Ethnographies of Transition in Eastern Europe and the Former Soviet Union*. Daphne Berdahl, Matti Bunzl, and Martha Lampland, eds. Ann Arbor: University of Michigan Press.

Burke, Al. 1998. *Nordic News Network*. http://web.archive.org/web/19981206222011/http://www.nnn.se/n.model.html. Accessed September 20, 2010.

Caplan, Jane, and John Torpey, eds. 2001. *Documenting Individual Identity: The Development of State Practices in the Modern World*. Princeton, N.J.: Princeton University Press.

Carlen, Stefan, and Sören Wibe. 1999. *EMU: Självbestämmande Eller Anpassning*. Umeå, Sweden: Umeå Forestry University Press.

Castle, Stephen, and Katrin Bennhold. 2010. "Dispute Grows over France's Removal of Roma Camps." *New York Times*. September 16.

Childs, Marquis. 1934. *Sweden: Where Capitalism Is Controlled*. New York: John Day.

———. 1936. *Sweden: The Middle Way*. New Haven, Conn.: Yale University Press.

———. 1947. *Sweden: The Middle Way*, 2nd ed. New Haven, Conn.: Yale University Press.

Chown, John. 1994. *A History of Money: From AD 800*. New York: Routledge.

Claeys, Gregory. 1994. *Utopias of the British Enlightenment*. New York: Cambridge University Press.

Cohen, Benjamin. 1998. *The Geography of Money*. Ithaca, N.Y.: Cornell University Press.

Comaroff, Jean, and John L. Comaroff. 1997. *Of Revelation and Revolution: Dialectics of Modernity on a South African Frontier*, vol. 2. Chicago: University of Chicago Press.

———. 2000. "Millennial Capitalism: First Thoughts on a Second Coming." *Public Culture* 12(2): 291–343.

Comaroff, John L., and Jean Comaroff. 1992. *Ethnography and the Historical Imagination*. Boulder, Colo.: Westview.

Corbett, Anne. 2005. *Universities and the Europe of Knowledge: Ideas, Institutions and Policy Entrepreneurship in European Union Higher Education Policy, 1955–2005*. New York: Palgrave Macmillan.

Coronil, Fernando. 1997. *The Magical State: Nature, Money, and Modernity in Venezuela*. Chicago: University of Chicago Press.

Crapanzano, Vincent. 2003. "Reflections on Hope as a Category of Social and Psychological Analysis." *Cultural Anthropology* 18(1): 3–32.

Cronon, William. 1991. *Nature's Metropolis: Chicago and the Great West*. New York: Norton.

Dahlerup, Drude. 1999. "Typiskt Svenskt!" *Bang* 3. http://www.bang.a.se/Amallar/torsk_intro.html.

Daly, Herman. 1996. *Beyond Growth: The Economics of Sustainable Development*. Boston: Beacon.

Darian-Smith, Eve. 1999. *Bridging Divides: The Channel Tunnel and English Legal Identity in the New Europe*. Berkeley: University of California Press.

Das, Veena. 2004. "The Signature of the State: The Paradox of Illegibility." In *Anthropology in the Margins of the State*. Veena Das and Deborah Poole, eds. Santa Fe, N.M.: School of American Research Press.

Daun, Åke. 1996 [1989]. *Swedish Mentality*. University Park: Pennsylvania State University Press.

Davies, Glyn. 1994. *A History of Money: From Ancient Times to the Present Day*. Cardiff: University of Wales Press.

Day, Sophie. 1999. "Hustling: Individualism among London Prostitutes." In *Lilies of the Field*. Sophie Day, Evthymios Papataxiarchis, and Michael Stewart, eds. Boulder, Colo.: Westview.

Day, Sophie, Evthymios Papataxiarchis, and Michael Stewart, eds. 1999. *Lilies of the Field*. Boulder, Colo.: Westview.

De Certeau, Michel. 1984. *The Practice of Everyday Life*. Berkeley: University of California Press.

Dickens, Charles. 1998 [1857]. *Little Dorrit*. New York: Penguin.

Dietler, Michael. 1994. "'Our Ancestors the Gauls': Archaeology, Ethnic Nationalism, and the Manipulation of Celtic Identity in Modern Europe." *American Anthropologist* 96: 584–605.

D'Oliveira, Hans Ulrich Jessurun. 1995. "Union Citizenship: Pie in the Sky?" In *A Citizen's Europe: In Search of a New Order*. Allan Rosas and Esko Antola, eds. Thousand Oaks, Calif.: Sage.

Dodd, Nigel. 2005. "Reinventing Monies in Europe." *Economy and Society*. 34(4): 558–583.

Donnan, Hastings, and Thomas Wilson. 1999. *Borders: Frontiers of Identity, Nation and State*. Oxford: Berg.

Douglas, Clifford Hugh. 1920. *Economic Democracy*. London: Harcourt, Brace and Howe.

Douthwaite, Richard. 1996. *Short Circuit: Strengthening Local Economies for Security in an Unstable World*. Devon, England: Resurgence.

Duffy, Ian P. H. 1985. *Bankruptcy and Insolvency in London during the Industrial Revolution*. New York: Garland.

Dumont, Louis. 1977. *From Mandeville to Marx: The Genesis and Triumph of Economic Ideology*. Chicago: University of Chicago Press.

du Monthoux, Pierre Guillet. 1987. *Läran om Penningen: Om Penningens Makt och Maktens Penning från Knapp till Friedman*. Stockholm: Norstedts.

Durkheim, Emile. 1984 [1893]. *The Division of Labor in Society*. New York: Free Press.

Ehn, Billy, Jonas Frykman, and Orvar Löfgren. 1993. *Försvenskningen av Sverige: Det Nationellas Förvandlingar*. Stockholm: Natur och Kultur.

Einaudi, Luca. 2001. *Money and Politics: European Monetary Unification and the International Gold Standard (1865–1873)*. New York: Oxford University Press.

Eklund, Jörgen, and Martin Ådahl. 1998. *Vad Betyder EMU?* Stockholm: SNS.

Ekström, Andreas. 1999. "Obetalbart—På Alla Vis." *Sydsvenskan*. June 10, p. A16.

Engels, Friedrich. 1978. "Socialism: Utopian and Scientific." In *The Marx-Engels Reader*. Robert Tucker, ed. New York: Norton.

ETC. 1999. *De Rika 2*.

———. 2000. "Letter to the Editor: Hej ETC-Redaktionen och Alla Läsare!"

European Union Commission. 1998. *The Raspberry Ice Cream War: A Comic for Young People on a Peaceful Europe without Frontiers*. Luxembourg: Office for Official Publications of the European Communities.

European Union. 1992. *Treaty on European Union*. Maastricht, The Netherlands.

Fajans, Jane. 1997. *They Make Themselves: Work and Play among the Baining of Papua New Guinea*. Chicago: University of Chicago Press.

Falkman, Ludvig B. 1986. *Minnen från Malmö*. Malmö, Sweden: Litos Reprotryck.

Finn, Margot C. 2003. *The Character of Credit: Personal Debt in English Culture, 1740–1914*. Cambridge: Cambridge University Press.

Finne, Arne. 2000. "Letter to the Editor: Gör EU till ett Skatteparadis." *Svenska Dagbladet*. July 13, p. 9.

Fisher, Irving (assisted by Hans R. L. Cohrssen). 1935. *Stabilized Money: A History of the Movement*. London: George Allen and Unwin.

Fleisher, Wilfrid. 1956. *Sweden, the Welfare State*. New York: John Day.

Fontaine, Laurence. 1996. *History of Pedlars in Europe*. Cambridge: Polity.

Forelle, Charles. 2008. "As Banking 'Fairy Tale' Ends, Iceland Looks Back to the Sea." *Wall Street Journal*. October 10, p. A1.

Foster, Robert. 1998. "Your Money, Our Money, the Government's Money: Finance and Fetishism in Melanesia." In *Border Fetishisms*. Patricia Spyer, ed. New York: Routledge.

Foucault, Michel. 1986. "Text / Context of Other Space." *Diacritics* 16(1): 22–27.

———. 1988 [1961]. *Madness and Civilization: A History of Insanity in the Age of Reason*. New York: Vintage.

———. 1995 [1977]. *Discipline and Punish*, 2nd ed. Translated by A. Sheridan. New York: Vintage.

Frankel, Jeffrey. 1998. *The Regionalization of the World Economy*. Chicago: University of Chicago Press.

Franzen, Bo. 1998. *Sturetidens Monetära System: Pant eller Penningar som Information i Köpstaden Arboga*. Stockholm: Almqvist and Wiksell International.

Frykman, Jonas, and Orvar Löfgren. 1996 [1979]. *Culture Builders: A Historical Anthropology of Middle-Class Life*. New Brunswick, N.J.: Rutgers University Press.

Gal, Susan, and Gail Kligman. 2000. *The Politics of Gender after Socialism*. Princeton, N.J.: Princeton University Press.

Gaonkar, Dilip Parameshwar, and Elizabeth Povinelli. 2003. "Technologies of Public Forms: Circulation, Transfiguration, Recognition." *Public Culture* 15(3): 385–397.

Gesell, Silvio. 1929. *The Natural Economic Order*. Berlin-Frohnau: Neo.

Gill, Tom. 1999. "Wage Hunting at the Margins of Urban Japan." In *Lilies of the Field*. Sophie Day, Evthymios Papataxiarchis, and Michael Stewart, eds. Boulder, Colo.: Westview.

Gmelch, George. 1977. "Economic Strategies and Migrant Adaptation." *Ethnos* 42: 22–37.

Graeber, David. 1996. "Beads and Money: Notes toward a Theory of Wealth and Power." *American Ethnologist* 23: 4–24.

Graubard, Stephen R. 1984. "Preface: The Nordic Enigma." *Daedalus* 113(1): v–xiii.

Greco, Thomas. 1994. *New Money for Healthy Communities*. n.p.: Thomas Greco.

Gregory, Chris A. 1996. "Cowries and Conquest: Towards a Subalternate Quality Theory of Money." *Comparative Studies in Society and History* 38(2) (April): 195–217.

Gupta, Akhil, and James Ferguson. 1992. "Beyond 'Culture': Space, Identity, and the Politics of Difference." *Cultural Anthropology* 7(1): 6–23.

Guyer, Jane. 2004. *Marginal Gains: Monetary Transactions in Atlantic Africa: Lewis Henry Morgan Lectures 1997*. Chicago: University of Chicago Press.

Hacking, Ian. 1990. *The Taming of Chance*. New York: Cambridge University Press.

———. 1998. *Mad Travelers: Reflections on the Reality of Transient Mental Illnesses*. Cambridge, Mass.: Harvard University Press.

Hall, Peter. 1998. *Cities in Civilization*. New York: Pantheon.

Hammarlund, Per. 2005. *Liberal Internationalism and the Decline of the State: The Thought of Richard Cobden, David Mitrany, and Kenichi Ohmae*. New York: Palgrave Macmillan.

Hannerz, Ulf. 1996. *Transnational Connections*. New York: Routledge.

Harmsen, Robert, and Thomas M. Wilson, eds. 2000. *Europeanization: Institution, Identities and Citizenship*. Atlanta, Ga.: Rodopi.

Harrington, Joel. 1999. "Escape from the Great Confinement: The Genealogy of a German Workhouse." *Journal of Modern History* 71(2): 308–345.

Hart, Keith. 1986. "Heads or Tails? Two Sides of the Coin." *Man* 21(4): 637–656.

———. 2001. *Money in an Unequal World: Keith Hart and His Memory Bank*. New York: Texere.

———. 2006. "Richesse commune: Construire une démocratie économique à l'aide de monnaies communautaires." In *Exclusion et liens financiers: "Monnaies sociales."* Jérôme Blanc, ed. Paris: Economica.

Harvey, David. 1989. *The Condition of Postmodernity: An Enquiry into the Origins of Cultural Change*. Cambridge, Mass.: Blackwell.

Heckscher, Eli. 1952. *Merkantilismen*, vols. 1 and 2. Stockholm: P. A. Norstedt and Söners.

Hegel, Georg W. F. 1985. *Reason in History*. Translated by Robert S. Hartman. New York: Macmillan.

———. 1991. *Elements of the Philosophy of Right*. Cambridge: Cambridge University Press.

Helleiner, Eric. 2003. *The Making of National Money: Territorial Currencies in Historical Perspective*. Ithaca, N.Y.: Cornell University Press.

Hellquist, Elof. 1922. *Svensk Etymologisk Ordbok*. Lund: C. W. K. Gleerups förlag Berlingska boktryckeriet.

Henriksen, Ingrid, and Niels Kærgård. 1995. "The Scandinavian Currency Union 1875–1914." In *International Monetary Systems in Historical Perspective*. Jaime Reis, ed. New York: St. Martin's.

Henriksson-Holmberg, Gustaf. 1913. *Socialismen i Sverge: 1770–1886*. Stockholm: Axel Holmströms.

Hermele, Kenneth, ed. 2003. *Allt du Inte Vill Veta om EMU om du Tänkt Rösta Ja*. Stockholm: Ordfront.

Herzfeld, Michael. 1997. *Cultural Intimacy: Social Poetics in the Nation-State*. New York: Routledge.

Hill, Christopher. 1972. *The World Turned Upside Down: Radical Ideas during the English Revolution*. New York: Viking.

Hobsbawm, Eric. 1969. *Bandits*. New York: Delacorte.

Holmes, Douglas. 2000. *Integral Europe*. Princeton, N.J.: Princeton University Press.

———. 2009. "Economy of Words." *Cultural Anthropology* 24(3): 381–419.

Holst-Nielsen, Svend, and Bent Larsen. 1999. "Ta Bort Hinder för Regional Identitet." *Sydsvenskan*. April 20, p. A2.

Humphrey, Caroline, and Stephen Hugh-Jones. 1992. "Introduction." In *Barter, Exchange, and Value: An Anthropological Approach*. Caroline Humphrey and Stephen Hugh-Jones, eds. Cambridge: Cambridge University Press.

Huntford, Roland. 1972. *The New Totalitarians*. New York: Stein and Day.

Idvall, Marcus. 1997. "Nationen, Regionen och den Fasta Förbindelsen: Ett Hundraårigt Statlig Projekts Betydelser i ett Territoriellt Perspektiv." In *Öresundsregionen: Visioner och Verklighet*. Lund, Sweden: Lund University Press.

———. 2000. *Kartors Kraft: Regionen som Samhällsvision i Öresundsbrons Tid*. Lund, Sweden: Nordic Academic Press.

Isaksson, Magnus. 2000. "Letter to the Editor: Med Hög Lön Kan Man Göra Rätt för Sig." *Sydsvenskan*. July 13, p. B7.

Jacoby, Russell. 1999. *The End of Utopia: Politics and Culture in an Age of Apathy*. New York: Basic.

JAK. 1998. "Ekonomi i Balans med Människa och Natur." Skövde, Sweden: JAK Medlemsbank.

Jakobsson, Ulf. 2003. *Därför Euron: Tio Ekonomer om Den Gemensamma Valutan*. Stockholm: Ekerlids.

James, Deborah. 2007. "Property and Citizenship in South African Land Reform." In *Making Nations, Creating Strangers*. Sara Dorman, Daniel Hammett, and Paul Nugent, eds. Leiden: Brill.

Jenkins, David. 1968. *Sweden and the Price of Progress*. New York: Coward-McCann.

Jevons, W. Stanley. 1919 [1875]. *Money and the Mechanism of Exchange*. New York: Appleton.

Johansson, Karin. 1999. "Snart Vet du Om du Bor Sunt." *Sydsvenskan*. February 23, p. A24.

Johansson, Karin, and Lasse Wierup. 1999b. "I Själ och Hjärta är Percy en Jävla Hyvens Kille." *Sydsvenskan*. June 13, p. A7.

Kaelberer, Matthias. 2004. "The Euro and European Identity: Symbols, Power and the Politics of European Monetary Union." *Review of International Studies* 30(2) (April 2004): 161–178.

Kaplan, Martha. 1995. *Neither Cargo nor Cult: Ritual Politics and the Colonial Imagination in Fiji*. Durham, N.C.: Duke University Press.

Kautsky, Karl. 1971. *The Class Struggle (The Erfurt Program)*. New York: Norton.

Kennedy, Magrit. 1995. *Interest and Inflation Free Money: Creating an Exchange Medium That Works for Everybody and Protects the Earth*. Okemos, Mich.: Seva International.

Kenner, Hugh. 1973. *The Pound Era*. Berkeley: University of California Press.

Keynes, John Maynard. 1960 [1930]. *A Treatise on Money*, vol. 2. London: Macmillan.

———. 1997 [1936]. *The General Theory of Employment, Interest, and Money*. Amherst, N.Y.: Prometheus.

Koch, Ragnar von. 1926. "Betänkande med Förslag till Lag om Behandling Av Vissa Arbetsovilliga och Samhällsvådliga, m. fl. Författningar." *Statens Offentliga Utredningar 1926: 9* (Socialdepartementet). Stockholm: Kungliga Boktryckeriet, P. A. Norstedt and Söner.

Kockel, Ullrich. 2002. *Regional Culture and Economic Development: Explorations in European Ethnology*. Aldershot, England: Ashgate.

Koerner, Lisbet. 1999. *Linnaeus: Nature and Nation*. Cambridge, Mass.: Harvard University Press.

"Konkurs." 2002. *Konsumentverket*. http://www.konsumentverket.se.

Kowaleski, Maryanne. 1995. *Local Markets and Regional Trade in Medieval Exeter*. New York: Cambridge University Press.

Kumar, Krishan. 1991. *Utopianism*. Minneapolis: University of Minnesota Press.

———. 1993. "The End of Socialism? The End of Utopia? The End of History?" In *Utopias and the Millennium*. Krishan Kumar and Stephen Bann, eds. London: Reaktion.

Langan, Celeste. 1995. *Romantic Vagrancy: Wordsworth and the Simulation of Freedom*. New York: Cambridge University Press.

Langholm, Odd. 1983. *Wealth and Money in the Aristotelian Tradition*. Oslo: Universitetsforlaget.

Larsen, Lotta Björklund. 2010. *Illegal yet Licit: Justifying Informal Purchases of Work in Contemporary Sweden*. Stockholm: Acta Universitatis Stockholmiensis.

Ledeneva, Alena. 1998. *Russia's Economy of Favors: Blat, Networking and Informal Exchange*. Cambridge: Cambridge University Press.

Lee, R. 1996. "Moral Money? LETS and the Social Construction of Local Economic Geographies in Southeast England." *Environment and Planning A* 28: 1377–1394.

Lefebvre, Henri. 1991. *The Production of Space*. Oxford: Blackwell.

Lemon, Alaina. 1998. "Your Eyes Are Green like Dollars: Counterfeit Cash, National Substance, and Currency Apartheid in 1990s Russia." *Cultural Anthropology* 13(1): 22–55.

Lester, V. Markham. 1995. *Victorian Insolvency: Bankruptcy, Imprisonment for Debt, and Company Winding-Up in Nineteenth-Century England*. Oxford: Clarendon.

LETS-Link Norden. 1999. *Nyhetsbrev* [Newsletter] 7 (March).

Levander, Lars. 1974 [1934]. *Fattig Folk och Tiggare*. Stockholm: Gidlunds.

Lietaer, Bernard. 2001. *The Future of Money: A New Way to Create Wealth, Work and a Wiser World*. London: Century.

Linde-Laursen, Anders. 1995. *Det Nationales Natur: Studier i Dansk-Svenske Relationer*. Lund, Sweden: Historiska Media.

——. 2010. *Bordering: Identity Processes between the National and the Personal*. Surrey, England: Ashgate.

Lindholm, Gunborg A. 1995. *Vägarnas Folk: De Resande och Deras Livsvärld*. Gothenburg, Sweden: Etnologiska Föreningen i Västsverige.

Lindquist, Johan. 2008. *The Anxieties of Mobility: Emotional Economies at the Edge of the Global City*. Honolulu: University of Hawaii Press.

Lloyd, T. H. 1982. *Alien Merchants in England in the High Middle Ages*. New York: St. Martin's.

Löfgren, Orvar. 1988. *Hej, Det Är från Försäkringskassan! Informaliseringen av Sverige*. Stockholm: Natur och Kultur.

——. 1999. "Crossing Borders: The Nationalization of Anxiety." *Ethnologia Scandinavica* 29: 5–27.

——. 2002. *On Holiday: A History of Vacation*. Berkeley: University of California Press.

Lucassen, Jan, and Leo Lucassen, eds. 1997. *Migration, Migration History, History: Old Paradigms and New Perspectives*. New York: Peter Lang.

Lucassen, Leo. 1993. "A Blind Spot: Migratory and Travelling Groups in Western European Historiography." *International Review of Social History* 38: 209–235.

Lundberg, Erik Filip. 1996. *The Development of Swedish and Keynesian Macroeconomic Theory and Its Impact on Economic Policy*. New York: Cambridge University Press.

Lundgren, Nils. 2003. *Europa Ja—Euron Nej! De Bästa Argumenten mot EMU*. Rimbo, Sweden: Fischer.

Lundh, Hans Lennart. 1997. "Den Skandinaviska Myntunionen: Tillkomst och Bakgrund." *Göteborgs Numismatiska Förenings Småskrifter* 24 (January): 628–656.

Magnusson, Erik. 1997. "Öresundsregionen en Utopi." *Sydsvenskan*. April 2, p. A16.

Malaby, Thomas M. 2002. "Making Change in the New Europe: Euro Competence in Greece." *Anthropological Quarterly* 75(3): 591–597.

Malkki, Liisa. 1995. *Purity and Exile: Violence, Memory, and National Cosmology among Hutu Refugees in Tanzania*. Chicago: University of Chicago Press.

Mann, Bruce. 2002. *Republic of Debtors: Bankruptcy in the Age of American Independence*. Cambridge, Mass.: Harvard University Press.

Marin, Louis. 1993. "Frontiers of Utopia: Past and Present." *Critical Inquiry* 19(3): 397–420.

Martinson, Harry. 1949. *Vägen till Klockrike*. Stockholm: Albert Bonniers.

Marx, Karl. 1973. *Grundrisse*. Translated by Martin Nicolaus. Baltimore, Md.: Penguin.

———. 1990. *Capital*, vol. 1. Translated by Ben Fowkes. New York: Penguin.

Maurer, Bill. 2005. *Mutual Life, Limited: Islamic Banking, Alternative Currencies, Lateral Reason*. Princeton, N.J.: Princeton University Press.

Mauss, Marcel. 1990. *The Gift*. New York: Norton.

McLellan, David, ed. 1988. *Marxism: Essential Writings*. Oxford: Oxford University Press.

Meikle, Scott. 1995. *Aristotle's Economic Thought*. New York: Oxford University Press.

Miller, William. 1990. *Bloodtaking and Peacemaking: Feud, Law, and Society in Saga Iceland*. Chicago: University of Chicago Press.

Milner, Henry. 1989. *Sweden: Social Democracy in Practice*. Oxford: Oxford University Press.

Mirowski, Philip. 1989. *More Heat than Light: Economics as Social Physics, Physics as Nature's Economics*. New York: Cambridge University Press.

Miyazaki, Hirokazu. 2006. "Economy of Dreams: Hope in Global Capitalism and Its Critiques." *Cultural Anthropology* 21(2): 147–172.

More, Thomas. 1993 [1516]. *Utopia*. New York: Cambridge University Press.

Munkhammar, Johnny. 2003. *Inför Euron! Rösta Ja Till EMU's Tredje Steg*. Avesta, Sweden: Pocky.

Munn, Nancy. 1986. *The Fame of Gawa*. Durham, N.C.: Duke University Press.

Narotzky, Susana, and Gavin Smith. 2006. *Immediate Struggles: People, Power, and Place in Rural Spain*. Berkeley: University of California Press.

Newell, Sasha. 2006. "Estranged Belongings." *Anthropological Theory* 6(2): 179–203.

Newman, Michael. 1996. *Democracy, Sovereignty and the European Union*. New York: St. Martin's.

Nielsen, Axel. 1911. "Den Tyske Kameralvidenskabs Opstaaen i det 17 Aarhundrede." *Danske Videnskaps Selskaps Skrifter* 7. Række, hist-filos. Afd. II: 2. Copenhagen.

Nietzsche, Friedrich. 1956. "The Genealogy of Morals." In *The Birth of Tragedy and the Genealogy of Morals*. Translated by F. Golffing. New York: Anchor.

Nilsson, Fredrik. 1999. *När en Timme Blir Tio Minuter: En Studie av Förväntan inför Öresundsbron*. Lund, Sweden: Historiska Media.

———. 2000. *I Rörelse: Politisk Handling under 1800-talets Första Hälft*. Lund, Sweden: Nordic Academic Press.

Nogaro, Bertrand. 1949. *A Short Treatise on Money and Monetary Systems*. New York: Staples.

Nordisk Familjebok. 1905. "Bysättning." Stockholm: Nordisk Familjeboks.

North, Peter. 1999. "Explorations in Heterotopia: Local Exchange and Trading Schemes (LETS) and the Micropolitics of Money and Livelihood." *Environment and Planning D* 17: 69–86.

O'Dell, Tom. 2003. "Øresund and the Regionauts." *European Studies* 19: 31–53.

O'Doherty, R. K., et al. 1999. "Local Exchange and Trading Schemes: A Useful Strand of Community Economic Development Policy?" *Environment and Planning A* 31: 1639–1653.

Olsson, Karl Vicktor. 1999. "Turistresan Går Allt Längre: Snart Åker Vi ut i Rymden." *Sydsvenskan.* June 3, p. B4.

Øresund Business Integration. n.d. *Two Countries—One Region.* Sydsvenska Industry och Handelskammaren.

Öresundskomiteen. 1998. "Skåne och Hovedstadsområdet i nära samarbete." *Öresund-skomiteen.* http://www.oresund.com/oresund/orecomm2.htm.

Palludan, Uffe. 1999. *Øresundsbroens Muligheder: Fra Vision till Øresundsregion?* Copenhagen: Fremad.

Papataxiarchis, Evthymios. 1999. "A Contest with Money: Gambling and the Politics of Disinterested Sociality in Aegean Greece." In *Lilies of the Field.* Sophie Day, Evthymios Papataxiarchis, and Michael Stewart, eds. Boulder, Colo.: Westview.

Pawnell, Charles. 1996. "The European Union: What's in It for Me?" Brussels: European Commission, Directorate-General for Information, Communication, Culture, and Audiovisual Media.

Peebles, Gustav. 1997. "A Very Eden of the Innate Rights of Man? A Marxist Look at the European Union Treaties and Case Law." *Law and Social Inquiry* 22(3): 581–618.

——. 2002. "Utanför Stängslet." In *Öresundsbro På Uppmärksamhetens Marknad.* Per-Olof Berg, Anders Linde-Laursen, and Orvar Löfgren, eds. Lund, Sweden: Studentlitteratur.

——. 2003. "The Search for Sound Currencies: An Anthropological Study of the European Monetary Union." Ph.D. diss., University of Chicago.

——. 2004a. "The Crown Capitulates: Conflations of National Currency and Global Capital in the Swedish Currency Crisis." In *Market Matters: Exploring Cultural Processes in the Global Marketplace.* Christina Garsten and Monica Lindh de Montoya, eds. London: Palgrave.

——. 2004b. "A Wicked Cheat: ATMs and the Neo-Feudal Economy." *Harper's Magazine.* June.

——. 2008. "Inverting the Panopticon: Money and the Nationalization of the Future." *Public Culture* 20(2): 233–265.

Perkmann, Markus, and Ngai-Ling Sum, eds. 2002. *Globalization, Regionalization and Cross-Border Regions.* New York: Palgrave Macmillan.

Posner, Richard. 1995. *Overcoming Law.* Cambridge, Mass.: Harvard University Press.

Quiding, Nils Herman. 1978 [1886]. *Slutliqvid med Sveriges Lag.* Stockholm: Gidlund.

Rabinow, Paul. 1995. *French Modern: Norms and Forms of the Social Environment.* Chicago: University of Chicago Press.

Raffles, Hugh. 2007. "Jews, Lice, and History." *Public Culture* 19(3): 521–566.

Rehn, Gösta. 1984. "The Wages of Success." *Daedalus* 113(2): 137–168.

Riksdagen [Parliament]. 1840–1841. Bihang till Samtlige Riks-Ståndens Protocoll vid Lagtima Riksdagen i Stockholm. Sjunde Samlingen, 2nd Afdelningen: Lag-samt Allm. Besv. och Oeconomie-Utskottens Gemensamma Memorial, Utlåtanden och Betänkanden. No. 12.

——. 1859–1860. Bihang till Samtlige Riks-Ståndens Protokoll vid Lagtima Riksdagen i Stockholm. Sjunde Samlingen, 1st Afdelningen: Lag-Utskottets Memorial, Utlåtanden Betänkanden. No. 41.

——. 1877. Bihang till Riksdagens Protokoll vid Lagtima Riksdagen i Stockholm. Åttonde Samlingen, 1st Afdelningen: Särskilda Utskottens Utlåtanden och Memorial N: 1–9. No. 2.

Risse, Thomas. 2010. *A Community of Europeans? Transnational Identities and Public Spheres*. Ithaca, N.Y.: Cornell University Press.

Roitman, Janet. 2003. "Unsanctioned Wealth; or, The Productivity of Debt in Northern Cameroon." *Public Culture* 15(2): 211–237.

———. 2004. "Productivity in the Margins: The Reconstitution of State Power in the Chad Basin." In *Anthropology in the Margins of the State*. Veena Das and Deborah Poole, eds. Santa Fe, N.M.: School of American Research Press.

———. 2005. *Fiscal Disobedience: An Anthropology of Economic Regulation in Central Africa*. Princeton, N.J.: Princeton University Press.

Ruth, Arne. 1984. "The Second New Nation: The Mythology of Modern Sweden." *Daedalus* 113(2): 53–96.

Sahlins, Marshall. 1972. *Stone Age Economics*. Hawthorne, N.Y.: de Gruyter.

Saint-Simon, Henri de. 1976. *The Political Thought of Saint-Simon*. Oxford: Oxford University Press.

Sampson, Steven. 1994. "Money without Culture, Culture without Money." *Anthropological Journal on European Cultures* 3(1): 7–29.

Santer, Jacques. 1998. "The Euro, Instrumental in Forging a European Identity." *InfEuro* 8 (May): 1, 8.

Sassen, Saskia. 1999. *Guests and Aliens*. New York: New Press.

Schivelbusch, Wolfgang. 1979. *The Railway Journey: Trains and Travel in the 19th Century*. New York: Urizen.

Scott, James C. 1998. *Seeing like a State*. New Haven, Conn.: Yale University Press.

Seabright, Paul, ed. 2000. *Barter Networks and Non-Monetary Transactions in Post-Soviet Societies*. New York: Cambridge University Press.

Shaw, Jo. 2010. "Citizenship: Contrasting Dynamics at the Interface of Integration and Constitutionalism." Florence, Italy: EUI Working Paper RSCAS 2010/60.

Shore, Cris. 2000. *Building Europe: The Cultural Politics of European Integration*. New York: Routledge.

———. 2005. "The State of the State in Europe; or, What Is the European Union That Anthropologists Should Be Mindful of It?" In *State Formations: Anthropological Perspectives*. Christian Krohn-Hansen and Knut Nustad, eds. Ann Arbor, Mich.: Pluto.

Simmel, Georg. 1978 [1907]. *The Philosophy of Money*. New York: Routledge.

Small, Albion W. 2001 [1909]. *The Cameralists: The Pioneers of German Social Polity*. Kitchener, Ont., Canada: Batoche.

Smith, Adam. 1976 [1776]. *An Inquiry into the Nature and Causes of the Wealth of Nations*, vol. 1. Edited by Edwin Cannan. Chicago: University of Chicago Press.

———. 1984 [1790]. *The Theory of Moral Sentiments*. Indianapolis, Ind.: Liberty Fund.

Sparbanken. 1997. *EMU: 99 Frågor och Svar*. Stockholm: Sparbanken Sverige.

Spohn, Willfried, and Anna Triandafyllidou, eds. 2003. *Europeanisation, National Identities and Migration: Changes in Boundary Constructions between Western and Eastern Europe*. New York: Routledge.

Sproul, Michael. 2003. "There Is No Such Thing as Fiat Money." Working Paper no. 830. Department of Economics, University of California, Los Angeles.

Stacul, Jaro, Christina Moutsou, and Helen Kopnina, eds. 2006. *Crossing European Boundaries: Beyond Conventional Geographical Categories*. New York: Berghahn.

Stallybrass, Peter, and Allon White. 1986. *The Politics and Poetics of Transgression*. Ithaca, N.Y.: Cornell University Press.

Stewart, Michael. 1999. "'Brothers' and 'Orphans': Images of Equality among Hungarian Rom." In *Lilies of the Field*. Sophie Day, Evthymios Papataxiarchis, and Michael Stewart, eds. Boulder, Colo.: Westview.

Strindberg, August. 1987 [1885]. *Utopier i Verkligheten: Fyra Berättelser*. Stockholm: Bonnier.

———. 1993. "Creditors." In *Plays: Three*. London: Methuen Drama.

Svallhammar, Stig. 1999. "När Människor Rätt Hette Pengar." *Spår* 78–102.

Svensson, Birgitta. 1993. *Bortom all Ära och Redlighet: Tattarnas Spel med Rättvisan*. Stockholm: Nordiska Museets Handlingar.

Tagesson, Pelle. 1999. "Björkegrens Öde Fortfarande ett Mysterium." *Sydsvenskan*. June 4, p. A8.

Taussig, Michael. 1997. *The Magic of the State*. New York: Routledge.

Taylor, Charles. 1989. *Sources of the Self: The Making of the Modern Identity*. Cambridge, Mass.: Harvard University Press.

Therborn, Göran. 1995. *European Modernity and Beyond*. Thousand Oaks, CA: Sage Publications.

Thompson, E. P. 1993. *Customs in Common: Studies in Traditional Popular Culture*. New York: New Press.

Thorne, L. 1996. "Local Exchange and Trading Systems in the United Kingdom: A Case of Re-embedding?" *Environment and Planning A* 28: 1361–1376.

Tilton, Timothy. 1990. *The Political Theory of Swedish Social Democracy: Through the Welfare State to Socialism*. New York: Oxford University Press.

Tingsten, Herbert. 1941. *Den Svenska Socialdemokratiens Ideutveckling*, vol. 1. Stockholm: Tiden.

Tolstoy, Leo. 1902. "What Is to Be Done?" In *The Novels and Other Works of Lyof N. Tolstoi*, vol. 18. New York: Charles Scribner's Sons.

Tomasson, Richard. 1970. *Sweden: Prototype of Modern Society*. New York: Random House.

Torpey, John. 1998. "Coming and Going: On the State Monopolization of the Legitimate 'Means of Movement.'" *Sociological Theory* 16(3): 239–259.

TT. 1999a. "Pilen Kritiserar Tågstöd över Sundet." *Sydsvenksan*. September 16, p. A30.

———. 1999b. "Fogden Tar Upp Jakten På Grevinnan." *Sydsvenskan*. March 13, p. A6.

Underdånigt Förslag till Förordning Angående Lösdrifveri, m.m. 1882. Gothenburg, Sweden: Göteborgs Handelstidnings Aktiebolags Tryckeri.

Verdery, Katherine. 1996. *What Was Socialism and What Comes Next?* Princeton, N.J.: Princeton University Press.

Virilio, Paul. 1986. *Speed and Politics*. New York: Semiotext(e).

Von Hoffman, Nicholas. 2005. "There's No Free Market at America's Airports." *New York Observer*. September 26, p. 4.

Wagner, Ulla. 1977. "Out of Time and Space: Mass Tourism and Charter Trips." *Ethnos* 42(1–2): 39–49.

Wallentin, Hans. 1989. *Lösdriveri och Industrialism: Om lösdrvierifrågan i Sverige 1885–1940*. Östersund, Sweden: Högskolan i Östersund.

Weber, Max. 1958. *The Protestant Ethic and the Spirit of Capitalism*. New York: Charles Scribner's Sons.

———. 1978. *Economy and Society*, vol. 1. Berkeley: University of California Press.

Wicksell, Knut. 1935. *Lectures on Political Economy,* vol. 2: *Money.* London: Routledge and Kegan Paul.

———. 1936 [1898]. *Interest and Prices: A Study of the Causes Regulating the Value of Money.* London: Macmillan.

Widen, Johan. 1906. "Om Hemortsrätt." *Fattigvård och Folkförsäkring* 2(1): n.p.

Wieslander, Anna. 1997. "Att Bygga Öresundsregionen: Från 1960-talets utvecklingsoptimism till 1990-talets lapptäcksregionalism." In *Öresundsregionen: Visioner och Verklighet.* Sven Tägil et al., eds. Lund, Sweden: Lund University Press.

Wilke, Björn. 1999. *Sätt Fart På Pengarna! Så Får du Ditt Kapital att Växa.* Täby, Sweden: Lille E. Bokförlaget.

Williams, C. C. 1996. "Local Exchange and Trading Systems: A New Source of Work and Credit for the Poor and Unemployed?" *Environment and Planning A* 28: 1395–1415.

Williams, Raymond. 1973. *The Country and the City.* New York: Oxford University Press.

Wilson, Thomas M. 2000. "Agendas in Conflict: Nation, State and Europe in Northern Ireland Borderlands." In *An Anthropology of the European Union: Building, Imagining, and Experiencing the New Europe.* Irene Bellier and Thomas M. Wilson, eds. Oxford: Berg.

Wimmer, Andreas. 2002. *Nationalist Exclusion and Ethnic Conflict: Shadows of Modernity.* New York: Cambridge University Press.

Woodburn, James. 1982. "Egalitarian Societies." *Man* 17(3): 431–451.

Woodruff, David. 1999. *Barter and the Fate of Russian Capitalism.* Ithaca, N.Y.: Cornell University Press.

Worsley, Peter. 1968. *The Trumpet Shall Sound: A Study of "Cargo" Cults in Melanesia.* New York: Schocken.

Zelizer, Viviana. 1997. *The Social Meaning of Money.* Princeton, N.J.: Princeton University Press.

INDEX

by, 94; pension plans, 149, 150; regional-
ization programs, 9–10, 25–26, 28–31,
86, 163n9, 166n24; sovereignty of, 29–31;
stabilization of currency by, 48–50. *See
also* Øresund Region; People's Home
Newell, Sasha, 172n2
Newman, Michael, 166n18
Nielsen, Axel, 80
Nietzsche, Friedrich, 124
Nilsson, Percy, 121–122, 125, 135, 138–139,
152
Nilsson Fredrik, 30, 37, 44, 163n6
Nogaro, Bertrand, 170n34
North, Peter, 164n14
Norway, 43, 44

O'Dell, Tom, 163n4
O'Doherty, R. K., 164n14
Olsson, Karl Vicktor, 110
Øresund Bridge. *See* bridge (Øresund Region)
Øresund Region, x; advertisements for, 35–
36; advocacy for, 7–8, 36, 86; as binational space, 156–157; commencement
of, 1–2; currency devaluation in, 56;
debt legislation, 122, 139; devaluations
of currency in, 56–57; labor force in, 34–
35, 95, 113, 117–118; leisure in, 95; monetary organization of, 2; Øresundskomiteen, 29, 36; population of, 4–5, 6;
statistical data on, 36; transnationalism
encouraged by, 4, 5, 6, 28–30; as utopian
space, 19–20, 31, 40, 41, 167n29. *See also*
Copenhagen; Malmö

Palludan, Uffe, 37, 168n34
pan-nationalism, 25–26, 31, 44, 166n24
Papataxiarchis, E., 96–97, 98, 112, 113–114,
119, 174n4, 175n10
paper currency, 42, 45–46, 54, 183n33
parasitism: indebtedness, 72, 73, 142, 143,
145; local-currency rings as opposed to,
115–116; stereotypes of, 118–119,
172n13; vagrancy as, 94–95, 101, 102,
103, 128, 159
passports, 121, 125, 153
Peebles, Gustav, 9, 41, 51, 57, 61, 81, 149,
151, 161, 168n8, 176n17

People's Home: attitudes toward vagrancy,
95, 96, 101–102, 104, 111, 125, 160; concealment of wealth, 129–132, 152,
180n11; consumption and the beginnings of, 49–50; equality as value of, 129,
163n8; indebtedness, 74, 77; markets
compared with homes, 16–18, 29, 58;
mobile populations, 57, 101; as model of
hothouse capitalism, 91; receipt transactions and, 84, 85; Sweden as, 15–18, 24;
as utopian space, 21, 24; welfare state,
15–16, 57, 104
Pepper Island (fictitious tax-free paradise),
151–152
Perkmann, Markus, 164n9
piracy, 138, 153, 181n23
Posner, Richard, 179n5
Pound, Ezra, 183n32
poverty, 104, 174n6
Povinelli, Elizabeth, 39
price indexes, 48, 49
prisons, 122, 124–128, 137, 138–139, 179n6,
180n9, 180n10
Protestantism, 174n6

quantity theory of money, 42, 61, 168n3
Quiding, Nils Herman, 21, 164n3

Rabinow, Paul, 90, 169n20
racial profiling, 118
Raffles, Hugh, 183n31
railroads, 30, 31–32, 86, 107, 108, 111,
177n25
receipt transactions, 69–73, 75–77, 82–85,
90
regionalization programs, 9–10, 25–26,
28–31, 86, 163n9, 166n24. *See also* Øresund Region
Rehn, Gösta, 169n18
Risse, Thomas, 164n12
Robbins, Joel, 38, 171n40
Roitman, Janet, xii, 15, 122, 138
Ruth, Arne, 21

sacrifice, rhetoric of, 9, 12, 14
Sahlins, Marshall, 96, 160, 172n9
Saint-Simonians (Saint Simon, Henri de):

Triandafyllidou, Anna, 164n12
tunnel construction, 30, 31, 167n29

unattached drifter (use of term), 104
utopianism: of EU (European Union), 25–
27, 166n17; in the modern age, 20–21,
164n4; Øresund Region as utopian
space, 19–20; Sweden as model society,
21–23, 164n5, 165n7, 165n9, 165n10. *See
also* Saint-Simonians (Saint-Simon, Henri
de)

vagrants and vagrancy: attitudes toward
money and savings, 96, 103, 111–112;
barter economy of, 103; debtors compared with, 125–126, 127, 128, 180n7;
foreignness of, 102, 103, 104, 117, 118–
119; in labor force, 98–99, 102–103, 112;
legislation, 99, 104, 128, 174n9, 175n11;
leisure travel as, 94–95, 100, 110–113; as
menace to society, 101–102, 114, 118–
119, 175n16; outlawry, 180n7; People's
Home on, 95, 96, 101–102, 104, 111, 125,
160; present-oriented lifestyles of, 97–98,
175n13; repatriation of, 111, 128, 178n30;
romanticization of, 111, 178n29; scientific reasons for, 158; societal attitudes
toward, 100–102, 104, 175n15, 175n16,
175n17; Swedish citizens in Copenhagen
as, 95, 110–111, 112–113, 117; terms for,
101, 174n9, 175n14, 175n15
VAT (value-added tax), 73, 74, 75, 78, 130,
172n11
Verdery, Katherine, 172n2

vinnarkonto, 131
Virilio, Paul, 32, 37, 167n30

Wagner, Ulla, 178n34
Wallentin, Hans, 175n17
wealth accumulation: changing definition
of, 96; concealment of, 129–132, 152–
153, 180n11; fame as non-monetary
credit, 131–132; games of chance, 130–
131, 180n14; Law of Jante, 35, 36, 129,
136, 148–149; magical wealth, 130, 131
Weber, Max, 103, 174n6, 178n31
White, Allon, 98
Wibe, Sören, 171n39
Wicksell, Knut, 41, 46–47, 48, 50, 51, 52,
53, 169n12, 169n21
Wierup, Lasse, 122
Wieslander, Anna, 167n28
Wilbe, Sören, 171n39
Wilke, Björn, 130, 149
Williams, C. C., 164n14
Williams, Raymond, 119
Wilson, Thomas M., 26, 164n12
Wimmer, Andreas, 103, 112
Woodburn, James, 169n22, 173n2, 174n3
Woodruff, David, 172n2
Work (Arbetet), 137
World Bank, 142
Worsley, Peter, 86

youth culture in Sweden, 33, 131–132

Zelizer, Viviana, 111, 142, 171n40

GUSTAV PEEBLES is Assistant Professor of Anthropology and Chair of Social Sciences in the Bachelor's Program at The New School in New York City.